The Great Caliphs

The Great Caliphs

THE GOLDEN AGE OF THE 'ABBASID EMPIRE

AMIRA K. BENNISON

Yale University Press New Haven & London

Published in the United States in 2009 by Yale University Press.
Published in the United Kingdom in 2009 by I.B.Tauris & Co. Ltd.

Typeset in Adobe Caslon Pro by A. & D. Worthington,
Newmarket, Suffolk.
Printed in the United States of America.

Library of Congress Control Number: 2009922520
ISBN 978-0-300-15227-2 (hardcover : alk. paper)
ISBN 978-0-300-16798-6 (pbk.)

A catalogue record for this book is available from the British Library.

10 9 8 7 6 5 4

Contents

Illustrations

✦ ✦

Acknowledgements

No book is ever written without incurring numerous debts of both a tangible and intangible nature. In this case, I am grateful to all those who taught me not only to examine the fine detail of Arabic texts but also to question and consider the history of the Islamic Middle East as a grand panorama. This includes not only lecturers and professors but also the undergraduates who have sat through my survey courses for over a decade and asked me many a stimulating and provocative question about the hows and whys of Islamic history. My thanks also to Alex Wright of I.B.Tauris who thought that I might be just the person to write this book and has patiently waited for it to be completed. While writing, I have had occasion to consult many friends and colleagues on all manner of points and I am grateful to them all, but special thanks are due to James E. Montgomery, who has offered consistent encouragement and invaluable references as well as making incisive comments on draft chapters, and to María Angeles Gallego, Christine van Ruymbeke and Ian Bennison, who also took the time to read and comment on various chapters. I also owe a debt of thanks to Theodore and Tshiami who have kept me sane and reminded me that there are other things to life than book-writing. Finally, in the words of the tenth-century geographer al-Muqaddasi, whom I have had frequent occasion to quote in the course of writing,

> Of course I do not acquit myself of error, nor my book of defect; neither do I submit it to be free of redundancy and deficiency, nor that it is above criticism in every respect.

Note on Transliteration and Arabic Conventions

Transliteration of Arabic into English poses a number of problems and it is impossible to be consistent. I have used the standard transliteration system employed by the *International Journal of Middle Eastern Studies*, but in order to avoid cluttering what is supposed to be an accessible text, I have chosen not to mark Arabic long vowels or emphatic letters. I have assumed that specialists know which letters are soft and which are emphatic and where long vowels fall, while the general reader does not need to be confused by a series of unintelligible lines and dots above and below letters. I have indicated the Arabic letter *ayn* and the glottal stop *hamza* with opening and closing quotation marks respectively.

With respect to place names, wherever possible I have used contemporary English forms for clarity, although this does lead to some anachronisms. For instance, for the Iberian peninsula I have used 'Spain', which really only applies to the Christian kingdom established in the fifteenth century, rather than more correct but less readily comprehensible terms. The same applies to 'Tunisia', 'Morocco' and other country names which were not regularly used in pre-modern times but direct the reader to the correct geographical area.

Pre-modern Arabic names consisted of several components in the form: father of (*abu*) someone, personal name, son of (*ibn*) someone, to which was often added an adjective indicating a tribe, place or profession and, for rulers, an honorific title. For example, the Prophet's full name was Abu'l-Qasim Muhammad ibn 'Abd Allah, to which one could add 'al-Hashimi', meaning 'of the clan of Hashim'. In keeping with usual academic conventions, I have abbreviated *ibn* to b. throughout the text except when it appears at the start of a shortened name, e.g. Ibn Khaldun. It is also conventional to describe caliphs and rulers using their honorifics, e.g. al-Ma'mun, with the exception of the Umayyads of Spain, who are generally known by their personal names.

꙰ ꙰

Introduction

For most of us the word 'Mediterranean' conjures up images of picturesque villages of whitewashed houses whose blue-painted shutters pick up the intense blue of sea and sky, or cream and ochre pillars topped with Corinthian capitals from Graeco-Roman times set against a backdrop of silvery green olive groves. Moreover the history of the Mediterranean from the Greeks and Romans to modern times is assumed to belong to 'Western civilization', a vague notion if ever there was one. In contrast the word 'Islam' triggers a very different set of associations: in recent times violent and confrontational, but previously an Orientalist pastiche of deserts, camels, turbanned warriors with swords, and women enveloped in black, casting coy and seductive glances from behind their veils. This seems to be a history which belongs to Arabia and the Middle East, the crossroads between Africa and Asia, the home of very different civilizations to those of the purported West – those of the mysterious Orient.

However, when viewed through the lens of the *longue durée* of history, preconceptions about what is East and what is West, familiar and alien, seem to have less secure foundations than before. For centuries, the Mediterranean was a Muslim-dominated sea and many of its shores are still inhabited by Muslims and, although it may come as a surprise, many of those Muslims in earlier centuries perceived themselves as heirs to the Mediterranean civilizations of Antiquity as well as the civilizations of Mesopotamia and Persia. Arabia, the homeland of the Arabs, had long historic connections with Greece, Rome and Persia before the conversion of the Arabs to Islam and their establishment of their own regional empire, and this book's main contention, which will be familiar enough to professional historians of Islam, is that Islamic civilization, as it came to flourish during the 'Abbasid era from the mid-eighth to the mid-thirteenth centuries CE, can legitimately be viewed as one in a succession of empires and civilizations which flowered in the Mediterranean. Some, like Rome, pushed further north and west into what became Europe, while others, like Islam, pushed into Asia and Africa, but to consider them as belonging to either East or West is a quite false dichotomy.

The Fertile Crescent was one of the cradles of human civilization which soon began to flower also in Egypt, Asia Minor and Greece, not to mention the Indus valley and China. However, European and Western scholarship until fairly recently insisted on dividing these civilizations into 'Western' and 'Eastern' categories which reflected whom the scholars in question perceived as the founders of Western civilization rather than any geographical reality. While Greece and Rome were indisputably of the West, Persia and Egypt stood for the East, and other peoples and civilizations needed to be assimilated to one or the other. To give but one small example: the Phoenicians, generally seen as 'Eastern', originated in the Levant and then set up a trading empire which stretched to Essawira, a small port on Morocco's Atlantic coast, which is further west than any part of Europe. On the other hand, the Seleucids, the descendants of the Macedonian Alexander's general, Seleucas Nicator, who established a series of city-states across the Middle East, are frequently popped on to the 'Western' list. These kind of attributions have little to do with geography and everything to do with cultural identity.

The Romans proved more able than any of their predecessors to bring the entire Mediterranean basin into a single empire which also incorporated northwestern Europe as well as parts of Asia and Africa. Rome's spectacular achievements – its apparently democratic form of government in the form of the Senate, its technical virtuosity symbolized by roads, aqueducts and amphitheatres, and its art and culture preserved in statues, mosaics and literature – have made it the supreme model for emulation by Western empire builders from the Holy Roman emperors to Napoleon and Mussolini. However, as it becomes more common to understand the Roman Empire from Augustus onwards as a monarchy with a court, so the earlier tendency to contrast Roman republicanism with the oriental despotism of Persia becomes less convincing; not to mention the fact that Rome also inspired the Muslim Ottomans, whose empire actually formed the closest match with the Roman Empire in terms of its geographical extent, its administrative complexity and its use of slaves.

The Muslim view of Rome as an eastern Mediterranean rather than 'Western' empire becomes even clearer with the transformation of the eastern Roman Empire into the Christian Byzantine Empire. This was a mostly Greek-speaking empire but the Byzantines called themselves 'Romans' and were so called by their Muslim neighbours, for whom 'Rome' was thus Constantinople and the Roman Empire a Middle Eastern rather than a

European power, its heartlands Syria and Turkey while Italy, Gaul and Britain were distant lands lost to all manner of Gothic, Vandal and Gaelic barbarians.

The same absence of East–West dichotomies is apparent when we turn to the history and civilization of classical Islam, which existed at a time when today's pre-eminence of the West was undreamed of and there was no need for either side to think in terms of today's polarities. Although the formation of Islam posed a serious challenge to Christianity, as to other religions in the Middle East, this did not gain any East–West connotations until the Crusades. Naturally, Latin Christendom during the Dark Ages was of little concern or interest to Muslims in the early Islamic era, except where they actually shared a frontier in northern Spain and the Pyrenees. Muslims were keenly aware of the myriad Christian sects in their own region and indeed conceptualized their faith as the final and best revelation in the series of such messages God had sent to the prophets of different peoples. Allah was the god of Abraham, Moses and Jesus as well as Muhammad, and Judaism and Christianity were therefore religions based upon Truth even if their practitioners had each in turn corrupted the message they had been sent, necessitating God's dispatch of a new revelation. In religious terms, therefore, Islam was no more 'oriental' than its Jewish and Christian predecessors, and all three communities shared the same territory alongside Zoroastrianism and even Buddhism further east.

In the realm of culture as in religion, Muslims entered into a discursive relationship with the past and their civilization came to draw on the Graeco-Roman, Byzantine and Sasanian heritages in various ways whilst also exhibiting its own separate and sparkling Islamic character. This is a particularly important point. It is fairly well known that some Greek science reached medieval Europe by way of the Arabs; however, it is less commonly recognized that Muslims actively engaged with the materials they had translated from Greek, Persian and Sanskrit into Arabic, and that they added a great deal of new material to the information they received. The Europeans of the Middle Ages therefore acquired not only Greek science but also the numerous important additions, improvements and criticisms of it made by generations of Muslim scholars from Baghdad to Toledo. This knowledge combined with many other developments within Western society itself to enable Europeans to embark upon the intellectual and physical voyages of discovery that formed the modern world.

It would be foolish to exaggerate the continuity between the different phases of Mediterranean history, but the link between Antiquity and Islam is usually neglected, if not actively denied, in favour of a concept of Orientalist and Enlightenment ancestry that Western Europe, and by extension the Western world, is the child of Greece and Rome, whilst Islam proceeds from an alien and exotic Eastern source. I have always found it striking the number of people who do not realize that Judaism, Christianity and Islam purport to come from the same Abrahamic source and that the founding fathers of our respective civilizations, 'the prophets of Israel and the philosophers of Greece', as the American scholar of religion Carl Ernst puts it, are shared.[1]

Civilizations are not, however, static, and this book cannot do justice to the entire sweep of Islamic history across three continents and 1,500 years. Instead I shall focus on the 'Abbasid era, which is generally considered the classical age of Islamic civilization and the formative century which preceded the 'Abbasid revolution in 750, during which the seeds of many of the achievements of the 'Abbasid age were actually planted. I shall end in 1258 when the Mongols marched into Baghdad and killed the last caliph. This marked the end of the classical era and the start of a new phase in Islamic history, often characterized as 'medieval' for want of a better word, during which the Muslim world was ruled by military men in alliance with coteries of religious scholars rather than by a caliph or his representatives. Some ruled no more than a city, others ruled vast territories but none claimed the universal mantle of the caliph until the rise of a new triad of empires – the Ottomans, Safavids and Mughals – the Muslim equivalents of the Habsburgs at the dawn of the early modern era in the sixteenth century.

Our story begins in the 630s CE when the Arabs, inspired by the new Abrahamic monotheism which came to be known as Islam, poured out of their harsh and rugged homeland in the Arabian peninsula and established a vast empire ruled by the Rightly Guided Caliphs (634–61) and the Umayyads (661–750) in turn. By 750 Muslims ruled most of the southern Mediterranean world and the ancient Persian lands to the east, and had extended their influence deep into the Sahara desert, the Central Asian steppe and India. Despite the scorn with which these often poorly clad wiry Arab tribesmen were originally viewed by their imperial Byzantine and Sasanian Persian opponents, they proved to be both militarily capable and politically adept. Within a short time, Christian contemporaries came to share the Muslims' own conviction that God was indeed on their side. A certain lethargy on the part of the subjects of both the Byzantines and the Sasanians, who were frequently over-burdened with taxes and at religious odds with their imperial masters, was also a contributory factor in the Arabs' success. Stories, almost certainly fictional, of Byzantine soldiers chained together to prevent their desertion convey the atmosphere of the times.

As the conquest proceeded the Arabs shifted their capital from the Prophet's city of Medina in the oases of western Arabia to Damascus, a city with an ancient pedigree stretching far back into Antiquity. Here the first caliphal dynasty, that of the Umayyads (661–750), presided over and fostered the birth of a new civilization, that of Islam, which imbibed the heady aromas of Greece, Rome and Byzantium whilst also retaining its own unique character. In fact, it is one of the most remarkable aspects of the Islamic conquests that this was so, and that the Arabs were not simply absorbed by the cultures they had politically subjugated, as was later the case with the Mongols in both China and the Middle East.

Instead they went from strength to strength despite the political and military turmoil created by the very process of empire-building itself. In 750 the 'Abbasid caliphs replaced their Umayyad predecessors and moved the imperial capital eastwards to the old Sasanian heartlands, where they constructed a new city which came to be known as Baghdad. This turned out to be a master stroke: Iraq, already the site of the thriving Muslim garrison towns of Kufa and Basra, quickly emerged as the centre not only of an empire but more importantly of a civilization which drew heavily on the foundations laid by Greece, Byzantium and Persia. The 'Abbasid caliphs themselves played an invaluable role in this process, welcoming at their court not only Muslim scholars, poets and artists but also Nestorian Christian and Jewish physicians, astrologers of all faiths, and pagan philosophers.

However, the importance of the 'Abbasid era for the flowering of Islamic civilization does not lie exclusively in the luxurious halls of the palaces of Baghdad or Samarra, the 'Abbasids' ninth-century capital, but in the society which developed outside the gilded corridors of power. From the outset, Muslims conceived of themselves as members of a single community, the *umma*. During the conquest period, the *umma* was a thin, predominantly Arab layer at the top of society, an elite held together by its Arab ancestry and differentiation from the masses of Christians, Jews and Zoroastrians over which it ruled. Although it would be naive to deny that Arab-Muslim ranks were, at times, deeply divided by tribal feuds and jostling for influence, some sense of common identity and origin persisted and was reinforced by the presence of Qur'an reciters, storytellers and poets who repeated the tales of Muhammad's life and doings and sang of the feats of the Arabs in the new *lingua franca* of Arabic in mosques, marketplaces and military camps from Cordoba in Spain to Merv in Central Asia.

Along with the new vivacious language of Arabic, the rituals of Islam also played a vital integrative role, especially as non-Arab populations began to convert to the new faith. The annual pilgrimage to Mecca, the *hajj*, which took place in the Muslim lunar month of Dhu'l-Hijja, was particularly important in this respect. The Ka'ba, a square building housing the famous black stone, was actually a pagan Arabian shrine where Arabs had congregated to pay their respects to the god Hubal and his consort al-'Uzza and other pagan deities such as the goddess Allat, worshipped at nearby Ta'if. Muhammad had transformed such pagan habits of pilgrimage into the Muslim *hajj* by asserting that the Ka'ba had actually been built by Abraham before it was defiled by the worship of pagan idols and was therefore the ultimate symbol of Semitic monotheism at which all Muslims should pay their respects at least once in their lifetime.

With the elaboration of Islam and the conversion of peoples who had no experience of Arabia, the pilgrimage served as a means of assimilation and created a sense of physical connectivity with the Muslim past for those who managed to make the often perilous and always time-consuming journey to Mecca and nearby Medina, the burial place of Muhammad. Many of those who undertook the pilgrimage were of an intellectual bent and dedicated many years to it, stopping in each city on their route to sit at the feet of its scholars who commented on the Qur'an and other texts in the shady arcades of the mosques. Such pilgrims all contributed to the emergence of a much larger *umma*, deeply rooted in local societies but also self-consciously part of a larger whole, the capacious *dar al-islam* or house of Islam.

The other crucial factor in the development of Islamic civilization in 'Abbasid times was commerce. Although the most usual stereotype is of the Arab as a desert nomad, in reality many Arabs came from the villages and towns of the Yemen (known as Arabia Felix by the Romans for its green steeply terraced valleys), the settled coasts of eastern Arabia and the Syrian towns on the northern fringe of the desert. The kingdoms of old Arabia supplied and received goods to and from Greece, Rome, Persia, Ethiopia and India. Even in the vast desert interior, sacred enclaves (*harams*), where tribesmen were obliged to enter unarmed, dotted the landscape and hosted important commercial fairs such as the gathering held at 'Ukaz near Mecca. Islam therefore developed in a semi-commercial environment and Muhammad worked as a commercial agent in his youth. This meant that despite the initially military character of the Islamic conquests, the Muslims were not slow to exploit the commercial opportunities opened up to them. The creation of a vast empire also enabled non-Muslims, Jews especially, to strengthen and extend their trade networks across the length and breadth of the Islamic world and develop new partnerships with Muslims to the mutual benefit of all those involved.

In the following pages, I shall draw a picture of the politics, society and culture of classical Islam with the two-fold aim of revealing its dynamic character and the nature of its relationship with the past and, to a lesser extent, the present. Chapter 1 provides a political overview of the 'Abbasid caliphate and its many ups and downs between its establishment in 750 and its destruction at the hands of the Mongols in 1258. At the outset, the caliphs controlled an impressive empire reaching from Tunisia to Afghanistan, but political problems in Iraq, where their capital, Baghdad, was situated, gradually allowed independent princes, provincial governors and finally rival caliphal lineages to take over much of the Islamic world. Warrior lineages masquerading as the caliphate's protectors took over in Baghdad, and then the Crusaders carved out their own principalities in the Levant. The history of the 'Abbasid caliphate is thus not simply the history of the caliphs themselves but also all those who sought to usurp their power and authority, control them or emulate them. This is why I have included references to the Fatimids of Egypt and Umayyads of Spain, who were rivals of the 'Abbasids from a political perspective but culturally connected to them in many ways.

Much of what we know about 'Abbasid times across the Islamic world relates to cities, and Chapter 2 therefore takes a look at classical Islamic cities as a development of earlier Middle Eastern urban traditions. The 'Islamic city' was one of the favourite themes of Orientalist scholarship, which tended to view such places as utter contrasts to the grand Graeco-Roman and Persian cities of more ancient times, and also defective in comparison with medieval European cities, which kept classical civic virtues alive in an attenuated form, and modern Western cities which had revived all the positive qualities of ancient cities. The cities of the early Islamic and 'Abbasid eras, however, did not really fit this negative stereotype and nor were they so wildly different from those of the Byzantine and Sasanian eras which preceded them. This chapter looks at how such cities were actually planned and built to serve the needs of rulers and the ruled, and the ebb and flow from previous eras.

Chapter 3 explores what life was really like for men and women, Muslims and non-Muslims, rich and poor, in this period. It is easy to assume that contemporary perceptions of what Muslim societies are like – which are themselves generally unrepresentative stereotypes – can be projected backwards in time, but this is often not the case. Like all pre-modern societies, Islamic society in 'Abbasid times was one in which upward social mobility was limited and a person's station in life was determined by his or her father's position. It was, however, a pluralistic society, which recognized ethnic and religious differences. Christians, Jews and Zoroastrians were allowed to practise their faiths as religious minorities, and Arabs, Persians, Turks and others competed for power and influence at the highest levels. Just as Roman citizenship was not based on ethnicity, neither was participation in the 'Abbasid elite. Service and merit were much more important. Public life was male dominated and women did not hold much formal power, although their rights to inheritance were rather better than in Christian societies of the time. However, the glimpses we have of their lives suggest a reality rather different from contemporary assumptions about the position of Muslim women in society.

In Chapter 4 I look at trade and industry, the lifeblood of the Islamic world, and the intimate relationship between these sectors and pilgrimage. Commerce kept the numerous cities, towns and ports of the Middle East and North Africa alive and also enabled the spread of commodities, ideas and people which created an 'Abbasid-influenced world much bigger than the area controlled by the caliphs themselves in a form of pre-modern globalization. The dynamism of the commercial sector reflected the Prophet's own commercial background, enshrined in his biography, and the early development of long-distance pilgrim routes from all over the Islamic world to Mecca in Arabia which doubled up as trade routes. As we shall see, pilgrimage and trade were often entwined and facilities provided for pilgrims could be used by merchants and vice-versa. Moreover many pilgrims supported their long journeys by buying and selling along the way, stimulating the market even more.

Chapter 5 explores the cultural production of the 'Abbasid era, what knowledge Muslims and scholars of other faiths considered important and which sciences they nurtured and developed in the eighth to thirteenth centuries, including their translation of a substantial number of ancient Greek works into Arabic. There is a strong tendency to divide Muslim knowledge into religious and rational categories and imply a sharp division between the two, an attitude rooted more in Enlightenment secularism than in Muslim definitions of the categories of knowledge. This chapter tries to present Muslim knowledge as a more integrated cultural package in which Islamic branches of study overlapped with areas of knowledge favoured by other civilizations, most notably Greek philosophy and medicine, but also mathematics, astronomy and astrology of Greek, Persian and Indian origin.

Chapter 6 concludes the story by looking at the processes of transmission which conveyed Arabo-Islamic knowledge and its Greek base into Latin Christendom, and justifies placing classical Islamic civilization on a continuum between the civilizations of Antiquity and modern Western civilization. Various facts, theories and concepts, not to mention literary styles, made their way slowly but surely from Muslim centres of learning to the frontiers of the Islamic world in the hands of scholars, traders and even warriors, where they were acquired by other peoples who took them in new directions. The avidity of scholars like Robert Ketton, a twelfth-century Englishman who spent his life in the Ebro valley south of the Pyrenees, translating scientific materials from Arabic, was as remarkable as that of the Arabs in Baghdad 400 years earlier, and equally significant in terms of creating a link between the empires and civilizations which preceded the 'Abbasids and those that succeeded them in the Middle East and in Europe.

It is probably obvious by now that this is a story of continuity and change, a pair of concepts which historians love to juxtapose as they study the transition from one era to another. In fact, it is simply a matter of common sense: how could a new regime, however revolutionary or apparently different, not owe some debt to the past? However, such common sense is sometimes lacking when it comes to viewing the transition from late Antiquity to the Islamic era, when a comfortable Christian world rooted in the Graeco-Roman heritage was suddenly and dramatically replaced by the apparently alien era of Islam, an interloper in both religious and cultural terms.

Many scholars have explored both the continuities and changes that occurred at this seminal moment in history, and I can only write this book because of their work. However, it seems to me important at this juncture, when the mere mention of the word 'Islam' conjures up a whole array of negative stereotypes, to try to capture the very different atmosphere of the classical Islamic era. It is not my intention to suggest that any single people or civilization is better than any other but simply to depict Islamic civilization at a moment when it was self-confident, tolerant by the standards of the time and open to influences from outside, and to point to the importance of this phase within the longer story of Mediterranean civilization. The Middle East has always been the physical bridge between Europe and Asia, but it has also functioned as an important link between past and present. As inheritors of at least a portion of the cultural wealth of Antiquity, Muslims presided over a new period of synthesis and creativity, the fruits of which Western Europeans came to share through various Mediterranean meeting points and frontiers before embarking upon their own age of discovery and creativity.

‌ᵃ⁂ᵃ

CHAPTER I

A Stormy Sea: The Politics of the 'Abbasid Caliphate

When the [Muslims] then set out to seek for themselves the royal authority held by the nations, there was no protection against them or refuge. They were granted the realms of the Persians and the Byzantines who were the greatest dynasties in the world at that time, and those of the Turks in the east, the European Christians and Berbers in the Maghrib and the Goths in Spain. They went from the Hijaz to the Sus in the far west, and from Yemen to the Turks in the north. They gained possession of all seven climes.[1]

This book is about culture rather than empire, but it would be fool-hardy to try to present the culture and society of this fascinating period without offering a rudimentary sense of the political frame-work within which the seeds of Islamic culture were scattered and where they so strikingly flourished. What follows is not a detailed account of the political history of the 'Abbasid caliphate or the intimacies of life at the 'Abbasid courts in Baghdad and Samarra, two tasks which have been admirably tackled already,[2] but rather a potted history of the period which preceded the foundation of the 'Abbasid caliphate and its subsequent politi-cal ups and downs as a backdrop to the story of the society and civiliza-tion explored in succeeding chapters. It inevitably simplifies often complex political events but flags up the key moments and *dramatis personae* from caliphs to rebels who together shaped the 'Abbasid world.

The 'Abbasids came to power in the 750s, 120 years after the death of the Prophet Muhammad in 632, on the crest of a revolutionary wave that swept away the Umayyad caliphs who preceded them and offered the promise of a juster universal Muslim society to the burgeoning number of non-Arab converts to the new faith. They started out with almost boundless author-ity, but the very size of their empire and the many competing for power, influence and recognition made caliphal politics turbulent and dramatic.

The real power of the 'Abbasids varied considerably over the next five centuries, sometimes encompassing little more than the palace in Baghdad, but the dream of a universal Muslim empire which they and their predecessors originally represented held the community together in myriad ways. It is this symbolic power of the caliphate, the Islamic institution of rule established after Muhammad's death, which is the key to understanding how the 'Abbasid paradigm continued to influence the Islamic world despite the caliphs' very mixed successes at ruling an empire and offering religious leadership.

Moreover, the patronage which the 'Abbasid courts at Baghdad and Samarra offered to scholars, artists, poets and many others ensured that Iraq exported cultural, architectural and intellectual models across the *dar al-islam* even after the 'Abbasids' political fortunes faltered and religious scholars wrested the right to define Islam from them. When the Fatimids in Egypt and the Umayyads in Spain threw down the gauntlet and challenged the 'Abbasids for the caliphate in the tenth century, they tried to outdo them rather than totally rejecting the precedents they had set, establishing a political competition measured by pomp and ceremonial which also involved the Christian Byzantines in Constantinople. It is thus perfectly possible to see the 'Abbasids and their Fatimid and Umayyad rivals, who emerged in Egypt and Spain respectively, as products of a common religio-political environment and proponents of variations on a single cultural theme, that of classical Islam.

The making of an empire

Much of the 'Abbasids' aura related to their possession of the caliphate, an institution which was not, in fact, equivalent to kingship or emperor-hood but denoted the unique and universalist inheritance of the mantle of the Prophet Muhammad as head of the Muslim community. Although sometimes likened to the papacy or the position of Holy Roman Emperor, neither fully encompasses the meaning of the caliphate. The Arabic word from which caliph is derived – *khalifa* – literally means a deputy or successor, and the term can be used in quite mundane administrative contexts. However, it was also adopted by the early Muslims to describe the Prophet's successor as leader of the nascent Muslim community after his death in 632 in Medina. Since we lack truly contemporary commentary, it is hard to say exactly what the Muslims of seventh-century Arabia meant by this title, and whether it was symbolic or simply descriptive for them. The ninth-century historian Abu Ja'far Muhammad al-Tabari (839–923) talks of the Muslims giving the first caliph, the gentle and fatherly Abu Bakr, their

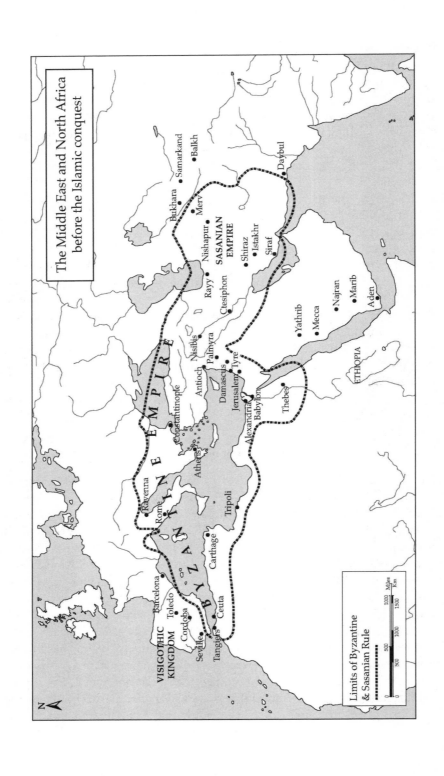

The Middle East and North Africa before the Islamic conquest

oath of allegiance without specifying his title, but he records 'Umar, who subsequently became the second caliph, saying in reference to Abu Bakr, 'I will not disobey the Prophet's successor (*khalifa*) twice in a day'.[3] If we turn to the Qur'an, the word 'caliph' appears twice, to describe Adam and then David:

> And when thy Lord said to the angels, 'I am setting in the earth a viceroy (*khalifa*)'. They said, 'What wilt Thou set therein one who will do corruption there, and shed blood while We proclaim Thy praise and call Thee holy?' He said, 'Assuredly I know what you know not.' And he taught Adam the names, all of them.[4]

> David, behold, We have appointed thee a viceroy (*khalifa*) in the earth; therefore judge between men justly, and follow not caprice lest it lead thee astray from the way of God.[5]

In the verse relating to Adam, the caliphate is comparable to God's bestowal of responsibility for the earth on humankind in Genesis, but in the second verse the status of caliph is given to a ruler, David, which provided a better underpinning for the development of the caliphate as an institution of religio-political power and authority in Muslim times. But were the caliphs the 'successors of God's messenger' (*khalifat rasul Allah*) or 'vicegerents of God' (*khalifat Allah*), and consequently what were the bounds of their role? Certainly the Umayyad and early 'Abbasid caliphs upheld the latter title, first attested for the third caliph, 'Uthman, who asserted that he would rather be crucified than 'give up the mandate of God Almighty and his caliphate', and regularly used by both dynasties because it conveniently endowed them with all-encompassing religious authority as God's representatives on earth.[6]

However, for those Muslims who wished to see religious authority in the hands of religious scholars (*'ulama'*) it was preferable to attribute such attitudes on the part of later caliphs to Byzantine and Sasanian concepts of divine kingship and to present the first four caliphs – Abu Bakr, 'Umar, 'Uthman and 'Ali – as upholding an original, pristine form of leadership as the successors of God's Messenger, which they had then passed to the scholars rather than to Umayyad and 'Abbasid 'kings'. The tenth-century Baghdadi political theorist al-Mawardi summed up the debate in the following words:

> He is known as 'caliph' because he is a vicar of the Messenger [Muhammad], God bless him and grant him salvation, in ruling his nation, and may be addressed as 'Caliph of God's Messenger' or simply 'Caliph'. There has been some difference of opinion whether he may be addressed as God's

Caliph, some allowing it on the grounds that he oversees what is owed God by his creation, in accordance with His words, glorified and exalted be His name. ... The majority of scholars, however, object to this view, regarding it as sinful to hold.[7]

The first four caliphs are known, at least by the Sunni majority of Muslims, as the Rightly Guided Caliphs, although consensus on this point actually took many centuries to form. They were all chosen from the ranks of the early Muslims by more or less consensual means for their precedence (*sabiqa*) within the community and their perceived ability to continue the Prophet's work, rather than their lineage. The range of duties expected of them is reflected in two titles which they routinely held – *imam* and *amir al-mu'minin*. The first, *imam*, means prayer leader and denoted the caliph's supreme religious leadership over the Muslim community, known as the *umma*. The second, *amir al-mu'minin*, which translates into English as 'commander of the faithful', was a more political and militaristic term which expressed the caliph's role as commander-in-chief of the Muslim armies. The Rightly Guided Caliphs resided in Medina and are generally accepted to have lived in a pious and simple manner akin to that of the Prophet but it is one of the great ironies of the period that three out of four died violent deaths in the political maelstrom created by the formation of an empire.

The first man to be chosen, Abu Bakr, was a close friend of Muhammad and one of the earliest converts to Islam. He was a softly spoken man committed to continuing the Prophet's work who dispatched the restive Muslim fighters in Medina to reconquer those Arab tribes that had seceded after the Prophet's death on the grounds that they had given their allegiance to Muhammad not to Islam. He also followed the Prophet's precedent by sending Muslim raiding parties into Byzantine Palestine and Syria, thereby laying the foundations for the conquest of that great symbolic prize, Jerusalem, a few years after his death. He was succeeded in 634 by 'Umar b. al-Khattab, a sometimes harsh man of firm convictions who plays a foundational role in Islamic historiography not dissimilar to that of Paul in Christianity, and presided over the first spectacular wave of Islamic conquest in Syria, Iraq and Egypt in the 630s and early 640s. He also established the military register known as the *diwan al-jund* which listed those eligible for campaigns and a share of the booty, with those who had joined the Muslim side earlier getting larger shares than latecomers, an important step in giving the conquests and the empire they spawned some kind of administrative underpinning.

In 644 'Umar was murdered by a resentful Persian slave, and 'Uthman b. 'Affan became caliph. Although an early Muslim himself, he came from the aristocratic Banu Umayya clan of the Quraysh tribe which had bitterly opposed Muhammad before finally converting to Islam after the Muslims' victory was assured. When he began to appoint members of his clan to positions of power, murmurs of discontent began to rumble. Al-Tabari presents 'Uthman as pious and well meaning but quite unable to cope with the tensions created by a quickly expanding empire and the vast torrents of booty which needed distributing fairly. He quite naturally relied on family but paid the price in 656 when disgruntled Muslims from Egypt assassinated him.

In the crisis leading to his murder, 'Uthman vacillated between the advice of his wife, his kinsmen and eminent Muslims before retreating to his home which was promptly besieged. Despite the protests of many in Medina, the caliph and his family were deprived of fresh water and food, and firebrands were thrown at his gates to enable his assailants to get in. The caliph meanwhile awaited his fate with dignity: 'he recited [his Qur'an] quickly and was not distressed by the noise. He proceeded without making an error or stuttering', and when the assassins fell upon him his blood spattered onto the holy book, creating a powerful icon for Sunni Islam enhanced by 'Uthman's own endeavours to prepare a definitive recension of the Qur'an.[8] The shamefulness of the situation was compounded by the killers' disrespect for his wife, Na'ila daughter of Farafisa, who tried to ward off the sword blows to her husband only to have her buttocks squeezed and dirty jokes made about his liking for such 'good things'.[9] There were mixed feelings about 'Uthman's assassination: afterwards 'the poets spoke about him – some in praise, some in derision, some in tearful lamentation, some in gleeful joy', but the political gravity of the situation is captured by the verses of Ka'b b. Malik:

The caliph's murder was something atrocious,
A terrifying calamity has arisen thereby.
Before the murder of the Imam the very stars bow down,
And because of it the sun is in eclipse.[10]

'Uthman was succeeded by 'Ali, the most tragic of the Rightly Guided Caliphs and, in many ways, the most influential in terms of later political and religious developments. 'Ali was the Prophet's cousin and son-in-law as a result of his marriage to Muhammad's eldest daughter, Fatima, who died six months after her father. Since Muhammad had no surviving sons, 'Ali, Fatima and their two sons, Hasan and Husayn, were his closest relatives, and some Muslims felt that 'Ali should have succeeded the Prophet immediately after his death and that his rights had been usurped by Abu Bakr, 'Umar and 'Uthman in turn. They were known as the 'Party of 'Ali' (*shi'at 'Ali*), which eventually developed into the Shi'i Muslim minority, and they strongly championed his elevation to the caliphate when 'Uthman was assassinated. However, others, including 'Aysha, the daughter of Abu Bakr and one of the Prophet's wives, popularly known as the 'Mother of the Believers', opposed 'Ali's choice as caliph. While no love was lost between 'Ali and 'Aysha, her vehement disapproval probably lay in, firstly, 'Ali's consistent criticism of economic, social and religious developments which he believed were against the spirit of Islam and, secondly, her fear that if he became caliph he would upset the emerging but still fragile social and political order of early Islam.

In order to secure his caliphate, 'Ali had to fight a coalition led by Talha and Zubayr, two eminent and early converts who shared 'Aysha's views. He managed to defeat his opponents at the Battle of the Camel, so called because of 'Aysha's attendance in a camel litter, only to be faced by a much greater threat to his power from the governor of Syria, Mu'awiya, a kinsman of 'Uthman, who insisted that the new caliph had not avenged his predecessor's murder as he should have. The armies of 'Ali and Mu'awiya met in 657 at Siffin in northern Syria. Although 'Ali might have won on military grounds, Mu'awiya was a consummate politician and reputedly halted the battle and called for a negotiated settlement by ordering his men to wave sections of the Qur'an on their spears. This proved to be disastrous for 'Ali: the arbitration process which took place the following year was inconclusive and 'Ali had to settle for control of Iraq while Mu'awiya ruled supreme in Syria and Egypt. The Islamic empire was temporarily divided into two and 'Ali's credibility among his own supporters was severely dented. Some of them felt that as caliph he should never have negotiated with a rebel such as Mu'awiya and that his decision to do so was such a gross misjudgement that it disqualified him from the caliphate. They left his camp and formed Islam's first sect, the Kharijites, who held the view that the caliphate belonged to the Muslim best qualified for the post, even if he was a black slave, according to a very frequently cited saying.

The Kharijites made their antipathy to 'Ali known by assassinating him in the great Mosque of Kufa in 661. This was a tangled affair of love, war and revenge according to al-Tabari, who recounts that the killer, Ibn al-Muljam, was spurred to put aside his reservations about killing 'Ali by the beautiful Qatami, whose brother and father had been killed in battle with 'Ali's men. She demanded 'Ali's death as part of her dowry and the befuddled Ibn al-Muljam hastened to perform the act.[11] He never came to enjoy his bride, however, because he was apprehended after the attack and put to death after 'Ali's stab wound proved fatal. The story inspired the following verses by a poet from Ibn al-Muljam's tribe:

I never saw a dowry provided by any generous man
Whether Arab or other, like that of Qatami:
Three thousand dirhams, a slave and a singing girl,
And the stabbing of 'Ali with the piercing blade.[12]

After 'Ali's death the caliphate passed to his rival Mu'awiya, despite the hopes of many that 'Ali's elder son, Hasan, would became caliph. Hasan was, however, a practical man and when he saw 'that rule was beyond his grasp' because he lacked sufficient support to fight Mu'awiya, he negotiated peace terms with him, including a substantial sum of money from the treasury of Kufa.[13] With hindsight, the death of 'Ali marked the end of the period of the Rightly Guided Caliphs and the start of a new era in which the caliphate passed to the Umayyad and then 'Abbasid dynasties, whose political ethos blended the original Medinese idea of the caliphate with various Near Eastern traditions of kingship. The Umayyads and 'Abbasids interacted with the Islamic and pre-Islamic pasts in distinct ways and presented themselves as picking up different strands of the story presented above but, such differences aside, the 'Abbasid edifice was constructed upon the foundations laid by the Umayyads, to whom we now turn.

The Umayyads: Islam's first caliphal dynasty

Like his second cousin, 'Uthman, Mu'awiya was a member of the aristocratic Banu Umayya clan from which the designation 'Umayyad' comes. He was the first caliph of a younger generation but had served as the Prophet's secretary late in the latter's life and was generally accepted by the community as a sensible choice of leader. He reunited the empire, which had been fractured by civil strife throughout 'Ali's caliphate, and the dynasty he established ruled it for the next 90 years. His successors constructed an imperial identity manifested in administration, architecture and coinage, and presided over the first phase in the creation of the Islamic culture and society which flowered under the 'Abbasids. The first important change which Mu'awiya made was to transfer the caliphal seat from Medina to Damascus in recognition of the shifting geopolitical centre of the Islamic empire. Despite its cachet as the city of the Prophet and the Rightly Guided Caliphs, Medina was a small city in remote Arabia from which it was impossible to adequately direct the conquests or administer an empire. Damascus, in contrast, was still in easy reach of Islam's birthplace to the south, but also placed the caliph in the heart of Byzantine Syria and within striking distance of Mesopotamia.

Damascus was also a city imbued with Byzantine and classical influences which inspired Mu'awiya's descendants to develop a new style of rule, using Byzantine models but also proudly Arab and Islamic. This was partly a matter of practicality: when the Umayyads came to power there was still a dearth of educated Arabs who could be recruited into the administration. The Umayyads therefore employed many from the pool of experienced Greek and Aramaic-speaking Christian administrators who had served the Byzantines and Sasanians and who worked very much as they had under their previous masters until the language of administration began to switch to Arabic in the 680s. Even then, many staff learnt Arabic to keep their jobs, and a high level of continuity still characterized administrative practices. At the same time, Muslims, both Arab and non-Arab, became part of the administrative community and contributed to the Islamization of a governmental culture of diverse origins. Although the Umayyad administration seems decentralized and rudimentary in comparison with that of their 'Abbasid successors, it is largely thanks to their efforts that the 'Abbasids could inherit an Islamic empire at all.

Despite their achievements, the Umayyads became notorious for a number of actions which irrevocably tarnished their reputation and paved the way for the 'Abbasid revolution in 750. The first of these was Mu'awiya's decision to nominate his son Yazid as his successor, thereby introducing hereditary rule to the caliphate. This may have been an honest decision in the sense that Mu'awiya might genuinely have felt that his legacy was safest with Yazid, but many Muslims felt uncomfortable with the very idea of Yazid's accession. Al-Tabari even has Mu'awiya's right-hand man, Ziyad, worrying about it and confiding to another advisor: 'Mu'awiya hopes for the people's agreement and asks for my advice. Support for Islam and its security is important, while Yazid is easy-going and neglectful, given his devotion to hunting!' This other advisor wisely suggested secretly informing Yazid of his father's quandary and recommending that he mend his ways, which he supposedly did.[14] However, according to a circular attributed to the 'Abbasid caliph al-Ma'mun (r. 813–33), and brought out of the archives again in the 890s as part of a drive against lingering popular respect for the Umayyads, this was Mu'awiya's most nefarious act, indicating his 'disdainful attitude to the religion of God, manifested in his calling God's servants to acknowledge the succession of his son, Yazid, that arrogant drunken sot, that owner of cocks, cheetahs, and monkeys'.[15]

Such vitriol was not really about Yazid but the anomaly of the caliphate becoming hereditary in a clan other than the family of the Prophet, the 'people of the house' (*ahl al-bayt*), which included not only 'Ali and Fatima's surviving son, Husayn, but also a plethora of cousins, uncles and nephews who were all part of the extended kin-group which Arabs of the time considered 'family'. When Yazid succeeded his father in 680, a reaction from 'Ali's younger son Husayn, now head of the 'Alid clan, was not long in coming, leading to the second Umayyad step towards infamy. Husayn decided to militarily challenge Yazid in an episode reminiscent of his father 'Ali's fateful encounter with Mu'awiya 23 years before and started a rebellion in Kufa. This time around, the Umayyad caliph did not personally participate but ordered the governor of Iraq to quell Husayn's uprising.

As the Umayyad force approached, Husayn's lukewarm supporters melted away, leaving him isolated with a few family and friends on the dry and dusty plain of Karbala', with the mirage of the Euphrates shimmering in the far distance, taunting the exhausted and thirsty band who had been prevented from drinking by Umayyad forces. Despite the hesitation of many of the soldiers when faced with the prospect of harming members of the Prophet's family, a massacre ensued in which the Prophet's grandson and many of his descendants were murdered in cold blood. The battle is recounted by al-Tabari as a series of shameful and tragic vignettes: Husayn's radiant sister, Zaynab, pleading for mercy as the women's tents were set on fire; his teenage nephew, al-Qasim, struck down by a sword blow to his head, carried off the field by his grieving uncle, 'the two feet of the boy leaving tracks in the ground while Husayn held his breast close to his own'; and, most poignantly of all, Husayn's infant son, killed by a stray arrow as he sat on his father's lap before the final onslaught in which Husayn himself died fighting bravely.[16]

Although Yazid is said to have wept when he discovered the extent of the killing and treated well the surviving women and children who were brought to Damascus, this act blackened the name of the Umayyads forever among the Shi'a and generated consternation and ambivalence among the Muslim community as a whole. That said, it is noteworthy that the amount of real political fall-out from this event was small, and a greater challenge to Yazid's authority came from the Hijaz, where Ibn Zubayr, the son of one of 'Ali's opponents at the Battle of the Camel, declared himself caliph in support of the Medinese rather than Umayyad version of the caliphate. Yazid died trying to evict Ibn Zubayr from Mecca, and his teenage son followed him to the grave shortly afterwards – divine retribution for his killing of Husayn in the eyes of some – but even this succession of blows did not destroy the Umayyad caliphate, which passed instead to the Marwanid branch of the clan who consolidated their hold on power. The Umayyads' tenacity suggests that despite their later vilification in the historical record and the later religious significance of Husayn's death as a martyr for Shi'i Muslims, their claim to the caliphate as the clan of 'Uthman was acceptable to many Muslims at the time, a view confirmed by repeated 'Abbasid attempts to discredit their predecessors for the next century and a half.

While the 'Alid and Umayyad clans competed for the caliphate, Muslim armies continued to bring more of the ancient world under Islamic rule. To the east, Muslim forces moved steadily across the Iranian plateau into Khurasan and crossed the Oxus into Central Asia, a region known in Arabic as *ma warra al-nahr* (that which lies beyond the river), an almost exact translation of its older Graeco-Roman name of Transoxania, the land across the Oxus. Traders and soldiers also advanced southeastwards into Sind in India, possibly following the trade routes already established in Sasanian times. To the west, the governor of Egypt initiated the conquest of Byzantium's North African holdings in Tunisia, which became the Muslim province of Ifriqiya, the Arabic word for Africa. Muslim forces then advanced slowly across the rest of North Africa to the Byzantine outposts of Ceuta and Tangiers. In the early eighth century they crossed the Straits of Gibraltar into Visigothic Spain which they captured in a series of campaigns from 711 to 714, stopping at the old Roman *limes* south of the rugged rain-swept mountains of Galicia and the Basque country. These conquests were often quite superficial, combining the capture of key settlements or the establishment of garrison towns with deals struck with local rulers – Visigothic nobles, Persian kings and Turkic warlords – which gave them autonomy in return for recognition and tribute. This light touch had its advantages and, despite extended periods of resistance in some areas, the conquests everywhere marked the inexorable advance of Islam and the ultimate fading away of the old ways during the ensuing 'Abbasid era.

The Umayyad century came to an end as a result of vicious infighting within the Umayyad clan itself and broader changes in the social and political circumstances of the now vast Islamic empire. The Umayyads' enemies accused them of developing delusions of grandeur, of styling themselves 'God's deputies on earth' in the manner of Byzantine emperors, whilst living dissolute and frivolous lives in their luxurious Syrian desert palaces, at odds with the piety and simplicity of the early Muslim community in Medina. There was some truth to these accusations: al-Walid II (r. 743–44) was notorious for his hedonistic lifestyle, his wine drinking in the company of beautiful young men and women, and his passionate poetry. His uncle, the dour but effective caliph Hisham (r. 724–43), is said to have greatly regretted his nomination as heir, and al-Tabari sums up the situation in the following tart lines:

> We have already given some account of al-Walid b. Yazid, mentioning his immorality, his wantonness and his flippant and frivolous attitude towards religion before he became caliph. When his accession came ... he only persisted all the more in his pursuit of idle sport and pleasures, hunting, drinking wine and keeping company with libertines.[17]

More seriously, al-Walid's negligence triggered disputes within the family, his own murder by his cousin Yazid and fatal internecine strife, but it would be quite unfair to ignore the underlying reasons for the replacement of the Umayyads by the 'Abbasids. The Umayyad rise to power had been a triumph for the Meccan aristocracy, and their regime had a strongly Arab as well as Islamic identity. Top positions were reserved for Arabs while their clients and other non-Arabs tended to be looked down upon. To preserve such an elitist attitude, the numerically small Arab ruling class would have needed to at least maintain its own cohesion but, as the empire expanded, tensions which had been present in Arabia from the pre-Islamic period coalesced in the form of a long-running feud between the northern Arabs, known collectively as Qays or Mudar, and the southern Arabs, known collectively as Yemen. Qaysi–Yemeni conflict is a recurrent trope in the sources and, although exactly what the Qays and Yemen labels meant changed according to the political circumstances in a particular locality, the division frequently caused damaging factionalism among the Arab elite.

While the Arabs fought among themselves, a much more potentially dangerous rift began to open between the Arab community as a whole and the ever-growing number of non-Arab converts to Islam whom the Arabs viewed in much the same way as the Greeks and Romans had viewed those whose mother tongue was neither Greek nor Latin. Muslims of Arab ancestry greeted the conversion of such people with a great deal of ambivalence. Contrary to the popular myth that Islam was spread by the sword, many Muslim Arabs believed that it was their mission to conquer the world, not change the faith of its inhabitants, and saw Islam as theirs, the religion of the ruling elite, not of their subjects. Although they wanted to convert all the Arabs, they showed little desire or compunction to convert the peoples of the other lands they had conquered, a sentiment reinforced by their belief that Islam was a sister religion to Judaism and Christianity, and that tolerance should therefore be shown to Jews and Christians who were categorized as fellow peoples of God's book, which had taken material form as the Torah, the Gospels and finally the Qur'an. Similar privileges were extended to Zoroastrians and other religious communities.

Muslim tolerance came at a price: non-Muslim communities were free to practise their faith as long as they submitted to Islamic political authority and paid a poll tax called the *jizya*. The basic principles of the covenant (*dhimma*) offered to them were derived from the Qur'an, but their elaboration is attributed to the second caliph, 'Umar, and his Umayyad namesake, 'Umar II, to whom the famous Pact of 'Umar (*c.* 717), outlining the regulations to which the Christians of Syria should adhere, is attributed. Interestingly enough, the many and varied medieval versions of this pact suggest that Umayyad and early 'Abbasid practice may well have been based on the Theodosian and Justinian codes on the one hand and Sasanian regulations on the other. Even this quintessentially Islamic institution was thus rooted in previous Middle Eastern ways of handling minorities. Both religious and financial considerations therefore encouraged the Arabs to conceptualize the Umayyad empire as one in which Arab Muslims ruled and taxed non-Arab practitioners of other faiths. Indeed, the association between Arab ethnicity and rule was so strong that they found it easier to offer tax exemptions to Arabs, regardless of their religion, than to non-Arab Muslims!

The one exception to this generally pragmatic approach was the Muslim response to belief systems they considered pagan, following on from Muhammad's long struggle against the pagans of Mecca which had led him to completely reject their beliefs as the very antithesis of Islam and a sure path to eternal damnation. When the Muslims encountered such 'pagans' in North Africa and Central Asia, the religious toleration they offered was much more limited than in predominantly Christian or Zoroastrian areas such as Mesopotamia, Syria or Spain. As is so often the case, there was a political dimension to this apparently religious distinction. In the sedentary heartlands of the Byzantine and Sasanian empires, Christian, Zoroastrian and Jewish communities were largely civilian and left warfare to the imperial armies. Therefore, people offered relatively little opposition to the Islamic conquests, which they appear to have viewed as the simple swapping of one set of masters for another. In contrast, the pagan fringe was for the most part tribal and every man – and some women – were armed and ready to fight rather than be subjected to any master at all. Just as the Arabs prided themselves on their freedom from servitude to either the land or other men, so too did the Berbers and Turks, and it was they who offered the most concerted resistance to the Arab-Muslim conquerors and elicited least tolerance for their beliefs in nature spirits and local deities. Not only were they denied religious freedom, they were also subjected to slavery if captured in war and required to pay their new masters in human tribute, often young women for the enjoyment of the Arab elite.

However, Arab chauvinism aside, Islam also contained a universalist impulse, and the Prophet had not limited conversion only to Arabs. While this did not mean that conversion was encouraged among those who submitted without a fight, it was offered to the many captives taken during military engagements across the Middle East and North Africa. Because the overlap between Muslim and Arab identity remained so pervasive, such captives were not simply converted but were also assimilated to the Arab tribal structure as clients (*mawali*) of individual Arabs or tribes. Even though capture and/or conversion were not absolutely essential to become an Arab client, the large numbers of people who did become clients by this route meant that *mawali* as a collective term quickly came to be a synonym for non-Arab Muslims. Clients were particularly prominent in the bureaucracy, because they had the clerical skills which Arabs by and large lacked, and in the army, where they either served in the entourages of their patrons or as recruits in their own right.

In some areas like Khurasan in northeastern Iran and North Africa, converted war captives and indigenous clients hugely outnumbered Arab Muslims. In the case of the Berbers, Christianity had made little headway outside Byzantine areas and Judaism was so modified by local beliefs and practices as to be almost indistinguishable from the paganism of the majority. Moreover the tribes fought bitterly against the Arabs and only submitted after their military inferiority had been repeatedly demonstrated. Once that had been achieved, however, whole tribes switched to the Muslim side, creating a huge pool of captives and clients of nominally Muslim faith. Some measure of the extent of conversion is provided by the sources describing the circumstances leading up to the conquest of Visigothic Spain in 711. The army is said to have numbered between 7,000 and 12,000 men but three years before, Musa b. Nusayr, the governor of Ifriqiya, who is sometimes described as an Umayyad client of eastern origin himself, left his Berber client Tariq b. Ziyad in charge of Morocco with fewer than 30 Arabs to whom he entrusted the task of instructing the Berbers in their new faith. Although the figures must be taken with a large pinch of salt, Berbers clearly outnumbered Arabs many times over.

The clients of eminent Arab commanders shared in the status of their masters and could hold positions of authority and power, as the example of Musa's client Tariq b. Ziyad highlights, but the Arabs considered clients in general to be of lower status than themselves and, as the Umayyad century proceeded, the latter began to resent the 'massive prejudice against them' and become amenable to Islamic doctrines which emphasized the equality of all Muslims – especially in matters of distribution of booty and taxation – and meritocratic forms of leadership over Arab monopolization of power.[18] Since identity in Muslim society at this time was determined solely by paternity, there were also many 'Arabs' whose mothers were non-Arab and who may have felt some affinity with the clients and with doctrines of Muslim egalitarianism, as well as an embryonic cohort of religious scholars who perceived Arab attitudes as contrary to the spirit of Islam.

One group promoting a more egalitarian approach were the Kharijites who had proved to be 'Ali's nemesis. Kharijite preachers from the garrison towns of southern Iraq, Kufa and Basra spread across the Umayyad empire and found a ready audience in the Muslim camp towns of North Africa, where hundreds if not thousands of Berber clients congregated under the command of a handful of Arabs. In this sort of environment, Kharijite discourse asserting the equality of all Muslims and the importance of choosing a caliph who was the best-qualified Muslim regardless of his ancestry was very appealing, and in 739 a major Kharijite revolt against the Umayyads erupted across North Africa, temporarily cutting off Umayyad Spain from the Middle East. Although the revolt simmered down after a year, the Umayyads never really managed to regain control of North Africa and, as they tried to reassert their authority over the wayward west, a new and more dangerous rebellion, the 'Abbasid revolution, began to brew in Khurasan on the northeastern frontier. It gained momentum in the late 740s soon after al-Walid II had begun to squander the Umayyad patrimony and create dissension in his clan.

The rise of the 'Abbasids

Broadly speaking, the appeal of the 'Abbasid revolution was the same as that of the Kharijite revolt in North Africa: it offered a fairer Islamic order in which Muslims, whatever their origin, would be able to participate on equal terms. However, the propagandists of the 'Abbasid movement asserted that this could only be achieved if the caliphate was held by a member of the Prophet's family, the *ahl al-bayt*, in contrast to the Kharijite position that the best man should be caliph regardless of his origin. The movement was highly successful because its chief representative in Khurasan, a client of the 'Abbasids called Abu Muslim, did not state which member of the Prophet's house would be elevated to the caliphate. This prevented squabbling and faction-fighting between supporters of the different scions of the *ahl al-bayt*, who included the male descendants of Hasan and Husayn and also more distant relatives of the Prophet such as the 'Abbasids themselves, who were the descendants of one of his uncles.

It is worth reiterating that the Muslims remained a minority of the population at this time, and although the 'Abbasid revolution involved individuals of mixed Arab and non-Arab parentage, given the substantial number of Arabs who had taken local women as wives and concubines and the presence of non-Arab-Muslim clients, it did not necessarily involve the population as a whole. It was decisive not because it was a mass movement but because it affected the key institution of the early Islamic empire – the army. Although there is some debate over the composition of the armies in Khurasan, and whether the Khurasani supporters of the 'Abbasid revolution were predominantly Arabs or Persian clients, the fact remains that by the late 740s they were marching west through Iran to Iraq with the black banners of the 'Abbasids aloft to seize power from the Umayyads in the name of the family of the Prophet and the integrity of Islam.

In 748 they captured Kufa, a garrison town with historically strong 'Alid sympathies, but the Umayyads retaliated by arresting and killing the head of the 'Abbasid clan, Ibrahim b. Muhammad, whose identity was probably betrayed by a disgruntled revolutionary. For a brief moment, supporters of the 'Alids and 'Abbasids competed for control of the revolution but in 749 'Abbasid agents successfully put forward Ibrahim's brother, Abu'l-'Abbas, as the new caliph. From a later perspective, the choice of the 'Abbasids over the 'Alids, who were much closer relatives of the Prophet, seems strange but, as the historian Hugh Kennedy has pointed out, their claim to the caliphate probably appeared quite strong at the time, given the broad understanding of 'family' current in the eighth century and their support from the Muslims of Khurasan which made their bid for power feasible.[19] It is also true that the assumption of power by the better-known descendants of 'Ali and Fatima would not have benefited Abu Muslim, who was the real leader of the Khurasani armies, and he remained committed to the 'Abbasids. However, the sidelining of the lineal descendants of 'Ali could not help but alienate their supporters and ensured that the 'Abbasids would face sporadic 'Alid opposition for many years to come. From the ideological perspective it also contributed to the evolution of a Shi'i sacred history, in which the line of 'Ali and Fatima repeatedly suffered martyrdom and betrayal at the hands of the Muslim majority.

Having consolidated their position in Kufa and proclaimed Abu'l-'Abbas al-Saffah caliph, the 'Abbasid armies marched north through Mesopotamia and defeated the last Umayyad caliph, Marwan II, in battle alongside the river Zab which flows into the Tigris. An eyewitness reported:

> We encountered Marwan at the Zab and the Syrians attacked us as if they were a mountain of iron. Then we crouched and extended our lances and they turned from us like a cloud of dust and God gave us their backs.[20]

Marwan himself fled to Egypt but was captured and killed six months later. Meanwhile the 'Abbasids took Damascus and massacred all the Umayyad men they could get hold of at Ramla in Palestine – 72 according to al-Tabari.[21] The most famous escapee was 'Abd al-Rahman, grandson of al-Walid II's predecessor as caliph, Hisham, who fled west in the hope of finding refuge amongst the Nafza Berbers, the people of his mother, one of the many Berber slave girls sent to the Umayyad court as concubines. Seven years later 'Abd al-Rahman crossed the Straits of Gibraltar to Spain, the furthest outpost of the Islamic empire, and after many years of internal fighting established an independent Umayyad principality which for the next 200 years neither recognized not rejected the hegemony of the 'Abbasids in the Middle East but remained culturally connected to their empire in myriad ways.

Once they had disposed of Marwan II and his Umayyad relatives, the 'Abbasids pushed west from Egypt into Ifriqiya, modern Tunisia, and in 761 recaptured the important garrison town of Qayrawan which was in the hands of Kharijites. Ifriqiya, however, proved to be the political limit of the 'Abbasid empire in the west. They were obliged to leave the immense fertile coastal plains, mountains and deserts of the rest of the Maghrib in the hands of a cluster of autonomous city-states which were the fruit of the Kharijite revolt two decades before. Instead the 'Abbasids turned their attention east to Iraq, Iran, Khurasan and Transoxania, from where they drew the majority of their military resources, and Syria, Egypt and Tunisia became their western Mediterranean flank.

Even in this area, however, the new caliphs faced challenges to their rule both from the pro-Umayyad Syrians and from their own client, the real leader of the revolution, Abu Muslim, whose immense popularity threatened their hold on power, especially in his homeland of Khurasan where 'the people are his men, completely obedient to him, and they hold him in the highest awe'.[22] Matters came to a head shortly after the accession of the second 'Abbasid caliph, Abu Ja'far al-Mansur (r. 754–75), when Abu Muslim performed the pilgrimage to Mecca and used it as a public relations exercise to win over the Arabs as well as the Persians by 'fulfilling the needs of supplicants, giving garments to desert Arabs and bestowing largesse upon whoever petitioned him' as well as digging wells and improving the road for pilgrims.[23] He then tried to return to Khurasan without giving his regards to the caliph. Al-Mansur was furious and sent his agents armed with all manner of blandishments to persuade Abu Muslim to come and make his peace. Despite his deep misgivings, Abu Muslim complied and the two met outside the old Sasanian capital of Ctesiphon in al-Mansur's tent where the caliph berated the 'Abbasids' most important supporter and then clapped his hands to summon the killers waiting outside who quickly butchered Abu Muslim with their swords. To prevent a Khurasani uprising after this audacious and treacherous act, al-Mansur quickly reassured the lords of Khurasan of his goodwill towards them and distributed largesse among the troops, leaving those with a conscience to lament that they had sold Abu Muslim for dirhams.

Having consolidated his political position, al-Mansur confirmed the new geopolitical reorientation of the 'Abbasid caliphate by transferring the caliphal capital from Damascus in Syria to Iraq, where it remained for the duration of the caliphate. After a series of false starts, al-Mansur initiated the construction of a new royal capital called rather optimistically the 'City of Peace' near the old Sasanian imperial agglomeration of Ctesiphon and a village called Baghdad, which ultimately became the name of the city itself. The new imperial establishment was economically supported by the Sawad, the rich alluvial plains of the Tigris and Euphrates, which were tilled by local inhabitants and black slaves, many of whom had the unenviable task of scraping the salt from the flood plains of the lower Euphrates to prepare it for the cultivation of sugar cane. The land of Mesopotamia had been tilled for millennia and the early 'Abbasids benefited greatly from the intricate irrigation systems and canals constructed by their Sasanian predecessors. They also used the excellent riverine communications in the vicinity of Baghdad to bring money, goods and food into the city from the rest of their empire.

The chequered political fortunes of the 'Abbasids over the next five centuries make it wise to divide their caliphate into several phases: the early 'Abbasid caliphate from the mid-eighth to the early ninth centuries; the middle 'Abbasid caliphate, when the caliphs created a new Turkish army and moved to Samarra for half a century; the so-called Shi'i century from the mid-ninth to mid-tenth centuries, during which the caliphs became virtual prisoners of Shi'i warlords called the Buyids, and the Shi'i Fatimids created a rival caliphate ruling Tunisia, Egypt and southern Syria; and the ensuing Saljuq sultanate, when the Saljuq Turks wielded effective power in Baghdad, relegating the caliphs to a ceremonial role. During this last phase the Fatimids continued to rule Egypt, but the Maghrib and Spain passed into the hands of the Almoravids, who somewhat unexpectedly acknowledged the 'Abbasids as their sovereigns, and then into the hands of the Almohads, who did not. Both the Almoravids and Almohads battled the rising power of Catholic Castile and Aragon on Islam's western frontier while the Latin Crusades to the Holy Land commenced in the 1090s. In the west, the great Muslim cities of Toledo (1085), Cordoba (1236) and Seville (1248) passed permanently into Christian hands. In the east, the Muslims turned the Christian tide and the Latins were finally expelled from Syria in 1291, 33 years after the death of the last 'Abbasid caliph in Baghdad, when the universal caliphate had become the stuff of legend and deep nostalgia.

The early 'Abbasid caliphate

The early 'Abbasid caliphate, between Abu'l-'Abbas al-Saffah's defeat of the Umayyads in 750 and al-Mu'tasim's transfer of the court from Baghdad to Samarra shortly after his accession in 833, was a time of Islamic political consolidation and centralization which built on Umayyad foundations to give the Islamic empire a sophisticated central government and provincial administration for the first time. The 'Abbasids presided over the maturation of the early Islamic empire from a state supported by the fruits of conquest – tribute, booty and slaves – to one supported by the taxation of land, produce and people. During this period revenues flowed into caliphal coffers and even the governors of the frontier provinces, who always insisted that they needed to spend taxes locally to adequately defend Islamic borders, felt obliged to show some deference in the form of remittances to their master in Baghdad. Much of this was made possible by the fact that the early 'Abbasids were able to supplement the now fractious Arab fighting force of the conquest era with a loyal and experienced army from Khurasan, which they dispatched to garrison every province and monitor the situation on behalf of the caliphs. Their control over the provinces was facilitated by their development of a fast and effective postal and intelligence service, the 'Abbasid *barid*, which was more sophisticated than any of its antique forerunners and whose relay stations still dot the desert landscapes between Syria and Iraq. The caliphs were frequently indebted to the riders who sped from one end of the empire to the other, getting a fresh horse at each stop, bringing vital communications back and forth, transporting money and important persons and even on occasion ice and exotic fruits for the caliph's table.[24]

Like the army, the new 'Abbasid administration was also heavily supported by eastern converts to Islam from Mesopotamia and Iran, who brought their experience of Sasanian government to complement the Byzantine strand already introduced by the Umayyads. Although Arabic remained the language of government as a whole, the 'Abbasids fulfilled their promise of a fairer society for Muslims of non-Arab origin by presiding over the emergence of a new governing elite composed of Muslims of all backgrounds. Arabized Persians fared particularly well as a result of their support of the 'Abbasid revolution, and lineages such as the Barmakids, descendants of the high priests of the Buddhist temple of Nawbahar near Balkh, played an important role in formulating a new Islamic statecraft imbued with Sasanian Persian elements. The counterside of the formation of a new Muslim government elite was a gradual decline in the number of Greek and Aramaic-speaking Christians, Zoroastrians and Jews in the civil service. This tendency did not reflect deliberately intolerant policies on the part of the 'Abbasids but the steady conversion of Christian, Zoroastrian and, to a much lesser extent, Jewish lineages to Islam. The reasons behind such conversions are opaque but, as the pool of potential Muslim government employees grew, non-Muslims probably felt pressure to convert in order to maximize their chances of a position.

Despite the firm administrative and military foundations of the early 'Abbasid caliphate, the caliphs were faced with a number of political difficulties. They needed to manage the ever thorny matter of the succession, maintain the loyalty and stability of the army, and quell or at least control the hostility of the supporters of the 'Alids – objectives which were in many ways interrelated. The succession to the caliphate had been a source of conflict since the death of the Prophet because of the potentially boundless authority it represented, both in this world and the next, and the lack of guidelines on the matter from Muhammad himself. It was not simply a question of who had the right to rule but also of how the right ruler should be selected and, increasingly, what political constituencies he represented. By the mid-eighth century, hereditary rule had been grudgingly accepted, but primogeniture had not. In tacit recognition of the necessity that a candidate should be suitable for the position, it was generally believed that the ruling caliph should designate which of his male relatives was to succeed him. The Umayyads had followed this principle of designation (*nass*) and it was also adopted by the Shi'i *imam*s.

The 'Abbasids took the same line, but this did not prevent challenges from other men in the family when a caliph died and his nominee assumed power. On occasion, 'Abbasid caliphs nominated two successors as an insurance policy in case the first nominee died or as a way of satisfying the ambitions of two potential heirs. This proved very counter-productive in practice, as new caliphs routinely attempted to undo the order of succession prescribed by their predecessor in favour of their own nominees – usually their sons – to which the ousted heirs did not always respond well. The stakes were made even higher by the fact that princes quickly became identified with competing regions of the empire, notably Iraq and Khurasan, and rival factions, usually the civilian bureaucrats versus the military commanders. As a result, succession struggles had empire-wide political significance and eventually led to civil war.

The first caliph, Abu'l-'Abbas al-Saffah, nominated his brother Abu Ja'far and named his nephew 'Isa b. Musa second in line to the caliphate, a decision opposed by his uncle 'Abd Allah b. 'Ali, who felt that his commitment and service to the revolution entitled him to the ultimate reward. When Abu Ja'far became caliph in 754, taking the regnal name al-Mansur, he altered the succession from 'Isa to his son Muhammad, who became caliph with the regnal title al-Mahdi in 775. 'Isa, assisted by a generous pay-off, had the good grace to let this pass. However, when al-Mahdi nominated his sons Musa al-Hadi and Harun al-Rashid as successive heirs it led to a barely masked struggle for power which culminated in Musa's suspicious death in 786 after just over a year as caliph, possibly at the instigation of his own mother, Khayzuran, who seems to have preferred his brother Harun. Although Musa may well have died of natural causes, al-Tabari also reports the gossip that the strong-willed Khayzuran had 'assumed sole control over matters of ordaining and forbidding'[25] during al-Mahdi's reign and expected to have the same influence over her son, who became increasingly frustrated by the tendency of the army chiefs to go to his mother rather than to him and by her overbearing attitude in his presence. A furious row erupted, after which Khayzuran uttered neither a 'sweet or bitter word' to Musa for the rest of his short life, which she was rumoured to have ordered a slave girl to terminate by smothering him with a pillow.

Harun succeeded his brother and proved to be more malleable, or tactful, towards Khayzuran until her death in 790. Harun al-Rashid was caliph for the period celebrated in *The Thousand and One Nights* and presided over the 'Abbasid empire at its height, when the word 'Baghdad' evoked opulence and splendour as far west as the court of the Carolingians. His plans for the succession, however, triggered the great 'Abbasid civil war between his sons Muhammad al-Amin and 'Abd Allah al-Ma'mun, which permanently altered the political character of the caliphate. The plan was that Muhammad al-Amin should become caliph and control Iraq and the western flank of the empire while 'Abd Allah al-Ma'mun would take over the governorship of Khurasan in the east and eventually succeed his brother as caliph. Harun al-Rashid made the arrangements public on a pilgrimage to Mecca accompanied by the two princes, who took oaths in the Ka'ba that they would uphold their father's wishes. A third prince, al-Qasim, was later added to the list and given the northern provinces on the Byzantine frontier to govern.

Any prince of the 'Abbasid clan who wished to compete for the caliphate naturally needed political allies and military backing. They sought them among the plethora of political players to be found in Baghdad and the provinces, of whom the foremost were from Khurasan. However, the Khurasani supporters of the caliphate had split into two factions after the foundation of Baghdad. On the one hand, many had moved to Baghdad with their families to serve as the caliph's standing army in the capital, where they were known collectively as the 'sons of the dynasty' (*abna al-dawla*). They were very keen to be supported by revenues from back home in Khurasan, and ensuring their remuneration and satisfaction was of paramount importance to any caliph. However, important local Khurasani families who had not migrated to Baghdad did not feel that their erstwhile countrymen should be able to draw revenues from the province at the expense of those who remained there, creating tensions between the elites of Khurasan and Iraq, despite their common origins. The civilian bureaucratic corps, composed of

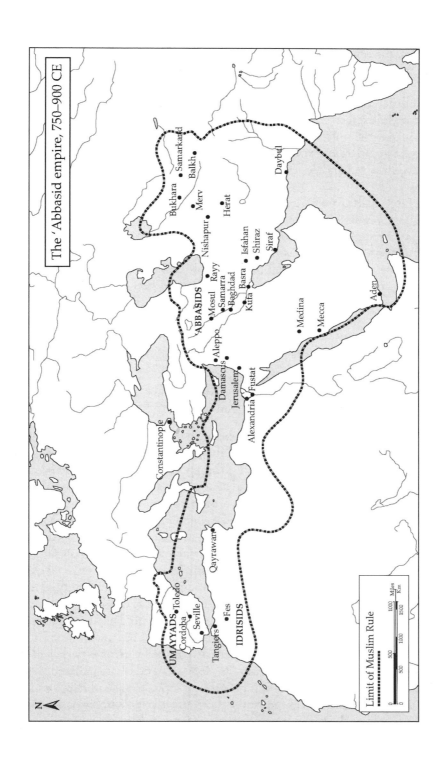

The 'Abbasid empire, 750–900 CE

ABBASIDS

UMAYYADS
IDRISIDS

Toledo
Cordoba
Seville
Tangiers
Fes
Qayrawan

Constantinople

Aleppo
Damascus
Jerusalem
Alexandria
Fustat

Mosul
Samarra
Baghdad
Kufa
Basra

Rayy
Nishapur
Isfahan
Shiraz
Siraf

Bukhara
Merv
Herat

Samarkand
Balkh

Daybul

Medina
Mecca

Aden

N

Limit of Muslim Rule

Miles
Km
0   500   1000
0   500   1000   1500

scribes, financial officials and ministers of varied background, was a third important political grouping whose leaders also wished to determine how the 'Abbasid empire was run. The precise political agendas of the bureaucrats differed, but generally they wanted revenues to come to Baghdad but not for the exclusive benefit of the military. Conversely the Arabs who had dominated the politics of the Umayyad caliphate were gradually absorbed into the population, except in such outposts of the Islamic world as Spain, where Umayyad and Arab identity remained pre-eminent for several centuries.

Harun al-Rashid endeavoured to avoid a clash by his elaborate division of labour between his sons, but in the process he made each the figurehead of a rival faction. Al-Amin had close ties to the civilian elite of Baghdad, while al-Ma'mun was the champion of the lords of Khurasan, and it was only a matter of time before trouble broke out. People differed in their opinions of Harun al-Rashid's dispensation: 'When he divided the earth between his three sons, some of the masses of the common people said, "he has made the fabric of the state firm", but others said, "On the contrary, he has given full rein to their propensities for clashing among themselves,"' or, in the words of a prescient contemporary poet:

And he has sown among them recurring warfare
And has made easy the way for their avoidance of each other
So woe to the subjects in the near future.[26]

When al-Amin became caliph in 809, he initially intended to uphold his father's wishes but, according to al-Tabari, his devious minister Fadl b. al-Rabi', who was on bad terms with al-Ma'mun, 'strove to incite' the new caliph against his brother and 'urged him to depose him and divert the succession to his own son, Musa'.[27] This forced al-Ma'mun into opposition and a full-blown civil war erupted. Al-Amin appeared to hold all the cards but al-Ma'mun had Tahir, a resourceful member of the Khurasani aristocracy, by his side, who proved his worth by defeating the army of al-Amin and successfully besieging Baghdad in 812–13. In the chaotic last days of the siege, al-Amin attempted to surrender but as he came from his palace in his caliphal robes and entered the skiff which was to take him across the Tigris, Tahir's men overturned the boat, captured the bedraggled caliph and had him ignominiously killed in a small cell. His death left al-Ma'mun as undisputed caliph. To begin with, he tried to rule the 'Abbasid empire from his governorial seat in Merv but, as chaos and anarchy enveloped Baghdad, he realized that to be caliph meant to reside in Iraq. He duly moved to Baghdad in 818 and has come to be remembered as one of the more effective and ambitious 'Abbasid caliphs, despite the regicide and fratricide committed in his name.

The war broke the power of the Khurasani faction in Baghdad and discredited al-Amin's civilian supporters. Henceforth the chief ministers of the caliphs wielded less influence, and lineages from the provinces, such as the descendants of Tahir, held a greater share of power. On the military front, the Khurasan contingents ceased to perform as satisfactorily as they had done, and al-Ma'mun and his brother, later the caliph al-Mu'tasim, began to rely on alternative military resources in the form of Turks, a large proportion of whom were slaves. This marked the beginning of a profound transition in the 'Abbasid military from a seasonal army of Arab tribesmen and non-Arab clients to a professional force of slave Turks whose commanders played a decisive role in caliphal politics during the ninth century.

Al-Ma'mun's most memorable policies, however, related to the relationship between the caliphate and the 'Alids on the one hand, and the caliphate's religious status vis-à-vis the increasingly cohesive community of religious scholars called the *'ulama'* on the other. 'Alid opposition was a political challenge which the 'Abbasids had faced from the outset and which duly manifested itself in a series of increasingly futile rebellions. The most threatening occurred in the early years of the reign of al-Mansur, when a descendant of Hasan called Muhammad b. 'Abd Allah rebelled in the Hijaz while his brother Ibrahim launched a sister rebellion in Basra. Like most rebellions centred in the now geographically peripheral cities of Mecca or Medina, Muhammad's revolt was crushed, but Ibrahim came close to success before being defeated a mere 60 miles from Baghdad by the caliph's nephew, 'Isa b. Musa. The stress of the moment is reflected in the description of al-Mansur by one of his officers, al-Hajjaj, who found him, 'like a solitary hawk, intensely concentrated, a man who has risen to meet the vicissitudes that have befallen him, facing up to them and contending with them'.[28]

The sixth Shi'i *imam*, Ja'far al-Sadiq, the foremost 'Alid of his generation, did not condone Ibrahim and Muhammad's two-pronged revolt and encouraged his followers to take a quietist path, but sporadic 'Alid rebellions continued to break out and challenge the 'Abbasids' right to the caliphate. Although the 'Abbasids did not hesitate to use a stick to break such rebellions when they occurred, they also tried a carrot from time to time. Al-Ma'mun took this the furthest when, in a striking departure from previous dynastic practice, he named the eighth Shi'i *imam*, 'Ali al-Rida, his heir in 817, and told his troops to swap their 'Abbasid black robes for green ones which symbolized Islam in a non-partisan way. The relationship between the two clans was sealed by betrothals between 'Ali and his son and two of al-Ma'mun's daughters. Although al-Tabari says that al-Ma'mun made his decision after he had 'given consideration to the members of the two houses of 'Abbas and 'Ali but had not found anyone more excellent, more pious, or more learned than 'Ali', it is not clear what he hoped to achieve by this move.[29]

On the one hand, 'Ali was not a young man and his chances of succeeding to the caliphate were slim, suggesting that the plan was designed to reconcile the 'Alids without any real cost. On the other hand, al-Ma'mun may have hoped that his goodwill gesture would affect a genuine reconciliation between the two families. His gesture was certainly taken seriously by those who opposed it, including other members of the 'Abbasid family, and in Baghdad itself his uncle Ibrahim set himself up as a counter-caliph in response. The situation was resolved in 818 when the unfortunate 'Ali 'ate an inordinate amount of grapes and suddenly died', or, as some sources would have it, was administered poison in a pomegranate at the command of a scheming or embarrassed al-Ma'mun.[30] In either case, the relieved population of Baghdad abandoned the counter-caliph Ibrahim, who was later discovered disguised as a woman and arrested, and renewed their oath to al-Ma'mun, who entered Baghdad shortly afterwards, having given up on the idea of ruling the empire from Merv.

Al-Ma'mun's forays into religious affairs were equally fraught. By the first decades of the ninth century, the question of the caliph's role, enshrined in the debate over whether he was God's deputy or the successor of the Prophet, was tipping towards the latter interpretation through the consolidation of a rather vocal and populist corps of religious scholars who believed that the interpretation of God's word and its application in all areas of life was their responsibility, not the caliph's. The scholars based their claim on their knowledge of the practice (*sunna*) of the Prophet, which had recently come to be recorded in a number of sayings (*hadith*). While no one disputed that the Prophet's example was important, the problem was that many *hadith* were fabrications and it was not always easy to sort the wheat from the chaff. Moreover the *hadith* scholars tended to be hostile to the fledgling group of Muslim theologians and philosophers who preferred to approach religion from a rational perspective, using tools acquired by the translation of Greek philosophical texts which had begun in earnest a few decades before.

Al-Ma'mun, an intellectual himself, encouraged the debates of theologians and philosophers at court in Baghdad but appears to have felt a deep distaste for the rabble-rousing *hadith* scholars outside the palace who not only threatened the theologians but also denied his right as caliph to pronounce on doctrinal matters. In 827 he threw down the gauntlet by declaring that all Muslims should adhere to the doctrine that the Qur'an was created. This doctrine was favoured by those of a more rational and philosophical bent on the grounds that to suppose the Qur'an was uncreated was to render it equal to God the Creator, an unsupportable proposition. The *hadith* scholars, however, upheld the view that the Qur'an was an eternal entity which had always been with God, and, in any case, contested the caliph's right to impose any doctrine at all, regardless of whether they agreed with it or not.

Shortly before his death in 833, al-Ma'mun went a step further and set up an inquiry (*mihna*) to insist that scholars and officials publicly adhere to the doctrine of the createdness of the Qur'an. Although often described as an inquisition, the *mihna* was nothing like as severe as the Spanish equivalent and did not routinely lead to executions – only one is recorded, and a few other scholars died in custody. During its 16-year course many hundreds of scholars were examined about their beliefs and the majority bowed to caliphal pressure but avoided giving a direct answer. The response of one such scholar, Abu Hasan al-Ziyadi, to the question, 'Is the Qur'an created?' may be taken as representative:

> The Qur'an is the word of God, and God is the creator of everything, all things apart from him are created. But the Commander of the Faithful is our Imam, and by means of him we have heard the whole sum of knowledge ... so if he commands us, we obey his orders; if he forbids us from doing something we desist; and if he calls upon us, we respond to him.[31]

The most famous dissenter was Ahmad b. Hanbal, founder of one of the Sunni schools of law, who was arrested and imprisoned by al-Ma'mun for reiterating that the Qur'an was the word of God rather than saying whether it was created or not, and answering 'I don't know' to further questions about the nature of God and His 'word'. He was later brought before al-Mu'tasim and a panel of theologians, jurists and other scholars to acknowledge the createdness of the Qur'an. According to al-Jahiz, he again avoided the issue by saying, 'I am no dialectition', and evaded the panel's questions until the frustrated caliph struck him.[32] His obstinacy before the caliph's men became legendary and was embellished as it was retold by Muslims receptive to such a trenchant parable about the brave resistance of the weak before the powerful, whatever their feelings on the doctrine of the createdness of the Qur'an.

The point at issue may seem rather abstract, but religion was a fertile ground for polemics in ninth-century Iraq and, just as complicated and subtly different positions on the nature of Christ had aroused furious passions in the fifth-century Byzantine church and state, so the exact relationship between reason and revelation and its implications for the nature of God was a bitterly fought point in Islamic intellectual life which also had ramifications for the status of the caliph. Al-Ma'mun's religious policy was an assertion of the caliph's right to be obeyed on doctrinal matters, but the *hadith* scholars argued that the Prophet's legacy was his practice, the *sunna*, as preserved in the *hadith* and that the caliphs' pretensions to be God's deputies on earth were an irreligious innovation introduced by the godless Umayyads. Ultimately the victory went to the scholars. Although al-Mu'tasim and his successor al-Wathiq did not officially back down, the inquisition was only occasionally enforced, and when it was quietly abandoned by al-Mutawakkil in the late 840s, the right to determine Islamic doctrine passed to the scholars, the representatives of the 'people of the *sunna*', or Sunnis, so called for their devotion to the *sunna* of the Prophet.

The Samarran interlude

In 833 al-Ma'mun died and his brother al-Mu'tasim became caliph after having served for several years as governor of Syria. Al-Mu'tasim was the architect of two major changes in the caliphate: the systematic recruitment of Turkish slave soldiers to replace the Arab and Khurasani troops of the early 'Abbasid era, and the transfer of the capital from Baghdad to a new site higher up the Tigris where he had the palatine city of Samarra built to house himself, the court and the new Turkish army. Although it is Baghdad which is synonymous with the 'Abbasid caliphate, for 60 years Samarra was its capital. It was an interlude which signalled the arrival of the Turks, alongside the Arabs and Persians as the makers of Islamic civilization and the start of a long process which transformed the 'Abbasid caliphs from rulers into figureheads.

The 'Abbasids' resort to slave soldiers has generated enduring controversy among historians who, working from the rather anachronistic perspective of the modern nation-state, have sought to determine why the Muslim 'nation' was forced to rely on outside military forces. Emphasis on the slave origins of the majority of the Turks and their coercion into the 'Abbasid army only heightens the contrast with more voluntaristic types of recruitment. However, the military use of outsiders, whether slaves or mercenaries, was hardly new to the Mediterranean and Middle East. What was distinctive in the 'Abbasid case was the almost complete substitution of the previous military structure, which depended on the military service of the Arab tribes and the Khurasani 'sons of the dynasty', with a new permanent army of Turkish cavalrymen, the majority of whom were purchased. The change was made more stark by the political role which the Turks also came to play, elbowing aside the civilian Persian ministers of preceding decades.

Turks had entered army ranks as clients from a very early period, but al-Mu'tasim decided to make much more extensive use of them at a time when the caliphate sorely needed good troops to resist Byzantine pressure on the northern frontier and to quell the numerous rebellions of the Khurrami-yya, a sect of Zoroastrianian parentage with an Islamic veneer, in Iran and Azerbayjan. He chose Turks for pragmatic reasons: they were skilful and hardy cavalrymen able to withstand enormous privations; they did not have commitments or loyalties to Muslim communities or factions which could interfere with their obedience to the caliph; and they were readily available in the slave markets of Transoxania. Most had been captured during the raids which were part and parcel of life in the Central Asian steppe but which seemed to have intensified during this era as a result of a rise of population in these high treeless lands. Competition for pasture was intense and Turkish tribes often came to blows, after which the vanquished continued their search for pasture, wandering southwards into Islamic territory while the victors carried their captives to slave markets in Merv, Samarkand or Bukhara. Conveniently these Turks were not Muslim at the time of their purchase. Although the Turkish tribes that journeyed south into Islamic lands often converted to Islam quite rapidly, the battling tribes of the steppe had their own shamans and spirits, and the captives were thus pagan, making their enslavement and sale legitimate according to Islamic law. The caliphate's appetite for Turkish youths and population pressure in the Turkish steppelands thus worked together to produce a steady flow of young and able cavalrymen into Iraq.

While the Turks were undoubtedly militarily effective, the creation of a majority Turkish army of non-Muslim origin had all kinds of unforeseen consequences, including the transfer of the capital from Baghdad to Samarra, the introduction of new politico-economic institutions such as land grants, and the insertion of a powerful new ethnic group into Islamic society. Soon after al-Mu'tasim began recruiting Turks it became obvious that the arrival of large numbers of rowdy cavalrymen in Baghdad was a recipe for disaster. The Khurasani 'sons of the dynasty' whom they replaced resented them, and the common people of Baghdad quickly reacted against their often drunken forays through the city:

> His Turkish slave retainers were continually finding [their comrades] …
> slain in their quarters. This arose from the fact that they were rough-mannered barbarians who used to ride their steeds and gallop through the streets of Baghdad, knocking down men and women and trampling children underfoot.[33]

The enraged old guard from Khurasan took matters into their own hands by dragging the Turks from their horses and accosting them, while an old man is said to have stood in al-Mu'tasim's path and accused him of bringing disaster to Baghdad by introducing his barbarians to the city. Meanwhile rebels of Indian origin in the Basra region, the Zutt, gloated over the discomfort of the Baghdadi population:

> You did not thank God for his previously vouchsafed goodness and were not mindful of His benefits, duly extolling Him.
> So summon help from the slaves, made up of the sons of your state, of Yazaman, of Balj, of Tuz,
> Of Ashnas, of Afshin, of Faraj, those [Turks] who are conspicuous in silk brocade and pure gold.[34]

The caliph himself was reluctant to see the Turks develop close links with the elite of Baghdad in case it undermined their loyalty to him and therefore decided to depart from his turbulent City of Peace and establish a new royal capital at Samarra where he, the court and his Turkish army could reside together, away from the tensions and nefarious influences present in Baghdad. In 834 his secretary Ahmad b. Khalid 'bought Samarra for 500 dirhams from the Christians who dwelt in the monastery' and 'purchased the site of the Khaqani garden for another 5000 dirhams plus a number of other places'.[35] Al-Mu'tasim gathered his slaves and left Baghdad in 835 and set up camp at the half-finished city of al-Qatul, started by his father Harun al-Rashid, before finally moving into the new palace at Samarra in 836 when the plaster was barely dry.

Samarra was a city of boundless grandeur which became a byword for royal splendour throughout the Islamic world. However, it also became a golden cage in which caliphs resided at the mercy of the Turkish *amir*s who commanded the loyalties of the troops and their families. Things began to go badly wrong in December 861 when the caliph al-Mutawakkil (r. 847–61) was assassinated after an evening of drinking in his palace by conspirators acting on behalf of his son al-Muntasir, whose unseemly haste to become caliph had caused his father to suggest that al-Musta'jil, 'the impatient', would be a better name than al-Muntasir, 'the victorious'. Four forgettable caliphs ruled in the next decade, brought to power and then brought down and often murdered by shifting alliances and factions of Turks.

The ability of the Turks to make and break caliphs during the Samarran interlude has been seen as a sign of the strength of the Turks but also of their insecurity and desperation to secure their wages. It was a vicious circle: a caliph who could pay was what the Turks craved, but as the caliphs became isolated and dependent upon their Turkish commanders their ability to extract revenues from the provinces decreased. At the same time, the fertile Sawad plains of Iraq were beginning to suffer from over-farming and yielded less than before. The main political outcome of the Samarran period was therefore not the strengthening of the caliphate through its possession of a strong and stable army but its weakening as provincial governors took the opportunity to assert their *de facto* independence from Iraq and establish local dynasties which acknowledged the 'Abbasids but paid them little practical heed. By the late ninth century the Samanids controlled Muslim Khurasan and Transoxania; much of Iran was ruled by a homegrown dynasty known as the Saffarids; in Egypt, the 'Abbasid governor Ibn Tulun ruled more or less autonomously; the Hamdanids controlled Aleppo and Mosul; and in Iraq itself, land exhaustion was exacerbated by a rebellion lasting from 869 to 883 which was supported by the Zanj, the black slaves who tilled the Sawad.

As a result, the 'Abbasid empire began to shift from a centralized to a more federal model, in which the caliphate was respected on a symbolic level but actual caliphs had limited political power beyond Iraq. This was perhaps a natural development given the vast size of the Islamic world by this stage but what stands out is the unstoppable cultural, intellectual and religious integration which proceeded alongside it, at least at the upper levels of society. Independent-minded governors still aped the culture of the centre, and when things went bad for people in Baghdad or Samarra they moved out to the provinces, taking the manners and customs of the capital with them. The most colourful example is Ziryab, an 'Abbasid court musician, who left Baghdad for Cordoba where he is credited with introducing urbane Iraqi haircuts, table manners and toiletries to the rough lords of the Umayyad court.

The Shi'i century

For much of the century after al-Ma'mun's brief flirtation with the idea of making 'Ali al-Rida his successor in 817, the Shi'a adopted a quietist stance, preferring to dissimulate their views than face persecution from the emerging Sunni majority. They had their own concerns to think about as they sought to elaborate their concept of Islamic leadership and develop a theology distinct from that of other Muslims. During this process their definition of the holy family narrowed down to the direct lineal descendants of Husayn, of whom one was designated by his predecessor as *imam* in each generation and was thus the true religious and political leader of all Muslims in contrast to the illegitimate Sunni caliph. However, this produced the unsettling prospect of the line dying out, a situation which first arose in the mid-eighth century when the sixth *imam*, Ja'far al-Sadiq, nominated his son Isma'il as his successor only to subsequently nominate another son, Musa, when Isma'il predeceased him. One group of Shi'is insisted that Isma'il's nomination could not be invalidated in this way and that the next *imam* should actually be Isma'il's son Muhammad and broke away from the rest of the community to form the Isma'ili or Sevener Shi'i sect. However, Isma'il's son, if he even existed, was a young boy and disappeared from sight shortly afterwards, apparently ending the line. The Twelver or Imami Shi'i majority faced the same problem a couple of generations later when their line of *imam*s died out with the disappearance of the twelfth *imam*, Muhammad al-Mahdi, in 874.

This proved unacceptable for both religious and political reasons and the Shi'is therefore asserted that the last *imam*, whether Muhammad b. Isma'il or Muhammad al-Mahdi, had not died but had left the earthly sphere to inhabit a divinely ordained space until his triumphant and messianic return to the world. For the Twelver majority the doctrine of the *imam*'s occultation (*ghayba*) legitimized the continuation of Ja'far al-Sadiq's quietist approach on the grounds that the Shi'is did not have a legitimate political leader on earth in the absence of the *imam*. The Isma'ilis, however, proved to be much more radical and militant and produced a number of movements in the late ninth to tenth centuries predicated on belief in the imminent return of their last *imam*, which greatly threatened the 'Abbasid caliphate.

The Isma'ilis burst on to the political stage in the late ninth century in the guise of an underground revolutionary movement dedicated to overthrowing the 'Abbasids on behalf of the soon-to-be-revealed *imam*. They were based in the Sawad of Iraq, the Arabian peninsula and Syria and known colloquially as the Qaramita after their leader and chief missionary Hamdan Qarmat. They gained support for their cause by sending out missionaries across the Middle East and North Africa. In the last days of the ninth century the mission split between the followers of Hamdan Qarmat and the mysterious 'Ubayd Allah, a figure accepted by his followers as the returned *imam* but described by others as merely a *hujja*, the *imam*'s representative on earth while he was in occultation. In order to avoid both the 'Abbasids and rival Isma'ilis, 'Ubayd Allah fled west into North Africa to the furthest reaches of the Islamic world, the oasis town of Sijilmasa on the edge of the Sahara in southern Morocco, founded by Kharijites 150 years earlier.

After 'Ubayd Allah's departure, the eastern Isma'ili movement splintered into several factions, but it went from strength to strength in the west where 'Ubayd Allah's most important supporter, the missionary 'Abd Allah al-Shi'i, successfully converted the Kutama Berbers of Tunisia to Isma'ili Shi'ism on his behalf. In 909 'Abd Allah collected 'Ubayd Allah from Sijilmasa for the long journey back across the desert edge to Qayrawan in Tunisia, which 'Ubayd Allah entered as the returned *imam* and true caliph of all Muslims. He and his descendants were known as the Fatimids to stress their true descent from Fatima, daughter of the Prophet, whatever their enemies might say to the contrary. It was their intention to conquer the entire Islamic world, replace the 'Abbasid caliphate with a Fatimid one, and introduce Isma'ili Shi'ism as the dominant form of Islam.

This was not to be. In the next decades, Fatimid expansion westwards into Morocco and Spain was countered by the Umayyads of Cordoba, who themselves assumed caliphal status in 929 as part of an ideological struggle with the Fatimids for the hearts and minds of the Berbers of Morocco and western Algeria. Fatimid expansion eastwards was more successful and their general Jawhar managed to secure Egypt in 969 and establish a base north of the great city of Fustat, which had developed from its origins as a Muslim garrison town into a thiving Mediterranean emporium. In 972 the entire Fatimid establishment was transferred lock, stock and barrel from Tunisia to Egypt and settled in al-Qahira, the Fatimid garrison town Jawhar had constructed north of Fustat. Over time al-Qahira, 'the victorious', rendered into English as Cairo, gave its name to the entire urban conurbation. It was the Fatimids' intention to use al-Qahira as the springboard for their conquest of Syria, Iraq and the Islamic lands further east, but they were unable to proceed beyond Palestine because of opposition from the Byzantines, who had taken the opportunity of the general anarchy in the Middle East to raid south from Asia Minor into Syria, regaining territories which had been in Muslim hands for two centuries. The Byzantines were resisted not by the might of the caliphal armies but by volunteer *mujahidun* who congregated in border towns like Tarsus, which was bursting with hostels built to house pious young fighters who wished to prove their devotion by defending the frontier.

The 'Abbasids were unable to offer any real opposition to either the Isma'ili Fatimids or the Byzantines, who together threatened to take over the entire western flank of their empire. In 892, shortly before the eruption of tribal discontent from the Arabian peninsula to Iraq and the Jazira orchestrated by the Qaramita, a new and able caliph, al-Mu'tadid, returned the capital to Baghdad and tried to repair the damage of the previous decades. He made overtures to the provinces and began to bring the Saffarids of Iran, the Samanids of Transoxania, the Tulunids of Egypt and the Aghlabids of Tunisia back into the fold. Shortly after his accession he arranged to marry the daughter of Khumarawayh, the Tulunid governor of Egypt, in an effort to mend bridges, and Ziyadat Allah of Tunisia sent gifts to Baghdad to acknowledge the new caliph's rights.

Although al-Mu'tadid and his son al-Muktafi (r. 902–08) were able to control the situation and even improve 'Abbasid fortunes, matters began to deteriorate with the accession of al-Muqtadir in 908, the year before 'Ubayd Allah marched into Qayrawan to establish the Fatimid caliphate. The problems of the next half a century were a combination of ineffectual caliphal leadership, fluctuating revenue receipts in Baghdad, financial mismanagement and over-spending and a breakdown in relations between the stakeholders in government – the military and the bureaucrats. The caliph's control gradually shrunk to encompass little more than his palace and gardens in Baghdad, while Turkish *amir*s competed for control of central Iraq and local lords struggled for power and precedence in the provinces.

This parlous situation nonetheless provided new opportunities for men of dynamism and vigour, and in the 930s and 940s 'Ali, Ahmad and Hasan b. Buya, the three sons of a fisherman from the remote mountainous frontier province of Daylam on the Caspian Sea, managed to build up a military following of Daylamite footsoldiers and establish themselves in the Iranian province of Fars in 934. In the next decade they endeavoured to consolidate their position in the hinterland of Rayy, an early Islamic city located close to the site of modern Tehran, and in Iraq. In 945 Ahmad b. Buya occupied Baghdad and the Buyid confederation came into being. He took the title of *amir al-umara'*, which may be loosely translated as 'commander-in-chief', previously held by the paramount Turkish commander in the city, and set himself up as 'protector' of the 'Abbasid caliphate.

What was anomalous about this situation was that the Buyids had strong Shi'i leanings, which by this time entailed the belief that the 'Abbasids were not the true leaders of the Muslim community, as this was a position reserved for the last *imam*, currently in occultation. The obvious explanation for this is that the Buyids were pragmatists and believed it to be in their political interests to maintain the 'Abbasid caliphate, given their own humble origins, while simultaneously encouraging and patronizing Shi'i scholars and thinkers. Certainly they did not treat individual caliphs well – they were kept under house arrest and sometimes deprived of even basic necessities – but nor did they dare to do away with them. However, the period of their domination certainly fostered an eclectic religious life in which Shi'i and Sunni views of various shades competed with and influenced each other, alongside mysticism and philosophy, ultimately contributing to the great intellectual and religious synthesis achieved in the late eleventh century.

By the mid-ninth century it thus appeared that Shi'i regimes of one kind or another – the Qaramita, the Fatimids and the Buyids – would succeed in dominating the Islamic world. By the end of the third decade of the tenth century, the 'Abbasids could not even count on unified Sunni support, as the Muslims of the far west – Spain and Morocco – acknowledged the Umayyads of Cordoba as their caliph and the representative of Sunni Islam. The political fortunes of the 'Abbasids had reached their nadir. From a cultural and intellectual perspective, however, not only did the Buyids encourage greater religious freedom in Iraq and Iran, but the attempts of the Fatimids and Umayyads to prove themselves as caliphs led to the wide circulation of models of government, legitimation and palatial architecture, originally developed by the 'Abbasids. Political fragmentation thus had the converse effect of encouraging cultural integration and the dissemination of knowledge and other cultural artefacts across vast territories, from which it would migrate again into Christendom through Spain, Sicily and the Levant.

The Saljuq sultanate and the 'Sunni revival'

In the end it was the Turks, who had created havoc at Samarra, who saved the day for the 'Abbasids as a dynasty. Al-Mu'tasim's creation of a large Turkish army from the 830s had been made possible by the abundance of young Turks in the slave markets of Transoxania, resulting from intertribal conflict over pastureland as the population of the steppe exceeded its capacity to feed them. Demographic pressure pushed some Turkish tribes to leave the Central Asian steppe for the lusher pastures of the Islamic south. As these tribes migrated they swapped their shamanistic beliefs for Islam, often of a mystical variety. One such group were the Ghuzz Turks, and in 1055 a leading Ghuzz clan, the Saljuqs, succeeded in 'rescuing' the 'Abbasid caliphs from their Shi'i Buyid 'protectors' and asserting their own control over Baghdad and eastern Islamic lands from Syria to Afghanistan. The Daylamite foot soldiers were unseated and Turkish cavalrymen once again dominated the military, but this time they were not the slaves of the 'Abbasids but their masters.

The 'Abbasids probably felt that in swapping the Buyids for the Saljuqs they had moved from the frying pan into the fire, but the Saljuq interlude proved to be of great significance for religio-political theory within Sunni Islam, and for Islamic cultural life too. For the second time, warriors from the fringe of the Islamic lands had taken control of the caliph but, rather like the barbarians in Rome and the Arabs at the time of the Islamic conquests, they had a healthy respect for metropolitan civilization. Nonetheless the relationship between the caliphs and the Buyids had been awkward because of the latter's Shi'i inclinations. The Saljuqs, however, professed to be Sunni, enabling the predominantly Sunni scholars and bureaucrats of Baghdad to come up with a rationalization of the political situation in a way they could not in the preceding Buyid century. This rationalization took the form of the creation of a new institution – the sultanate – as a complement to the caliphate. Prior to this period, the word *sultan* simply meant power or a powerholder, but in the pages of the legal thinkers of the Saljuq era it came to denote a Muslim ruler whose assumption and maintenance of power by military means was legitimized by the dedication of his financial and military resources to defending the faith.

In 1063 the first Saljuq sultan, Tughril, passed away. He was succeeded by his nephew Alp Arslan (r. 1063–72), and the latter's son Malikshah (r. 1072–92), who together presided over the consolidation of the Saljuq empire and the formation of a centralized administration. The new relationship between the 'Abbasid caliph and the Saljuq sultan was sealed by marriages between Alp Arslan's daughter and the son of the reigning caliph, al-Qa'im bi-Amr Allah, and the later and less successful union between the next caliph, al-Muqtadi, and the daughter of Malikshah. The other great achievement of the early Saljuqs was the first flourishing of a new Sunni educational system. While it is unlikely that the Saljuqs themselves came up with the idea of founding a series of theological colleges for the promotion of Sunnism, they willingly patronized the initiatives of their Sunni chief minister, the famous Nizam al-Mulk, and put up the money for the building of several new colleges (*madrasa*s) which greatly enhanced educational opportunities for able but poor students by providing them with free board, lodging and education. It was hoped that the provision of such assistance would reconcile scholars to the reality of military rule and that those who benefited from Saljuq largesse would become a cohort of amenable clerics committed to the promotion of Sunnism. Ibn al-Athir's comments on Alp Arslan's qualities sum up the deal that was done:

> [Alp Arslan] had a merciful heart and was a friend of the ulema (scholars). … He was generous with alms. During Ramadan he would give 15,000 dinars. His administration kept the names of a vast number of religious mendicants throughout all his realm who received pensions and donations. … He was extremely strict about protecting his subjects' property from the soldiery.[36]

The Saljuqs also made good on their religious obligations by leading a new offensive against the Byzantines to drive them out of their newly acquired Syrian territories in the name of the 'Abbasids. Their Turkish warriors were so successful that the Byzantines relinquished their Syrian holdings and retreated to Asia Minor, only to face sustained pressure from the land-hungry Turks there too. In 1071 Alp Arslan and his warriors defeated the Byzantines, led by the emperor Romanus IV Diogenes, at Manzikart (Malasgird), in a battle dramatized by Ibn al-Athir as a *jihad* of the same epic proportions as the Prophet's own battles against the pagan hordes of Mecca, in an attempt to translate the brute force with which the Saljuqs had subjected the Islamic heartlands not only into a virtue but also into their religious *raison d'être*:

> [Alp Arslan] moved towards the Greeks and they moved towards him. When he was close to them, he dismounted, rubbed his face in the dust, wept and prayed long. Then he mounted and charged and the troops charged with him. The Muslims broke into their centre, and the dust kept them concealed. The Muslims dealt out death to them at will. God sent down His helping hand to them and the Greeks fled.[37]

A decade later a renegade Saljuq prince, Sulayman, established the subsidiary Saljuq sultanate of Rum, whose capital was Konya (Iconium), deep in Asia Minor. For the first time in centuries, the Byzantines were on the defensive in their own lands, and the Saljuqs could justly claim to have dedicated their arms to the Islamic cause. For Islamic historians the Battle of Manzikart stands as a watershed, marking the moment when the Turks started to enter Asia Minor in significant numbers, thus initiating its ultimate transformation into modern-day Turkey. It set the Turks on the path to Constantinople, which they would ultimately capture, in fulfilment of the Prophet's hopes, in 1453 under Ottoman leadership. Manzikart was also a personal disaster for Romanus IV, who was captured by Alp Arslan, ransomed and ultimately put to death by a rival imperial faction in Constantinople.

The Saljuqs' ability to wage war against the Byzantines in Syria and push them back to Asia Minor, their liberation of the 'Abbasids from Buyid clutches and their support for Sunnism against Shi'ism made them legitimate Islamic sovereigns and validated the concept of the sultanate. This political and cultural package came to be known as the Sunni revival and was a decisive moment in the formation of the Muslim community as we know it today. In many ways the long Shi'i century from 945 to 1055 had proved conclusively that the idea of a single unitary caliphate controlling the entire Islamic world was not realistic. Three different caliphates had competed for universal acknowledgement but none had achieved more than regional religious and political authority. The 'Abbasids found it difficult to control even the eastern part of the Islamic world; the Fatimids could not advance significantly out of Egypt and lost effective control of Tunisia once they had left it; and the Umayyads of Cordoba were unable to impose direct control on Morocco as well as Spain despite years of diligent effort. There would be no more great Muslim empires until the rise of the Ottomans, Safavids and Mughals in the early sixteenth century.

The new institution of the Saljuq sultanate, however, provided a political alternative which was still Islamic but not universalist, thereby allowing numerous sultanates to coexist side by side and the Islamic world to move to a pluralistic understanding of political life. The formalization of the sultanate also marked a grudging recognition of a separation between religion and politics, which it is so often claimed Islam does not make, and the acknowledgement of this in Islamic political theory. Although sultans were expected to show deference to the Islamic values which the religious scholars purveyed and the caliphs stood for, they had no personal religious authority or status by virtue of being sultans. The dream of a universal Islamic empire remained, but Muslims had taken a significant step towards accepting that in reality the Islamic world was ruled by several different sultans and the caliph was a benign figurehead.

With the exception of a few outstanding figures, the caliphs of this

Fig. 1. Saljuq Minaret of the Great Mosque of Aleppo. (Author's photograph)

period lived in shadowy obscurity in Baghdad, venerated for their lineage and their nominal religio-political headship of the community but isolated from the real business of governing. The decline of the 'Abbasid clan was so acute that when al-Qa'im bi Amr Allah's son Muhammad predeceased him in 1056, the caliphate almost petered out:

> The people were convinced that it was the end of the line and the caliphate would pass from the line of al-Qadir [al-Qa'im's father] to some other and they did not doubt that affairs would be in chaos after al-Qa'im because all those not of the house of al-Qadir had mingled with the common people in the city and were living the life of petty tradesmen.[38]

Luckily al-Qa'im's son had left behind a pregnant Armenian slave girl, Urjuman, and she duly gave birth to the boy who later became the caliph al-Muqtadi when his grandfather died in 1074. Meanwhile the sultanate as an institution rapidly spread across the Islamic world because it enabled a wide variety of different regimes to claim legitimacy on the grounds of achievement — their proven dedication to Islam — which could be manifested through successful war against Islam's enemies, or generous contributions to religious scholars, or the endowment of a wide range of urban facilities including *madrasas*, which became hugely popular after the Saljuq initiative.

The Crusades and the twilight of the caliphate

The two centuries from the establishment of the Saljuq sultanate in 1055 to the demise of the 'Abbasid caliphate in 1258 witnessed the decisive retreat of Isma'ili Shi'ism from the centre of the political stage and the resurgence of Sunnism, supported now not solely by the 'Abbasid caliphs but by the Saljuqs and similar politico-military elites whose leaders claimed to be sultans acting on behalf of the caliph. However, Saljuq successes were quickly overshadowed by the occupation of the Levantine coast by Crusaders from France, Flanders and other northern European countries. The Crusades were triggered by the Saljuq victory against the Byzantines at Manzikart in 1071 and the establishment of the sultanate of Rum in the 1080s, which persuaded the Byzantine emperor Alexius Comnenus to swallow his natural distrust of Latin Christians and appeal to Latin Christendom for military assistance. He probably had in mind mercenaries who would do his bidding, but instead Pope Urban II responded by preaching the First Crusade and Alexius found himself face to face with the much more ambitious and much less malleable Crusaders. The Byzantines would live to regret their appeal to their Western co-religionists.

On the Muslim side the Crusades were totally unexpected and quickly revealed that the Saljuq empire was, in some ways, a rather shaky edifice. The military prowess of Turkish tribal cavalrymen was offset by their reluctance to submit to authority and their constant search for pasturelands for their flocks which could make them disruptive and unreliable. At the same time, there were tensions within the Saljuq clan itself. According to Turkish political norms, possessions belonged to the clan and not to an individual; therefore the empire did not belong to the sultan but to his clan, the members of whom expected their share. As a result the sultans had to parcel out the eastern Islamic lands between numerous relatives who then became independent potentates on their own patch. This led to a high degree of political fragmentation within the Saljuq realm, which was exacerbated by the fact that the Turks' warrior lifestyle meant that many princes died young leaving their fiefs to infants or minors in whose name regents known as *atabey*s ruled. By the onset of the Crusades in the late 1090s, Greater Syria had been parcelled out to several mutually suspicious Saljuq princes and *atabey*s who saw no reason to cooperate when the Crusaders did appear in the north. Moreover in the years immediately preceding the First Crusade almost every major Muslim political figure had died – the Saljuq sultan Malikshah, his chief minister Nizam al-Mulk, the 'Abbasid caliph al-Muqtadi, and his Fatimid rival al-Mustansir – creating a complete political vacuum in the Middle East.

The Saljuqs quickly dissipated the infamous People's Crusade led by Peter the Hermit, which had expended most of its energy on massacring Jews across Europe, but they were defeated by the knights of the First Crusade at Dorylaeum in 1097. Baldwin of Boulogne then diverted east and insinuated himself into the court of Edessa in northern Mesopotamia, which was ruled by a Christian Armenian lord called T'oros. In the strangest story of the First Crusade, Baldwin persuaded the childless ruler and his wife to adopt him by means of a bizarre ceremony during which he pretended to suckle from the ageing queen. Soon after, he murdered his unfortunate adoptive parents and became lord of Edessa. Various Crusaders held the County of Edessa until 1144, when the city was captured by the Muslims.

The other Crusaders proceeded south from Asia Minor into Syria and besieged Antioch. Dissension among the Saljuq princes and their regents prevented a relief force having any effect, and after six months the city fell when an armourer surreptitiously let in the Crusaders. In contravention of the specified aim of the Crusade – the liberation of the Holy Land from Muslim control – and oaths the Crusaders had taken to Alexius Comnenus, Bohemond I took Antioch as his appanage and left the rest of the Crusaders, led by Raymond of Gilles and Godfrey de Bouillon, to proceed south.

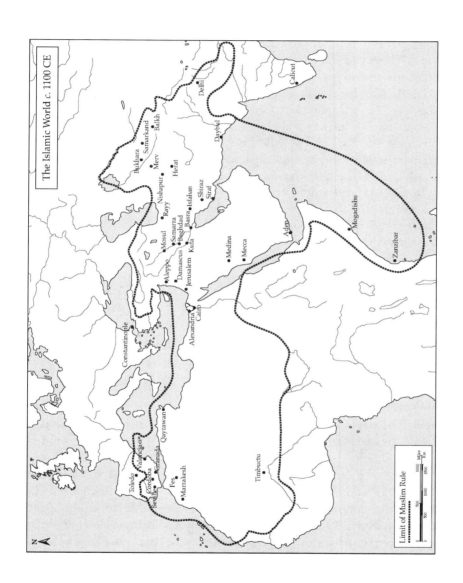

The Islamic World c. 1100 CE

Calicut
Delhi
Daybul
Samarkand
Bukhara
Merv
Balkh
Herat
Nishapur
Rayy
Shiraz
Siraf
Mosul
Samarra
Isfahan
Baghdad
Basra
Aleppo
Kufa
Damascus
Jerusalem
Medina
Mecca
Mogadishu
Aden
Zanzibar
Alexandria
Cairo
Constantinople
Qayrawan
Valencia
Granada
Toledo
Córdoba
Seville
Fes
Marrakesh
Timbuctu

Limit of Muslim Rule

0   500   1000 Miles
0   500   1000   1500 Km

N

In 1097 the most sinister and notorious event of the Crusade took place, the sack of the small town of Ma'arra where, as Radulph of Caen later admitted, 'our troops boiled pagan adults in cooking pots; they impaled children on spits and devoured them grilled'.[39] Jerusalem was finally taken in 1098, its Muslim and Jewish inhabitants slaughtered by the vengeful Crusaders. A horrified Ibn al-Athir recorded that the Jews of the city were barricaded in their synagogue and burnt to death while a massacre of the city's Muslim inhabitants ensued, causing the streets literally to run with blood. Godfrey de Bouillon became custodian of the holy city on behalf of the pope, and Raymond, the only eminent Crusader not to have acquired a fiefdom, hastened north to make good his claim to Tripoli on the Levantine coast.

By 1100 the map of the Middle East had become a mosaic of small principalities clustered around the notional centres of Baghdad, where the 'Abbasids and Great Saljuqs held court, and Cairo, the capital of the Fatimids. In the Levant the handful of Crusaders who remained established a precarious foothold, dependent on supplies brought by the ships of the Italian city-states of Genoa and Pisa. West of Egypt, a new Berber regime, the Almoravids, had emerged from the Sahara desert below Morocco to create an empire encompassing parts of West Africa, the Sahara, Morocco and the southern Iberian peninsula. Somewhat ironically given the political disintegration in the Middle East, the Almoravids chose to pledge their allegiance to the 'Abbasids and thus technically brought North Africa and Spain into the 'Abbasid fold for the first time. Although the 'Abbasids held no real power in the west, the fact that the Almoravids believed that offering them their loyalty and service would be politically useful shows the power of the caliphal idea even in such testing times.

The Muslim response to the Crusades was initially muted and disunited. The inhabitants of the region were shocked by the incursions and horrified by the violence and barbarous habits of the newcomers, but those with the military skills – the Saljuq princes and their *atabeys* – could not surmount their political differences to fight against them. The impassioned plea of the religious scholar al-Sulami, who went to Baghdad to beg the Saljuq sultan and 'Abbasid caliph for assistance, fell on deaf ears. It was not until the ambitious *atabey* of Mosul and Aleppo, Imad al-Din Zangi, and his son Nur al-Din began to create a larger Muslim enclave straddling northern Syria and Iraq that a counter-offensive conceptualized as a *jihad* began. During the late 1120s Imad al-Din consolidated his control over his domains. By the 1130s he was pushing southwards in Syria and northwards towards the Crusader county of Edessa. Its fall in 1144 triggered the Second Crusade in 1148, which failed to achieve its main goal, namely the capture of Damascus. Instead the Zangids managed to consolidate their control of

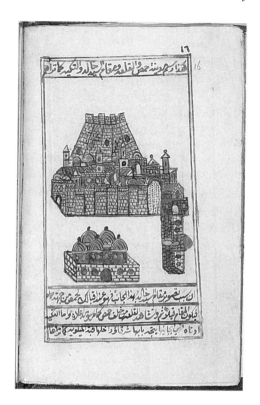

Fig. 2. Illustration of the Ayyubid citadel of Homs from a *History of the City of Homs* written by Constantine b. Da'ud in 1863 at the behest of the French consul. (Manuscript Add 338, p 16. Reproduced by kind permission of the Syndics of Cambridge University Library)

the Orontes valley from Aleppo down to Hama, Homs and finally Damascus, creating a unified Muslim bloc adjacent to the Crusader principalities on the coastal strip of the Levant.

In the 1160s both the Crusaders and the Zangids began to view Egypt, where the Fatimid caliphate was fading fast, as the next prize. During the early 1160s Amalric, the Latin king of Jerusalem, threatened Egypt repeatedly but was forced back by the approach of Zangid forces each time. In 1167 the Zangids tired of the game and Nur al-Din sent one of his Kurdish commanders, Shirkuh, into Egypt to occupy it. He was accompanied by his nephew, Salah al-Din al-Ayyubi, better known in Europe as Saladin. When Shirkuh died soon after, Salah al-Din assumed the Zangid command in Egypt. He consolidated his position by assuming the role of chief minister to the Fatimid caliph but soon, under pressure from Nur al-Din, he suppressed the Fatimid caliphate. In 1171 the sermon at the Friday Prayer in Cairo was dedicated to the Zangids, Saljuqs and 'Abbasids after over two centuries during which it had been offered to the Shi'i Fatimids. The termination of the Fatimid caliphate was the end of an era: the Umayyad caliphs of Cordoba had been gone for over a century, their palaces alternately sacked by unpaid Berber soldiers and irate Cordoban townspeople, while the 'Abbasid caliphs resided in the twilight world of Baghdad and left the real business of government to politico-military dynasts such as the Zangids. It was only a matter of time before they too would disappear from the Muslim political stage.

In Egypt power passed to Salah al-Din and his descendants, the Ayyubids, who soon extended their control over Syria at the expense of their former Zangid patrons and the Latin kingdoms. In 1187 Salah al-Din achieved his greatest victory when he defeated the Crusaders at the Battle of Hattin and recaptured Jerusalem. The fall of Jerusalem triggered the Third Crusade (1190–92), which engendered the romantic European image of the encounter between Richard the Lionheart and Salah al-Din but, in fact, led to little gain for either side. In the truce of 1192 the Muslims kept Jerusalem but the Crusaders retained their strategically more important coastal base of Acre. Salah al-Din died the following year. Although he was eulogized as a holy warrior by some of his contemporaries, in subsequent centuries other heroes loomed larger: his Zangid master Nur al-Din, and the later Ayyubid slave soldier Baybars, who helped halt the Mongol advance through Syria in 1260 and then, having become Mamluk sultan, dedicated annual military campaigns from Egypt to dislodging the last remaining Latins from the Levantine coast until his death in 1277. The task was finally completed when the Mamluk sultan Qalawun recaptured Acre in 1291.

During the last decades of the caliphate the 'Abbasids made a startling comeback in the shape of al-Nasir (r. 1180–1225), an ambitious caliph who attempted to claw back some real power from the various condottieri who passed through Baghdad and extricate himself from Saljuq clutches. On the political front he managed to ally himself with the rulers of Khwarazm in Transoxania and kill the last Saljuq sultan, Tughril, and then avoid Khwarazmian 'protection' by making an alliance with the Ghurids of Afghanistan. Having achieved some freedom of political action, he set about restoring the authority of the caliphate by developing an integrative version of Islam which brought together Sunnism and Shi'ism under the umbrella of Sufism (Islamic mysticism). He gave his religious programme an institutional framework in the form of the *futuwwa*, a term literally meaning 'young men' but used in this era for groups of men bound by a common moral or honour code and loyal to a particular master or leader. In some contexts *futuwwa* were little more than urban gangs or militias, but al-Nasir reformed the organization, took over its headship himself, and made it into an empire-wide hierarchy, a military order in the service of the caliph.

However, al-Nasir could not turn back the clock. It had become normal throughout the Islamic world for locally based warrior sultans to rule in the place of the universal caliph, who had become a symbol rather than a reality for the majority of Muslims. In other words, political plurality had become a fact of life. It is for this reason that the final demise of the 'Abbasid caliphs in 1258 at the hands of the invading Mongols did not cause more distress. The Mongols had arrived in force in Transoxania in 1222, a few years before the death of al-Nasir, to punish the ruler of Khwarazm for having killed a Mongol ambassador. Chinghiz Khan swept through Transoxania and Khurasan, burning, pillaging and destroying cities. Their inhabitants were given a choice – surrender or die – and those who thought the Mongols were bluffing did not live to tell the tale. Although the numbers of deaths given in the chronicles are hugely inflated, they convey the utter desolation caused in the region by this punitive attack. The Mongol conquest of the Middle East, which was directed by Chinghiz Khan's grandson Hulegu, took place 30 years later. As the Mongols advanced, most cities surrendered quickly to avoid the fate of those who had paid the penalty for resisting the clan of Chinghiz Khan. The Mongols reached Baghdad in 1258, took the city and killed the 'Abbasid caliph. A member of the 'Abbasid family made it to Cairo, where the new Mamluk sultan willingly set him up as a latter-day caliph, but his status was not widely recognized outside Mamluk domains in Egypt and Syria.

The arrival of the Mongols radically altered the political geography of the Middle East by drawing a line through the heartlands of the 'Abbasid caliphate. The eastern Islamic lands from Iraq through Iran to Khurasan and Transoxania became part of the vast Mongol empire, while the western half of the region, Syria, the Arabian peninsula, Egypt and the rest of North Africa were divided up between a number of Muslim regimes, the majority of whom accepted that they were sultans rather than potential caliphs. The cultural legacy of earlier centuries nonetheless lived on, and it is to the society and culture of the 'Abbasid age that we now turn.

CHAPTER 2

From Baghdad to Cordoba:
The Cities of Classical Islam

Baghdad is the metropolis of Islam. ... Its people have distinctive characteristics of wittiness, charm, refinement and correct scholarship. The climate is mild, and all that is good and beautiful is found there. Every heart yearns for it, every battle is fought over it, and every hand is raised to defend it.[1]

Cordoba is the capital of al-Andalus; I have heard it said that it is a more important town than Baghdad. The evidence is clear and the people agree that it is an important metropolis, friendly and attractive, where one finds justice, wisdom, political sense, benignity, obvious prosperity, and religion.[2]

Much of what we know about the 'Abbasid era comes from the pens of those who lived in the countless cities or towns of the caliphate and neighbouring regions, and who migrated to its thriving intellectual, political and commercial centres: Baghdad, Kufa, Basra in Iraq; the great Transoxanian cities of Merv, Samarkand and Bukhara; Damascus and Cairo, capitals of Syria and Egypt respectively; and in the vast province of the Maghrib, Qayrawan in Tunisia and Cordoba in Spain, to name only the best known. Although some of these cities were new Muslim foundations, many were already ancient when the Muslims conquered them, and urban life is one of the many facets of Mediterranean and Middle Eastern society which shows both continuity and change as classical Islamic civilization came into being. Although it was tempting for nineteenth- and early twentieth-century travellers to North Africa and the Holy Land to lament the passing of the great Graeco-Roman cities of Antiquity whose ruins provided dramatic *memento mori* from Volubilis in Morocco to Apamea and Palmyra in Syria, the impact of the rise of Islam on city life was a rather more nuanced affair which involved both loss and gain.

Figs. 3–5. Two of the many Graeco-Roman sites that inspired early Muslim architects and city planners, Apamea in Syria (left) and Palmyra in Syria (top right, bottom right). (Author's photographs)

We need not dwell on the insidious Orientalist tendency to consider the twisting, narrow and apparently illogical alleys of pre-modern Islamic towns and cities as material manifestations of the irrational mind of the 'Oriental'. Suffice to say that when such renowned French Orientalists as the Marçais brothers, George and William, or Jean Sauvaget set out to define the 'Islamic city' they tended to assume that the early twentieth-century 'old towns' which they studied in North Africa and Syria could provide a model more or less relevant for all cities in the Islamic world at all historical periods. Based on their own sense of European modernity which was showcased by cities such as Paris, redesigned by George-Eugène Haussman in the 1850s–60s at the behest of Napoleon III, these scholars saw pre-modern towns in Muslim regions as poor, dirty and cramped. They called them 'medinas' from the Arabic word for a town or city, suggesting the antithesis they perceived not just between old and new but also between East and West. To replace such medinas was an intrinsic objective of modernization and Haussman's design for new Cairo, a series of elegant circuses with straight streets radiating from them like the spokes of a wheel, was a much-applauded step in that direction. Orientalists also saw Muslim urban communities as lacking in the civic values and institutions which, they believed, had defined the Greek *polis*, Roman *civis* and European cities from medieval times onwards. Islamic cities were, from the perspective of Orientalists, not only the physical obverse of modern European towns but also their conceptual opposite, an attitude which is now commonplace in the constant but often exaggerated juxtaposition of Western versus Islamic values.

The truth is less polemical and more mundane and abounds in shades of grey rather than stark contrasts. In the last decades, urban historians have shown that many of the features attributed to Islam a century ago when Orientalist and imperialistic narratives dominated actually began to appear centuries before the Arabs launched the Islamic conquests. Byzantine Syria, for instance, already presented an urban profile very different from that of a few centuries before. In Damascus the Basilica of St John nestled in the inner sanctum of the vast enclosure of the Temple of Jupiter-Haddad, and Byzantine parishes prefigured the urban quarters of Islamic times. The Temple of Baal at Palmyra similarly housed a church which utilized only its Holy of Holies, leaving much of the sanctuary derelict. Decades of Byzantine–Sasanian war had already undermined the thriving towns of northern Syria, and villages, shrines and hermit's retreats were more common than the grand civic architecture of the past. Moreover some of the changes which occurred after the Islamic conquest owed less to the arrival of Islam than to natural phenomena, such as the recurrent plagues which had already depopulated Syria and the earthquake which the region suffered in 749.

As the new religion gained sway over the centuries, there were both obvious and subtle changes to city life, but the traditional concept of an unchanging 'Islamic city' at loggerheads with the rational and expansive urbanism which preceded it is patently wrong, as both archaeology and the many detailed descriptions of cities and towns to be found in Muslim and non-Muslim writings from different eras show. Rather we see a situation in which a relatively small number of Arab Muslims founded a limited number of new settlements and took control of numerous others of Byzantine and Persian pedigree. In the Umayyad period, Arab-Muslim urbanism reached its apogee but also moved in fresh directions using a new imperial idiom derived from Byzantine prototypes. With the rise of the 'Abbasids, Persian concepts of city planning were added to the pot and a mature urban model began to emerge. As rising numbers of urban Christians, Zoroastrians and other non-Muslims began to convert to Islam and 'Abbasid models were adopted across the Islamic world by their governors and political rivals, the difference between new Muslim foundations and pre-Islamic cities started to fade and the town descriptions of Muslim geographers began to converge in their content.

Such descriptions show that in terms of size and facilities, cities in the 'Abbasid era did not compare badly with their antique predecessors, and they greatly outstripped their medieval European counterparts. Only in China were there cities to rival those of Islam in wealth, size and sophistication. Although Muslim towns of the eighth century had relatively few identifiable public buildings beyond a mosque, a governor's residence and a marketplace, by the twelfth century important cities possessed myriad mosques, theological colleges (*madrasas*), shrines, hospitals, markets and, usually, sophisticated water supply and sewage systems as well as 'green spaces'. Although the civic institutions of the Graeco-Roman Mediterranean city disappeared, different forms of community emerged out of a synthesis between early Arab Islamic values and the existing urban traditions of Byzantium and the Sasanian Empire. What, then, was the Muslim contribution to urbanism in the lands of the caliphate, how did it evolve in the period contemporary with the Dark Ages in Europe, and what was it like to live in the cities of classical Islam?

Arab urbanism at the dawn of Islam

As with most aspects of this story, the 'Abbasid era did not initiate a new form of city life but brought to fruition trends apparent from the establishment of an Islamic empire in the mid-seventh century. Like the northern barbarian Huns, Vandals and Goths who carved up the western Roman Empire, the Arabs had a healthy respect for the mores of the sedentary imperial lands they conquered and sought to perpetuate and appropriate them rather than cast them aside. Their attitude to the ancient cities of the Near East was therefore one of qualified appreciation which was rooted in centuries of interaction with the neighbouring great powers and a ready understanding of their urban aesthetics. Moreover the Arabs, especially those of south and east Arabia, had their own deep-rooted urban traditions which they could export from the Arabian peninsula to conquered lands, adding a new layer to an already diverse urban landscape.

Although there are several Arabic words for cities and towns, the most common is *madina*, a noun denoting a place of religion and exchange which conveys the importance of the mosque and the market to Muslim urban life, a feature reflecting the centrality of pagan shrines and fairs in pre-Islamic Arabia. However, the city was also something more to the Arabs, it was an oasis, a well-watered verdant garden which nurtured not only the body but the soul. For Muslims paradise is a garden, but that garden is not one of untrammelled nature but an orderly walled garden in an urban setting, as the renowned mosaics of the great Mosque of Damascus unequivocally

show. The Arabs acquired and developed these early notions of the city in
Arabia itself. Although we often imagine them as quintessential nomads
from the deserts of Inner Arabia – a view cultivated by some of the 'Abbasid
Arab elite at more lyrical moments and satirized by the Persians – Islam
actually developed in the small commercial towns of the Hijaz – Mecca and
Yathrib (Medina). These towns were way stations on the trade routes which
snaked up from Yemen, the mythical land of Sheba, a fertile region of oasis
towns and villages watered in Antiquity by the tail-end of the monsoon
rains, trapped by the great and ancient Marib dam which finally collapsed
in the early seventh century CE.

According to the standard account, Muhammad began his career as a
commercial agent for a rich widow, Khadija, who later became his wife, and
his message addressed the social inequalities which had begun to emerge
in the increasingly urbanized environment of the Hijaz as some men grew
wealthy on the proceeds of trade and others struggled to scrape a living on
the margins of society. However, Mecca's trade was probably more limited
and nondescript than this account implies – leather and raisins rather than
frankincense and myrrh – and the 'town' itself consisted of dusty rammed
earth houses clustered around the shrine known as the Ka'ba, the only stone
building in town, the precinct of which operated as the town's main public
space. In fact it was the wide recognition of the Ka'ba as a sacred pilgrimage site that drew Arabs into Mecca, and its economy depended as much
on offerings made at the shrine as on the trade fairs which took place in
the area under the protection of al-'Uzza and her sister goddesses Allat and
Manat. Nonetheless the inhabitants of Mecca were by no means bedouin,
constantly roaming the deserts from one encampment to another, as the
poetic image of the pre-Islamic Arabs suggests.

Yathrib, the settlement where the Islamic community first came into
being as an autonomous political and social unit, was a very different kind of
'town' to Mecca. Rather like the red and ochre mud villages of the southern
Moroccan valleys today, it was made up of several rammed earth forts, each
inhabited by a clan or tribe, nestling in an oasis of palm trees. Its inhabitants lived by trade and agriculture and included several Jewish tribes. There
were other oasis settlements of this type in the Hijaz, including Khaybar,
another predominantly Jewish settlement. When Muhammad was forced
to leave Mecca by the persecution of his pagan opponents in 622CE, he
moved to Yathrib where he established his archetypal Muslim community
amidst its shady palms. The settlement came to be known simply as 'The
Illuminated City' (*al-madina al-munawwara*) or 'The City of the Prophet'
(*madinat al-nabi*) from which we get its abbreviated name, al-Medina, 'The
City', in itself a statement of the association between Islam and urban life,

understood as a controlled environment of buildings, greenery and water.

The Prophet founded the first mosques in Medina, the most important of which was simply a large compound attached to his living quarters, and it was here that the ritual and social obligations of Muslims were first articulated and applied to daily life. The Prophet's mosque was also a gathering place where Muslims could discuss and debate political and military matters, in keeping with the varied uses to which the Ka'ba enclosure in Mecca had been put in pagan times. More subtly, descriptions of this first mosque also evoked Solomon's temple in Jerusalem and raised Medina to the status of a Semitic holy place, one stage in the fostering of a Judaeo-Christian-Muslim sacred geography that extended the traditional Judaeo-Christian Holy Land southwards into the Hijaz.

The early community's choice to establish its most crucial religious space within its new oasis town not only played a pivotal role in transforming pagan Yathrib into Muslim Medina, it also offered a paradigm which could be adhered to in the physical layout of other cities and referred to in numerous foundation myths. Many of the accounts we have of the formative moments in the early Islamic community's life in seventh-century Medina were written down in the early 'Abbasid era and reflect not only historical memory but also an Islamic city of the imagination which affected how the establishment and workings of other cities were later understood by Muslims themselves. In the legends told of the foundation of Baghdad, Samarra, Qayrawan, Fes and other cities, the transformation of a wilderness to a civilized urban space and the replacement of paganism with Islam are prominent motifs which pointed to the definition Muslims themselves had of the city, based on their understanding of the Medinese paradigm with its varied associations to Arabian and wider Semitic precedents.[3]

Although Mecca and Medina figured large in the Muslim imagination, many other Arabs who converted to Islam also came from urban or semi-urban backgrounds and contributed to the ways in which Muslim settlements actually developed. Some had already had contacts with the Roman and Persian worlds for centuries, and on the eve of the Islamic conquests both powers were heavily involved in trying to colonize Arabia's eastern coast and Yemen. The kingdom of Kinda, perched on the edge of the empty quarter in southwest Arabia, which flourished in the third and fourth centuries CE, had extensive enough contact with the Graeco-Roman world for its people to embellish their homes with frescoes of frankly Hellenistic inspiration, the most famous of which depicts a nobleman as a curly-headed Greek youth with a bunch of grapes dangling above his head. At Najran, 300km further south, Byzantine merchants eagerly promoted Christianity while pro-Persian elements tried to prevent the region becoming an outpost of either Christian Ethiopia or Byzantium. In the process, Najran gained a cathedral, the remains of which still stand today.

To the north of the Hijaz, where the Arabian desert blends imperceptibly into the Syrian steppe, stood the elegant Nabataean cities of Petra, Busra (Bostra) and Palmyra, as well as the later settlement of Hira (Hatra), ruled by the Lakhmids – Christian Arabs who acted as border guards for the Sasanian Persians – all of which combined Graeco-Roman, Persian and Arabian elements. The Byzantines also had Christian Arab clients in the century before the rise of Islam, the Ghassanids, whose royal enclosure stood near the Romano-Byzantine city of Rusafa (Sergiopolis) in northern Syria. These Arab clients were not simply condottieri, but also aspired to the culture of their masters. At the court of Mundhir b. Harith, a client of Byzantium in the time of Justinian, an observer witnessed 'ten singing girls, five of them Byzantines, singing Greek songs to the music of lutes, and five from Hira who had been presented to the king Jabala by Iyas b. Qabisa, chanting Babylonian melodies', in addition to Arab singers from Mecca.[4] Although some of these peoples, in particular the Nabataeans and Sabaeans, were not Arabs in the strict pre-Islamic sense of the term, in a broader sense they came from the Arabian milieu, and men of their tribes and towns participated in the construction and settlement of the first purpose-built Muslim cities in the Near East.

The first Muslim towns

The early Muslims who surged forth from the Arabian peninsula in the seventh century thus came from a mixed environment of oasis towns, shrine centres, mountain villages and desert encampments. They might have set themselves up as land owners in the Fertile Crescent, but it was one of the features of the conquest era that they did not settle on the land but clustered in garrisons located near to existing towns or in new purpose-built settlements known in Arabic as *amsar* (sing. *misr*), a decision attributed in the Islamic sources to the second caliph, 'Umar b. al-Khattab, and maintained by the Umayyads. 'Umar's reasons were supposedly a pious dislike for the effete and luxurious ways of the cities of Antiquity and a pragmatic sense that it was essential for the survival of Islam and its nascent empire to keep the army together and focused on conquest, concerns which are clearly expressed in al-Tabari's account of the foundation of Kufa in Iraq.

The Arabs initially settled in the old Sasanian capital, Ctesiphon, but soon their stomachs grew paunchy and their faces sallow, to which 'Umar responded, 'no land suits Arab tribesmen except that which suits their camels'.[5] The local commander then found a suitable site close to the

Euphrates and the old Lakhmid city of Hira on the desert fringe. The Arabs of both Kufa and Basra petitioned 'Umar to allow them to build in reeds rather than simply raise their tents, to which he rather reluctantly replied, 'living in an army camp is easier for you to mount your military operations from and is more convenient, but I do not like to disagree with you'.[6] The settlers duly constructed their homes of local reed, but soon after a huge fire raged through the town, causing them to petition 'Umar yet again to permit them to build in brick. He acquiesced but with the proviso that, 'no-one built more than three rooms for himself and do not let anyone build higher houses than the other'.[7]

'Umar's preferences may also have reflected concern to keep the Arabs away from areas of plague that struck both Syria and southern Iraq during the conquests, but in the longer term his insistence that Muslims should live together and apart from the subject population could be how a small and hugely over-extended cohort of Arab conquerors managed to retain their identity and reshape regional civilization according to an Islamic framework rather than being absorbed into the Byzantine or Persian worlds around them.

The best known of these early Arab settlements were the aforementioned Kufa and Basra in Iraq, Fustat (later Cairo) in Egypt and Qayrawan in Tunisia. They acted as springboards for further conquests but also as an environment in which an Islamic lifestyle began to be articulated and developed based on the foundations laid down in Medina. While the administrative and military function of these settlements is contained in the term *misr*, their religious function was expressed by an alternative denomination, *dar al-hijra*, meaning a 'place of migration' and thus a settlement for Muslim emigrants rather than just soldiers. This was an evocative term for Muslims which recalled the Prophet's own migration (*hijra*) from Mecca to Medina in 622 and encouraged all Muslims to think of themselves as participating in the foundation of new communities like that of Medina.

A typical *misr* began its life as little more than a campsite whose topography was determined by two principles – Islam and tribalism. At the centre of the site stood a mosque which was often makeshift at this stage, demarcated by no more than 'a line of scattered ashes, a reed fence, a shallow ditch and the like'.[8] The Mosque of 'Amr in Fustat, for instance, was initially no more than a rectangular brushwood stockade around a muddy pitch where the faithful jostled with livestock for precedence when it was founded in 641–42. The situation was only remedied in 673 when a permanent mosque was constructed using the abundant classical building materials available in the area. Additional arcades supported by columns from derelict churches were added in 827. Although time and crass restoration have made their mark on the Mosque of 'Amr, the south wall still sports some wooden architraves decorated with a Hellenistic frieze from the seventh century. The first great mosque in Kufa had no more than a ditch to indicate its perimeter, but its interior was supposedly made a little more grand with marble columns from Byzantine churches taken from a Persian palace in or near Hira where they had already been re-used once.[9] The residence of the commander or governor was generally near the mosque and was surrounded by a large plaza that served as a useful space for gathering the troops or setting up market stalls. This became its standard location through the Umayyad century and into the early 'Abbasid period.

When it came to the rest of the camp-city, tribalism was the main organizational principle: although not all Arabs were nomads, the vast majority were tribesmen and they were allocated space in a *misr* by tribe. Over time these tribal plots became less makeshift and developed into residential quarters built using the traditional construction methods of each area: in Iraq, rammed earth and mudbrick, in Tunisia, re-used Roman blocks of masonry. Each urban plot was roughly equal in size and therefore tribal groups were sometimes modified to 'fit' standard plots: larger tribes might be subdivided into clans, and smaller tribal groups might be placed together in a single plot. These plots included some of the elements of later urban quarters – a mosque or prayer space and other amenities. Soon plots were allocated to clients of non-Arab origin, the *mawali*, and to the non-Muslims who offered services to the Muslim soldiers and their families.

These early settlements quickly developed market areas which grew in size and importance as their military functions diminished and their commercial role developed. Although it is a common trope that the markets cluster around the great mosque in Muslim cities, the placement of markets was practical rather than ideological. In Basra the famous Mirbad market-place was located on the western desert side of the city to receive caravans from Arabia, but as riverine trade became more important the main markets gradually moved towards the Tigris. In Kufa the market area did develop around the great mosque, a pattern also evident in Fustat, although the latter seems to have had other markets as well. In Qayrawan the market developed along the main street in a manner reminiscent of Graeco-Roman cities. Finally, in contrast to the familiar walled cities of later periods, these settlements were generally not walled and were spacious rather than cramped in their layout, with cultivated garden areas dotted throughout the urban fabric in the tradition of the oasis settlements of Arabia. Although they were not as rigorously planned as Hellenic or Roman cities, they did have fairly straight and wide arterial streets leading out from the central mosque and governor's residence to the periphery, or simply bisecting the town.

Fig. 6. East Gate of Damascus, constructed in Graeco-Roman times and restored by the Muslims. (Author's photograph)

It was in the pre-existing Byzantine cities of the region – Aleppo, Damascus, Jerusalem – where space was already at a premium that denser and more convoluted street plans were to be found, already overlaid on Hellenistic grids and encroaching upon the Roman *decumanus maximus* and *cardo maximus*. It was also in these cities that continuity was most evident: despite many changes over the centuries it is still possible to walk on the 'Street called Straight' in Damascus down to the classical and Islamic eastern gate where Saul of Tarsus entered the city, blind and on the verge of his transformation into St Paul, and visit the house where he supposedly sought refuge. In these cities, the Arabs trod gingerly, taking over some urban quarters or homes for their own use and negotiating with local Christians to share their churches, another indication of Islam's strong self-identification as a religion predicated on essentially the same revelation as that sent to the Jews and Christians in the past. A similar process occurred in the Christian cities of Visigothic Spain. Even Orientalists such as von Grunebaum admitted that the Muslim Arabs 'consummated' a process already underway in the second century CE rather than initiating the 'degradation' of an intact Graeco-Roman city.[10]

In the old Sasanian Empire, which had stretched from Mesopotamia across Iran and into Central Asia, a similar pattern is evident. Although some Persian cities had experienced a Hellenic phase as a result of Alexander's journeys of conquest and the subsequent establishment of the Seleucid Empire in Asia by his general Seleucas Nicator, the majority of cities in

Sasanian lands did not have a grid plan. Instead the norm was a citadel within a walled enclosure, the 'inner city' (*shahristan*), which served governmental and administrative functions, and an 'outer city' (*birun*) where the residential and market areas were located and which encircled or abutted the *shahristan*. An outer wall or rampart protected the settlement and any outlying gardens in their entirety. This form had also existed, of course, in pre-Hellenic Syria, as the ancient citadel mounds of cities like Aleppo and Hama testify.

During the conquests of Persianate areas, the Muslims tended to take over the citadel or inner city, or establish new settlements known as 'suburbs' (*rabad, arbad*) alongside the old, as at Merv. On occasion Zoroastrian temples became mosques: the people of Istakhr in southern Iran assured the tenth-century geographer al-Muqaddasi that the reason there was an image of a cow on the top of each mosque pillar was that it had previously been a 'temple of fire'.[11] One of the few instances of recorded destruction occurred at Rayy, situated near modern Tehran, where the old Sasanian city was replaced by a new Muslim foundation. Nonetheless there is no indication of major disturbances to the existing Sasanian urban fabric, although there was a gradual but conclusive drift of population towards the new Muslim parts of most settlements, and by the tenth century the older parts of many Persian cities were in ruins.

Umayyad urbanism

Prior to the Umayyad period, then, Muslims either congregated in army settlements, whose plan reflected the organization of the army itself into tribal units and an aversion to unnecessary luxury, or settled into the fabric of existing Byzantine and Persian cities with minimum disruption. We only see a more distinctive Islamic urban ethos begin to appear under the Umayyads who initiated a shift towards a more grandiose and imperial style of Islamic building which drew heavily on Romano-Byzantine precedents, changing the profile of some ancient cities and embellishing new settlements with grand mosques and palaces. The Umayyads wanted to be seen as equals of the empire builders of the past and present, and it is not coincidental that Mu'awiya (r. 661–80) is said to have rebuilt his wooden Damascene residence in stone at the prompting of a Byzantine ambassador, an individual whom the sources clearly perceive as a suitable arbiter of imperial taste.

The artistic debt of the Umayyads to Rome and Byzantium has long been recognized, but so too has the stunning self-confidence with which they utilized the cultural resources of the conquered. 'Abd al-Malik (r. 685–

705) set the tone with his experiments at minting money based on Byzantine prototypes, with the caliph in place of the emperor and legends in Arabic rather than Greek script. Moreover he constructed the first Islamic monument, the Dome of the Rock, on Mount Moriah in Jerusalem, which utilized the form of a Byzantine *martyrium* to create a shrine which allowed Muslims to circumambulate the sacred stone on which Abraham was believed to have laid his son for sacrifice and from which Muhammad had ascended to heaven during his miraculous night journey from Mecca to Jerusalem on his winged steed Buraq, 'whose every stride carried it as far as its eye could reach'.[12] Ibn Ishaq's report of this miracle in his hagiography of the Prophet clearly linked the three Abrahamic faiths, while also signalling Islam's new ascendancy:

> The apostle [Muhammad] and Gabriel went on their way until they arrived at the Temple in Jerusalem. There he found Abraham, Moses and Jesus among a company of the prophets. The apostle acted as their imam in prayer.[13]

The Dome of the Rock translated these sentiments into marble and stone, it added a new Muslim layer to the sacred Judaeo-Christian landscape of Jerusalem and it created a Muslim monument which echoed and competed with the nearby Byzantine Church of the Anastasis.

'Abd al-Malik's son al-Walid I (r. 705–15) continued his father's initiatives with the reconstruction of the Prophet's mosque in Medina and the building of hallmark Umayyad mosques in Jerusalem, Damascus, Aleppo and smaller Syrian cities such as Hama. The Umayyads' appreciation of Syria's Byzantine heritage finds no better expression than the story, recounted in numerous Arabic sources, that when al-Walid I decided to build an imperial mosque in Damascus, he not only located it on the site of the Byzantine cathedral of St John but also asked the Byzantine emperor for 200 skilled craftsmen to work on the project. At the same time, the mosque was highly competitive: two centuries later, al-Muqaddasi remarked to his uncle that Umayyad money might have been better spent on roads, but his uncle replied:

> Al-Walid was absolutely right. ... For he saw that Syria was a country settled by Christians, and he noted there their churches so handsome with their enchanting decorations, renowned far and wide. ... So he undertook for the Muslims the building of a mosque that would divert their attention from the churches, and make it one of the wonders of the world.[14]

Fig. 7. Byzantine-inspired mosaics on the treasury in the Great Mosque of Damascus. (Author's photograph)

The Umayyads also continued to build new settlements such as 'Anjar in Lebanon and their famed desert palaces in Syria and Jordan which used the forms of *castrum* and *villa* as well as such large amounts of classical *spolia* that early excavators sometimes assumed that they were Roman or Byzantine sites. In Spain the most noted accomplishment of the otherwise fairly nondescript Umayyad governor Samh al-Khawlani was to reconstruct the Roman bridge over the Guadalquivir river at Cordoba, and when a great mosque was finally established in that city in the 780s by the refugee Umayyad 'Abd al-Rahman I it followed the precedents set not only by the great mosques of Umayyad Syria but also by the inspiring Roman remains at Mérida to the north. He and his successors also built numerous country estates outside Cordoba on the sites of the Roman and Visigothic villas which preceded them.

However, to perceive the Umayyads as slavish imitators of Roman and Byzantine styles would be a great mistake. Just as their coins triumphantly signalled their appropriation of the classical heritage by stamping it with their own Arabic mark, so they embellished the Dome of the Rock with the earliest known band of Arabic Islamic calligraphy in a triumphant statement of their conquest of the region and acquisition of its heritage for their own purposes. While Umayyad mosques were often built on sites already sanctified by centuries of worship, comparisons of Umayyad sites across greater Syria shows that there were Arabian planning principles at work. The archaeologist Donald Whitcomb has mooted that the position-

Fig. 8. Umayyad city of 'Anjar in Lebanon, originally thought to be a Graeco-
Roman site. (Author's photograph)

ing of institutions, including the great mosque, the governor's residence,
the baths and a revenue office, reflected an arrangement already evident in
pre-Islamic towns of Arabia including Mecca and Zafar, capital of Himyar,
in the south.[15]

To these Arabian and Byzantine influences must be added that of the
Sasanian Persian cities of Mesopotamia, which reached its apogee under
the 'Abbasids but began with the Umayyads. From Roman times the Arabs
had absorbed cultural influences from Persia, as well as Greece and Rome,
to create their own unique urban heritage which can still be seen at Hira
(Hatra), Petra and Palmyra, seat of the famous queen Zenobia, who challenged the Romans in the third century CE only to find herself paraded
through the streets of Rome as a captive, a fate which Cleopatra, whose
descendant she claimed to be, had only narrowly escaped. However, it is
Palmyra's delicate pinkish stone carvings of Persian inspiration which are
of interest here: aristocratic men and women recline on funerary panels,
draped in Persianate textiles, and the formality of classical columns, capitals and arches is gently mocked by rows of delicately worked flowers which
could equally well grace the border of a silken robe. In very much the same
spirit, the Umayyads commissioned exuberant Persianate decoration for the
great stone portal of Qasr al-Hayr al-Gharbi, one of their numerous country estates in the now arid Syrian steppe, which now graces the entrance to
the Damascus Museum.

Fig. 9 (top). Umayyad desert palace of Qasr al-Hayr al-Sharqi. (Author's photograph)

Fig. 10. Tomb of Elibol at Palmyra. (Author's photograph)

'Abbasid imperial cities and their imitators

When the 'Abbasids came to power and established themselves in Iraq with the aid of the armies of Khurasan, one of the four divisions of the old Sasanian Empire, the influence of Persia naturally became stronger. In comparison to the Umayyads, the 'Abbasids are usually seen as adopting a more Persian style of planning, construction and statecraft, influenced by the Sasanian legacy in Mesopotamia and the integration of Persian converts to Islam at the highest echelons of government. This shift was exemplified in the siting and plan of Baghdad, their new capital, founded by the second 'Abbasid caliph, al-Mansur, in 762. Although the early garrison towns and Umayyad settlements were to an extent planned, Baghdad was the first of several showy purpose-built imperial capitals which were culturally influential, albeit not always successful as cities. According to the sources, its site on the fertile, well-irrigated land between the Tigris and Euphrates was carefully chosen for its strategic and agricultural virtues and personally approved by the caliph, who was reassured by a local Christian hermit's prophecy that the city would be prosperous and by local monks' endorsement of the favourable climate. One of al-Mansur's advisors, having noted the agricultural fertility of the immediate environs, summed up the felicity of the site:

> Supplies would also come to you up the Tigris in ships from China, India, Basra and Wasit. Finally stores would reach you from Armenia and those adjacent areas via the Tamarra canal connecting to the Zab [river] as well as from Byzantium, Amid, the Jazira and Mosul down the Tigris. You would be among waterways where no enemy of yours could reach you except by a floating or fixed bridge. … You would be near land, sea and mountain. … The proper organisation of cities requires you to make walls, moats and forts but the Tigris and Euphrates shall be the moats for the Commander of the Faithful.[16]

At the same time, the site's proximity to the old Sasanian capital of Ctesiphon symbolized the substitution of one imperial regime by another, while the Taq-i Kisra, the enormous great arch of the abandoned Sasanian palace's audience hall, posed a challenge for the Muslim architects to meet. Al-Mansur apparently paid as much attention to the city's plan as to its site:

> He commanded that its outline be drawn in ashes. He then proceeded to enter through each gate and to walk among its walls, its arcades, and its courtyards, all of which were outlined in ashes. … Having done that, he ordered cotton seeds placed on this outline and oil poured on it. Then he watched as the fire flared up, seeing the city as a whole and recognising its full plan.[17]

Satisfied, he gave the order for construction to begin. The city that emerged was circular in the Persian tradition, with the caliph's palace at its very centre, a symbolic statement of the universal centrality of the 'Abbasid caliphate which echoed the concept of the Persian monarch as pivot of the universe. The well-known Islamic art historian Robert Hillenbrand goes so far as to describe the city as a 'reworking of Sasanian themes'.[18] The caliph's throne room at the heart of the entire ensemble was topped by a green dome, a sign of imperial authority and a symbol of heaven borrowed from the Umayyads who had themselves adopted it from the Byzantines. A great mosque a quarter of the size of the palace was built adjacent to it and both were located in a huge open plaza called the *rahba*, their exclusivity enhanced by the vast area around them which was sometimes used for parades or as a camping ground but which was also often simply an empty space that highlighted 'the megalomania of the entire conception'.[19]

The other parts of the city were located in concentric circles, crowded into the space between the plaza and the outer walls. There was an inner ring of residences inhabited by princes and high officials and then an outer ring of less sumptuous dwellings for the caliph's Khurasani army, their families and assorted serving staff. Four thoroughfares cut through these rings from the central plaza to four city gates located in the outer double walls. Although the four gates were generally located at the cardinal points in Sasanian round cities, the 'Abbasid plan was Islamized by locating them at regular intervals from the Kufa Gate, which pointed southwest not only towards Kufa but also, more symbolically, towards Mecca. The city's markets were located along these main streets in the vicinity of the gates until 773 when a Byzantine prelate serving as ambassador expressed shock at the way the daily ingress and egress of market folk compromised the caliph's security. He told al-Mansur, 'I saw a beautiful building but your enemies with you in the city ... the market people.'[20] Just as an earlier Byzantine ambassador had goaded the Umayyad Mu'awiya to action, the 'Abbasid al-Mansur was now prompted by this comment to move the markets to the already flourishing extramural southern suburb of al-Karkh. He also built the Khuld Palace, a summer residence enwrapped in verdant gardens, outside the walls of the 'Abbasid 'Forbidden City'.

Although named Madinat al-Salam, the 'City of Peace', the new settlement quickly came to be known as Baghdad, the name of a small village in the same locality. Originally intended to be a residence for the caliph, his family, his advisors and his army, Baghdad was also the capital of a vast Islamic empire stretching from Tunisia to India, and as such a magnet for migrants and settlers of all kinds. Although the older Iraqi cities of Basra and Kufa were very important to intellectual and religious developments,

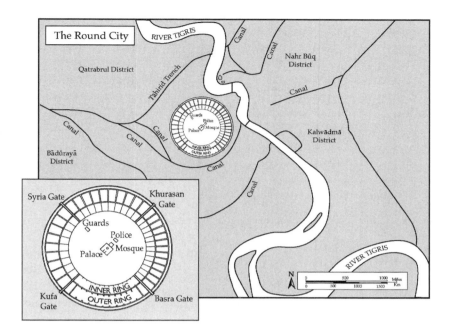

Plan of Baghdad. (After Lassner, *The Shaping of 'Abbasid Rule*, pp 186, 190)

Baghdad quickly became a commercial and industrial metropolis with numerous suburbs outside the round city of Madinat al-Salam, where the residential, commercial and manufacturing areas were located. Everything which the empire had to offer could be made or found in Baghdad, and its huge population lived off the produce not only of Iraq but of the empire as a whole: grain from the fertile farmlands of the north was shipped from Mosul downriver, dates and fruit came from the Hijaz, Syria and many other regions by caravan, while the 'Abbasids raised horses on northern Persian stud farms and imported richly embroidered ceremonial fabrics from the southern Persian province of Khuzistan. The wealthy denizens of the city – including princes and princesses of the blood – constructed luxurious secluded homes sheltered by high walls along the Tigris, and in later centuries the caliphs themselves moved out of the round city to riverside palaces away from the hustle and bustle of the city centre.

Despite the undoubted success of Baghdad as the chief metropolis of the Islamic world, political and religious differences between the inhabitants of the city and the 'Abbasids persuaded the caliph al-Mu'tasim (r. 833–42) to embark on a new imperial urban project intended to provide an appropriate residence for his new Turkish army and a haven from the scholars who opposed the 'Abbasids' imposition of the doctrine of the createdness of the Qur'an. The outcome was the establishment of Samarra on the banks of the Tigris about 70 miles north of Baghdad between 834 and 836. Al-Mu'tasim did not choose his site quite so carefully or fortuitously as al-Mansur. The area was watered by the Sasanian-built Nahrawan canal and was primarily good for hunting rather than agriculture, and although there had been a Sasanian hunting lodge and perhaps a Roman fort in the vicinity, previous regimes had not built a town there. Victualling Samarra was thus a permanent problem.

The succession of Samarran palaces, including Jawsaq al-Khaqani built for al-Mu'tasim himself, Balkuwara built for al-Mu'tazz, and several similar foundations, were designed for maximum effect but not for longevity. They were huge, so huge that it was often necessary to ride a donkey or mule from one area to another, and were built of rammed earth, mudbrick and occasionally baked brick so that they could be raised as quickly as possible. Their humble building materials were then disguised with every kind of decorative facing available in the Islamic world – marble panels, tiles, mosaics, carved stucco, wall paintings and inlaid precious wood and metal – to create a dazzling spectacle. The plan of each palace varied but the architects conveyed the power of the caliph by placing an audience chamber at the end of a series of courts, often on a higher plane with a splendid view, conveying the idea of the monarch as master of all he surveyed. Water and gardens also figured largely in the plans, as did polo grounds and horse-racing tracks to keep the Turkish cavalry's skills honed and provide entertainment for the court.

The city's name is probably the Arabic form of Sumra, the Syriac name of an earlier village in the area, but poets of the 'Abbasid court gave it a rather more florid etymology, positing that it was the abbreviated form of the Arabic phrase *surra man ra'a*, which literally means 'it delights whoever sees [it]' or, more elegantly, 'the delight of the beholder'. Despite Samarra's brief period of glory from the 830s to early 890s, this poetic rendering of its name points to the profound impact it had on imperial urban planning across the Islamic world, an impact in fact much greater than that of Madinat al-Salam in Baghdad which was not replicated in other places. Its vast and splendid array of riverside palaces, boulevards and soldiers' homes set the standard for planned royal cities across the Islamic world from Afghanistan to Spain. Even though it was finally abandoned by the caliphs in 892, it possessed a similar aura to such legendary sites as Persepolis, Constantinople or even Rome. In Egypt the 'Abbasid governor Ibn Tulun established his own royal city called al-Qata'i' alongside Fustat (Cairo) in emulation of Samarra. Its great mosque, the Mosque of Ibn Tulun, is still one of the

Fig. 11. Baghdad Gate in Raqqa showing the typical monumental brickwork of the 'Abbasid era which originally graced Baghdad and Samarra. (Author's photograph)

Fig. 12 (above). 'Abbasid-style Mosque of Ibn Tulun in Cairo. (Author's photograph)

Fig. 13. Great Mosque of Qayrawan which achieved its current form under the Aghlabids who ruled Tunisia in the name of the 'Abbasids. (Author's photograph)

foremost monuments in Cairo and one of the most stunning examples of 'Abbasid brick mosque design outside Iraq – its minaret a sister to the minarets of the great mosques of al-Mutawakkil and Abu Dulaf at Samarra, whose unusual coiled design may have been inspired by the ziggurats of Mesopotamia.

It was not only 'Abbasid governors who followed the architectural lead of the caliphs. In the next century both the Umayyads in Spain and the Fatimids in North Africa also adopted the idea of a royal city and constructed their own versions: the Umayyads at Madinat al-Zahra' outside Cordoba, and the Fatimids at Mahdiyya in Tunisia and al-Qahira (Cairo) in Egypt. These were imitative and competitive acts that expressed in urban form the claims of the Fatimids and Umayyads to caliphal status. In the case of the Umayyads, the influence of 'Abbasid Baghdad and Samarra began to be felt in the ninth century when 'Abd al-Rahman II decided to replace the rough and ready character of palace life in Cordoba with more appropriate etiquette and protocol modelled on that of the 'Abbasids. When 'Abd al-Rahman III changed his title from 'prince' (*amir*) to the caliphal 'commander of the faithful' (*amir al-mu'minin*) in 929, Umayyad engagement with eastern 'Abbasid models started to go much further.

In practical terms 'Abd al-Rahman III's revival of an Umayyad caliphate marked his successful restoration of Umayyad power throughout the Muslim parts of the Iberian peninsula, and as tax revenues from all quarters began to flow in he turned to the construction of a royal capital befitting his new status to replace the old royal residence in Cordoba next to the great mosque. With the assistance of his son al-Hakam II, who directed the project, a south-facing site was selected at the base of a small range of hills with a panoramic view east across an agricultural plain to Cordoba and the Guadalquivir river, where the Umayyads and their courtiers already had several suburban estates at least partially built on Romano-Visigothic foundations.

The new city was rectangular, with an outer wall 'laid out in the Roman and Byzantine fashion' which evoked the specific heritage of al-Andalus and, perhaps, the Umayyads' previous home in Syria, while its arrangement on three tiers, according to the Arab authors, gave the caliph commanding views across the plain to Cordoba, just as the Samarran palaces of the 'Abbasids were designed to provide the caliphs with sweeping vistas across the Tigris. The top tier abutting the back wall was the site of the royal palace itself; receptions halls, gardens, government offices and the residences of important officials were located on a second slightly lower tier; while the 'public' part of the city, including the great mosque, ordinary residences and a hunting park stocked with animals, occupied the third and

Fig. 14. Umayyad royal city of Madinat al-Zahra' outside Cordoba.
(Author's photograph)

lowest tier which was much larger than the upper ones.

Although by no means physically the same as Samarra, Madinat al-Zahra' spoke a similar language of power and gave the Umayyads a stage on which they played out their claim to be the foremost Sunni Muslim monarchs in the world before their own subjects, Muslim ambassadors, and visitors from Constantinople, the Christian principalities of north-ern Spain and the Frankish lands further north. The late Umayyad histo-rian Ibn Hayyan describes the visit of a deputation from Barcelona to the caliph al-Hakam II, who waited immobile, seated in a large arched niche at the end of his eastern audience hall which looked out on the gardens, surrounded by his glittering court. A caliphal guard escorted the embassy to Madinat al-Zahra', accompanied by Cordoban Christian translators, and they were made to wait in an antechamber before finally being admitted to the caliph's presence, and, 'when they reached the entrance of the hall inside which the throne was located, they fell to the ground in prostration … until they drew close to the caliph's hands which they kissed'.[21] Stunning architecture, extensive protocol and the massed subjects of the caliph all combined to intimidating and impressive effect.

Madinat al-Zahra' was, however, very different to Samarra in one respect: while the 'Abbasids had sought to get away from Baghdad, the old and new Umayyad capitals enjoyed a symbiotic relationship. The caliphs themselves travelled backwards and forwards and ensured that their visitors

Fig. 15. Portal of the Fatimid Great Mosque of Mahdiyya which evokes the Roman arches dotted across the Tunisian landscape. (Author's photograph)

did the same. Embassies followed a complicated ceremonial route to Madinat al-Zahra', which always included Cordoba. Moreover many Cordobans attended court at Madinat al-Zahra' and the Umayyads offered them financial incentives to build residences and shops along the highway connecting the two. Ibn Hawqal, who wrote two geographical surveys of the Islamic world in the late tenth century, commented:

> 'Abd al-Rahman [III] built to [Cordoba's] west a city known as [Madinat] al-Zahra' at the foot of a mountain called Jabal Batlash. He laid out markets, built baths, caravanserais, palaces and garden retreats. He attracted the common people to build there by ordering his town criers to announce that anyone wishing to build a house or take up residence near the ruler would receive four hundred dirhams. The people hastened to build and the town quickly increased and became busy. The construction almost reached from Cordoba to [Madinat] al-Zahra'.[22]

Madinat al-Zahra' flourished for less than a century. When the Umayyad caliphate of Cordoba collapsed between 1008 and 1031, Madinat al-Zahra' collapsed with it, sacked and pillaged by the unpaid troops of the Umayyads and the factions involved in the civil wars which erupted. However, the process of political fragmentation which occurred in Islamic Spain at

Fig. 16. Roman arch at Sbeitla in Tunisia. (Author's photograph)

this time had a rather similar result to earlier periods of political collapse in the 'Abbasid heartlands – the wider dissemination of metropolitan cultural norms to the provinces. In the ensuing decades Seville, Toledo and Saragossa all became the sites of new palace complexes modelled on Madinat al-Zahra', whose memory was celebrated in poetry and song, and lesser potentates competed to cultivate courts worthy of the Umayyad era and, by extension, the 'Abbasid golden age in Baghdad.

When the Isma'ili Shi'i Fatimids came to power in Tunisia in 909 they also emulated the 'Abbasid paradigm by constructing a series of planned cities, the best known of which is Mahdiyya, a heavily fortified royal enclave on a coastal promontory which protected the Shi'i Fatimids from the hostile Sunni population whose base was Qayrawan, originally a *misr* and centre of the 'Abbasid administration in the area. Its great mosque, however, harked back to Antiquity, with its grand portal reminiscent of a Roman triumphal arch, of which there were several in what is now Tunisia and Libya. After quelling a major rebellion, the Fatimids emerged from Mahdiyya and constructed a round city in the Baghdad mode called al-Mansuriyya, 'The Victorious', near Qayrawan. Like the Umayyads, the Fatimids were rivals of the 'Abbasids, but as fellow 'easterners' they enhanced and deepened the diffusion of Persian cultural influence into the Islamic west and indeed into

Fig. 17 (top). Fatimid Mosque of al-Hakim in Cairo. (Author's photograph)

Fig. 18 (middle). Fatimid al-Aqmar Mosque in Cairo. (Author's photograph)

Fig. 19 (bottom). The Fatimid Gate of Victory and minaret of the Mosque of al-Hakim, Cairo. From David Roberts, *Egypt and Nubia* (London, 1846–49), vol. 3, plate 3, tab. b.19. (Reproduced by kind permission of the Syndics of Cambridge University Library)

Mediterranean culture as a whole, as the stunning ceiling paintings depicting dancers and musicians in the Norman Capella Palatina in Palermo testify.

The Fatimids' best-known city, however, is al-Qahira, from whence the name 'Cairo' is derived, which they built north of the existing city of Fustat and its neighbouring 'Abbasid complex al-Qata'i'. Although al-Qahira was originally a camp-city in the tradition of the *amsar*, the Fatimids' failure to conquer Syria and invade Iraq meant that it became their capital. Unlike the *amsar* it was walled from the outset to protect the invading army, but like them it had a fairly simple plan: a main street bisected the camp from north to south, straddled by the eastern and western palaces between which stood an open area that loomed large in later Fatimid ceremonies. A large outdoor prayer area (*musalla*) was demarcated north of the walls, and the famous al-Azhar Mosque was founded south of the eastern palace. The rest of the area enclosed by the walls was divided and allocated to different ethnic units of the Fatimid army, which was dominated at first by Kutama Berber tribesmen from Tunisia but also included black troops from Zawila in the Sahara, Turks and Daylamites.

After the transfer of the Fatimid caliph, his family and court to Cairo in 972, al-Qahira became a royal city of the 'Abbasid and Umayyad type. Its resounding success as a city related to its quick development of an intimate economic relationship with Fustat to the south, whose merchants rented shops and sold their wares within its walls in contravention of its original politico-military exclusivity. Although al-Qahira was the caliph's residence and the place in which Fatimid public ceremonies took place, it seems not to have maintained such a separation of functions as either Samarra or Madinat al-Zahra'. A few years after the Fatimids arrived, al-Muqaddasi, who appears to have been a Shi'i, revelled in the joint elevation of Cairo and Fustat, saying:

> It is the seat of the Commander of the Faithful. ... It has superseded Baghdad, and it is the glory of Islam, and is the market place of all mankind. It is more sublime than the City of Peace. It is the storehouse of the Occident, the entrepot of the Orient, and is crowded with people at the time of the pilgrimage festival. Among the capitals there is none more populous than it, and it abounds in noble and learned men.[23]

Set at the base of the Nile delta, Cairo was supported by the toil of the peasants of the delta to the north and the Nile valley to the south, and, like Baghdad, canals facilitated the development of riverine traffic which connected Cairo to Alexandria on the Mediterranean and to the Red Sea ports which channelled pilgrims and trade to Arabia and the Indian Ocean beyond. Its favourable situation meant that the passing of the Fatimids in 1171 did not compromise its existence. Instead it went from strength to strength and, as the economic foundations upon which Baghdad depended crumbled away and it became an 'effaced ruin', its truest successor as the foremost metropolis in the Islamic world was indeed Cairo.[24]

Provincial cities in the 'Abbasid age

The ninth and tenth centuries were the era of the Islamic palatine city *par excellence*, but the great capitals of the Islamic world were only the most outstanding cities in a flourishing urban network which also included provincial capitals, market towns, holy cities, ports, border posts and, of course, countless substantial villages, most of which were rather less transient than their more glamorous cousins. In contrast to the Sasanian Empire which had nurtured and revered the land and built the canals which watered so much of Iraq, Muslims conceptualized their empire as a series of highways connecting an endless chain of cities, towns and villages. Many of the 'Abbasid-era geographers speak in just this way, describing the Islamic world in terms of journey stages from town to town which could take a traveller from the southern foothills of the Pyrenees to China or India. Although sometimes frustratingly brief in their actual descriptions of towns and cities, it is these meticulous catalogues of the classical Islamic world and the personal travel accounts which began to proliferate in the later centuries of the 'Abbasid caliphate that allow us to glean something of the nature of ordinary cities and the way they worked.

One of the best such geographical accounts, and incidentally one which very much views the Islamic world as a single cultural unit, is *The Best Divisions of Knowledge of the Regions* written by the tenth-century geographer Abu 'Abd Allah Muhammad al-Muqaddasi (*c.* 945–1000), whose foreword explains his rigorous scientific method and emphasis on observation, which he amply demonstrates in his subsequent orderly account of every 'province' of the Islamic world starting from its symbolic heart in Arabia, and then covering the Arab provinces, including North Africa and Spain, followed by the non-Arab provinces from Iran to Sind.

It is evident from al-Muqaddasi's narrative and from the later travel accounts of Nasir-i Khusraw and Ibn Jubayr, dating from the eleventh and twelfth centuries respectively, that the great mosque and the marketplace were the two foremost institutions in the mature 'Abbasid cityscape, whether a city was of Islamic or pre-Islamic origin. Both served a wider range of functions than their primary purposes suggest: the great mosque was much more than a religious building and the market was by no means limited to

Fig. 20. Minaret of the Almohad Great Mosque of Seville. (Author's photograph)

retail. In his description of the Great Mosque of Damascus, al-Muqaddasi notes that the arcades at one gate were 'the place of the secretaries', while 'astrologers and other such people' sat at the next gate and 'notaries and the like' sat at a third plying their trade.[25] Although great mosques may have been commissioned sparingly in the early centuries of Islam, the vast majority of towns and cities possessed a great mosque by the tenth century and, as cities expanded, many suburbs acquired one too. This became ever more necessary as the Muslim population went from being an elite minority to the majority, and older Christian and Zoroastrian communities dwindled or disappeared. Al-Muqaddasi lists seven congregational mosques in Cairo by the late tenth century, while Nasir-i Kusraw – who is sometimes given to exaggeration – claims that it had as many as 15 congregational mosques for its burgeoning Muslim population in the next century.[26]

The great mosque's institutional importance derived from the pivotal role it played not only in communal religion but also in the recognition of the political authorities. Whether founded on virgin land or on the site of a previous church or temple, the great mosque was the most trenchant sign of Islam's presence in a city and the venue where the Muslim population publicly stated their religious and political allegiances. Every male Muslim was (and is) required to attend the communal noon prayer on Friday as a religious duty. It is meritorious but not obligatory for women to attend. Attendance at the Friday prayer was an obligation which early Muslims took seriously and historians frequently estimate the Muslim population of cities in this period using the number of adult males the great mosque could accommodate as a starting figure. When the number of worshippers exceeded the space available, they crowded into adjacent areas. Al-Muqaddasi was unsure whether to believe reports in Fustat that the congregation of the Mosque of 'Amr was 10,000 but he was convinced by the following incident:

> Being late one day, I was strenuously repairing to the Friday prayers, and I found the lines of people in the markets extending to more than a thousand cubits from the mosque. And I saw, moreover, that the mercantile establishments, and the places of worship, and the shops around the mosque were filled on everyside with worshippers.[27]

The Almohads who ruled Spain and North Africa in the twelfth century faced a similar problem in Seville and responded by replacing the small congregational mosque, which had been built in Umayyad days, with a new larger one, the minaret of which still survives as the famous Giralda bell tower of the cathedral:

> The great mosque of Seville, known as the Mosque of 'Adabbas, had become too small for the population and they prayed in its surrounding plazas and courtyards and in the parts of the market adjacent [to the mosque] which distanced them from the call signalling the obligation [of prayer], and perhaps invalidated their prayers.[28]

The Friday prayer, in contrast to all other ritual prayers, was accompanied by a sermon (*khutba*) which was dedicated to the political master of the area – the caliph and his local representatives – and thus an affirmation of loyalty to those authorities. Refusal to make this acknowledgement or to replace the caliph or governor's name with that of a rival was a trenchant statement of rebellion involving or implicating a substantial proportion of the adult male population. The political authorities also used the occasion of the Friday prayer to inform the congregation of military victories or other noteworthy achievements, or to threaten unruly subjects with dire punishments.

Fig. 21. Courtyard of the Almohad Great Mosque of Seville planted with orange trees. (Author's photograph)

Up until at least the eleventh century, the great mosque played important civic, educational and judicial roles in the absence of designated buildings for these purposes, emphasizing its composite character as a public space. It was also the hub of public social life. It is very easy to project the later and more sacred character of great mosques back in time, but for much of the 'Abbasid era the expansive courtyard of a great mosque was the Muslim equivalent of the forum, a place where men gathered for political exchanges, to resolve legal disputes, listen to the words of the scholars and meet friends, as well as to pray. The colonnaded courtyard and prayer hall offered a venue for scholars to instruct the pupils gathered at their feet in a time-honoured Mediterranean fashion which did not greatly differ from the image we have of students listening to Socrates or Plato. The Muslim judge, the *qadi*, would pronounce on cases in the congregational mosque, even though much of the work associated with a case took place in less formal and constrained circumstances, including the judge's own home. Many hawkers and minor tradesmen did a roaring business in great mosques, and it was by no means unknown for people to bring their animals into its precincts, where they wandered at liberty among the worshippers.

Jurists and indeed caliphs sometimes viewed this askance and attempted to limit the activities taking place in the mosques. In 892 the caliph al-Mu'tadid, who was sensitive to the subversive possibilities of mosque culture, instructed the Baghdad authorities to decree 'that no popular preachers, astrologers or fortune tellers should sit [and ply their trade] in the streets or the Friday mosque'.[29] In July 897 he issued a similar directive that storytellers should not sit in the congregational mosques or by the roadside, and 'groups studying legal opinions and other people were also prevented from sitting in the two Friday mosques and vendors were prevented from sitting in their stalls [in the mosques]' to prevent the circulation of pro-Umayyad sentiments which the caliph found contrary to 'Abbasid interests, despite the absence of any Umayyad threat except in far away Spain.[30]

The reverent air we associate with religious buildings was further compromised by people shouting greetings, coughing and even spitting. Women also came into the mosque, some to sell their wares, others to attend the prayer in areas specially designated for them. Beggars were another common sight in the vicinity of the mosque, although the official responsible for public order and decency, the *muhtasib* (market inspector), was expected to make sure that they did not importune the faithful during prayer. The mosque courtyard was used rather like a public garden or plaza. Some courtyards did indeed have grassed areas or trees enhancing this impression: the congregational mosque of Acre was 'partially paved in stone and partially planted with grass'.[31] Even today it is not uncommon to see couples strolling across the spacious courtyards of mosques, groups of children playing under the watchful eye of their mothers, and elderly men snoozing in the shade of the arcades in a manner reminiscent of Ibn Jubayr's comments about the courtyard of the Great Mosque of Damascus in 1184: 'This court is one of the most beautiful and splendid of sights. Here the population congregate for it is their place of care-dispelling and recreation.'[32]

Given the great mosque's central or prominent location in any city, the fact that every male Muslim was required to frequent it on at least a weekly basis and that people mingled there regularly, it is hardly surprising that the markets were often located in close proximity to it as well as in other economically viable locations, such as close to ports or other transport routes. As Paul Wheatley puts it, while '*suqs* might appear in almost every possible location', the vicinity of the mosque was a favoured location because everyone had to pass that way.[33] Markets also came in all shapes and sizes – open squares where people could set up stalls or lay out mats piled high with their wares, elegant streets of shops often roofed to keep out the sun, and market halls for specific commodities which could be locked at night to protect the merchandise within. For instance, the tenth-century Buyid ruler 'Adud al-Dawla built a 'great edifice with four gates, within it another structure where the clothes were sold' in the Persian city of Kazarun.[34]

The *suq* or bazaar was an integral part of the life of most cities in the 'Abbasid era and provided a second public space for people – primarily men – to gather and communicate as well as buy and sell. With the exception of a few towns whose *raison d'être* was that of a shrine, exchange was the lifeblood of the urban network in the *dar al-islam* and it is noteworthy that the grand planned cities of princes rarely survived unless they developed a stable commercial sector: while Baghdad and Cairo were success stories in that respect, Samarra, Madinat al-Zahra' and Mahdiyya all faltered, although Samarra developed a new more limited role as a Shi'i shrine city thanks to the death and burial there of 'Ali al-Hadi (d. 868) and his son Hasan al-'Askari (d. 874), the tenth and eleventh Shi'i *imam*s.

The main market area of any city was not only the locale for buying and selling but also for manufacture. Small producer-retailers tended to work in close proximity to other producers of the same or similar items, making and selling their own products. Markets of this type included those of the shoe-makers, tentmakers, brassworkers, carpenters, jewellers and numerous other craftsmen. Other goods were imported either from local rural producers or from further afield – rich textiles, ceramics, perfumes and spices – and sold in city shops. Agricultural produce destined for the mouths of hungry urbanites came from nearby villages and was often sold at weekly markets by the city gates. Caravans bearing goods were also unloaded at convenient points outside the city and their products brought into urban warehouses on mules and other beasts of burden.

Although the dimly lit, narrow lanes of the markets of Istanbul, Cairo or Fes, stuffed to bursting point with gleaming brass lamps, multi-coloured silk robes and richly patterned carpets, give a hint of the markets of the past, they are a poor reflection of the *suq*s which offered the consumer almost all the products of the civilized world, in surroundings more often described as splendid and palatial than cramped and dusty. The Buyid 'Adud al-Dawla constructed fine markets in Ramhurmuz, which al-Muqaddasi eulogized in the following words: 'I have never seen more admirable than them in cleanliness and elegance. They have been decorated, ornamented, paved and covered. Gates have been constructed on the markets and are locked each night.'[35] When the Persian traveller Nasir-i Khusraw visited Tripoli in Lebanon in the mid-eleventh century, he noted that 'the lanes and bazaars are so nice and clean you would think each a king's palace'.[36] He was partic-ularly enraptured by Cairo and described one of the markets of Fustat situ-ated north of the Mosque of 'Amr in the following fulsome terms: 'No-one ever saw such a bazaar anywhere else. Every sort of rare goods (sic) from all over the world can be had there.'[37] Slightly later, Ibn Jubayr considered Alexandria's markets 'magnificent' and its streets broad.[38]

Two additional references show that well-appointed markets were very much the norm and were believed to have a ancient heritage. Al-Muqaddasi thought it worth a particular note when markets were not well designed and criticized Shiraz in Iran sharply for its 'narrow markets' where 'it is not possible for two beasts of burden to go side by side'.[39] Furthermore when the Syrian al-Shayzari wrote an influential manual on regulating the market in the twelfth century, he explicitly linked the physical character of the Muslim market to Antiquity:

> The markets must be situated on an elevated and spacious site as they were in ancient Rome. If the market is not paved, there should be a pavement either side of it for the people to walk on in winter. Nobody is permitted to bring a shop bench from the roofed passageway into the main thoroughfare as this obstructs passers by.[40]

The market was also a cultural melting pot. The most famous example of this is Basra, the home of one of the early 'Abbasid age's most unique men of letters, al-Jahiz, who recounted that his education took place not only in the Great Mosque of Basra but also in the Mirbad marketplace west of the city where he joined with the storytellers to collect Arabic 'verses by madmen and Bedouin brigands ... [and] works by Jewish poets'.[41] In so doing he attempted to preserve Arabic language and lore in a city which was the meeting point between Arabic and Persian speakers and cultures and he contributed to the formulation of an important strand within Arabic *belles lettres*. The market area of any city was also the place where visitors could find accommodation in the form of the *funduq*, a hostelry related in name and function to the earlier Byzantine *pandocheion* and the inns of the Holy Land, known in Aramaic as *pundaq*.

Busy main streets connected the public parts of the city, represented by the great mosque and the markets, to the outer periphery, which generally acquired walls and gateways during the 'Abbasid era, if not before. Although these streets were not always straight or particularly wide, they were lined with shops and stalls. Numerous residential quarters were located in between. Most such quarters had their own local mosque, a bath house, a water fountain, a communal oven where people could bring their bread to be baked for a small sum, and some stalls or shops where daily essentials such as utensils and food could be purchased. Classical Islamic urban living was often one of fast food bought outside the home, especially for the poorer inhabitants of cities who lacked their own cooking facilities: al-Shayzari lists numerous types of prepared food available in twelfth-century Syria from meat pasties, sausages and fried fish to candies and honey pastries. In some cities high-rise living was common, and families maximized their space by building roof gardens with orange and banana trees and herbs in tubs. Al-Muqaddasi talked of 'towering houses' of teakwood and brick in Siraf on the Persian Gulf and remarked that in Fustat 'their buildings are four of five stories high, just as our lighthouses; the light enters them from a central [courtyard]'.[42]

In his more hyperbolic description of Fustat in the eleventh century, Nasir-i Khusraw claimed that there were tenements of seven and even 14 storeys high, and 'bazaars and lanes where lamps must always be kept lit because no light ever falls on the ground'.[43] The houses of al-Qahira were a more modest five or six storeys high, but they were 'magnificent and fine' detached residences, 'so that no-one's trees or outbuildings are against anyone else's walls'.[44] Tripoli in Lebanon boasted buildings four or five storeys high.[45] Allowing for some exaggeration on the part of the author, it is still obvious that these towns and cities had high-rise buildings which call to mind Roman *insulae*, although no direct link between the two can be made.

Nasir-i Khusraw's descriptions recall to mind the importance of the Arab image of the city as a garden which was reinforced by the Persian tradition of including gardens and water within the city limits. Although walls were not an integral part of the first Muslim towns, they increasingly became the norm. Unsympathetic analysts have tended to see the extensive areas encircled by city walls as a sign of faulty planning or excessively grandiose expectations, but these walls may also indicate forethought for possible growth in the city population and a desire to include gardens within rather than outside the city for the pleasure and sustenance of its inhabitants. Wherever they were located, it is clear from the comments of geographers and travellers that gardens and orchards were as much part of the normal urban environment as mosques and markets and that there was no rigorous separation between town and country. To take a fairly random sample, al-Muqaddasi described Shahrastan in southern Iran as 'a delightful place with gardens and copious springs' and Balkh in Khurasan as 'an attractive metropolis, prosperous, agreeable. ... Streams cut through its streets, gardens and trees encircle it.'[46] Nasir-i Khusraw later characterized Caesarea in Palestine as 'a nice place with running water, palm groves, orange and citron groves and a fortified rampart with an iron gate', while he says of Qazvin in Iran, '[It] has many orchards with neither walls nor hedges, so that there is nothing to prevent access to the gardens.'[47]

The above references to streams and springs remind us that water is always crucial to city life. For Muslims, flowing water was an integral part of their image of a garden and paradise itself. In the often hot and arid lands of Islam, the provision of water for the thirsty was a sacred duty and water was also essential for performing the required ritual ablutions before prayer. The practical, ritual and symbolic importance of providing water manifested itself in the Muslims' considerable devotion to hydraulic engineering, an area in which they showed ingenuity as well as expertise. Water was transported to cities by all manner of aqueducts, canals and deep-bored wells. All great mosques had ablution areas and often public lavatories and every urban quarter had one or more bath houses with hot and cold water on tap. These facilities either used stored water from cisterns or, where possible, natural springs within cities. At Mayyarfariqin in northern Mesopotamia, the congregational mosque had an impressive sanitation system:

> Briefly, the ablution pool faces forty chambers, through each of which run two large channels, one of which is visible and for use, while the other is concealed beneath the earth and is for carrying away refuse and flushing the cisterns.[48]

Nearby Amid sported a large round pool the height of a man with a brass waterspout in its great mosque courtyard, and in Tripoli the great mosque had 'a marble pool with a brass fountain' and 'in one of the bazaar streets, water spil[t] out from five spouts for people to draw water'.[49] Meanwhile baths with hot and cold running water were such a common feature in cities that they were rarely described in detail. In his account of Baghdad, Ibn Jubayr claims that the baths 'cannot be counted, but one of the town's sheikhs told us that in the eastern and western parts together, there are about two thousand', despite his initial comment that the 'Abbasid capital of 1184 was a shadow of itself, 'a remain washed out, or the statue of a ghost'.[50]

By the eleventh and twelfth centuries the religious infrastructure had diversified to include schools and colleges of various kinds, shrines, as well as numerous local and great mosques. Free hospitals and libraries founded by rulers and wealthy urbanites had also become common. The majority of these urban institutions were supported by pious endowments, known as *waqf* in Arabic, which meant that a benefactor had legally bequeathed some property or revenue, usually rents from land or shops, to support a mosque, school, shrine or college in perpetuity. Rich individuals, including rulers who wished to show their dedication to the welfare of the community, often paid for the construction and upkeep of whole buildings, but less wealthy individuals made smaller contributions, dedicating money for oil to keep lamps alight, bread for hungry students and beds for pious visitors. This system was private in the sense that no individual was obliged to make a pious endowment, but it was highly communal and heavily supported by those in positions of power and authority, giving it a public social aspect and ensuring that education, the poor, the sick and travellers were supported by the community either free of charge or for nominal sums.

One of the most important institutions which had grown up was the *madrasa*, a school or theological college which provided free living quarters and teaching space to students of the religious sciences, especially law. The idea of having Muslim centres of higher learning originated in Baghdad with the *bayt al-hikma*, or house of wisdom, founded by the caliph al-Mansur in the eighth century, which acted as a site for the translation of the knowledge of the ancient Greeks and Persians into Arabic and its study. A more religiously focused *dar al-hikma* or *dar al-'ilm* (house of wisdom or knowledge) was constructed by the Fatimids in Cairo to train Isma'ili propagandists as well as promote learning more generally. These initiatives promoted the spread of libraries and then other institutions of learning like the *madrasa*, which became popular in eastern Islamic lands during the second half of the eleventh century. Its popularity was due to the Saljuqs who are generally considered patrons of the *madrasa* and responsible for its diffusion across the Islamic world. The most famous *madrasa* was the Nizamiyya, founded in Baghdad in 1165 by the Saljuqs' chief minister Nizam al-Mulk, who may well have been the originator of the idea of creating state *madrasa*s in the first place and who founded several similar institutions in other eastern Islamic cities such as Merv, Nishapur and Isfahan. It spread through Syria in the eleventh century and into Egypt, finally reaching Morocco and Spain in the fourteenth century.

For those whose preferences were mystical rather than juridical, there was the *khanqah*, an institution often physically very similar to a *madrasa* but dedicated to the teaching of Islamic mystical doctrines and practices. The term *khanqah* is Persian in origin and appeared in the tenth century to denote a lodge for ascetic and militant Muslims in frontier areas, but during the eleventh century it came to mean a Sufi retreat. The otherworldly interests of the denizens of a *khanqah* were signalled by the frequent location of such buildings in cemeteries, away from the bustle of city life and on the very threshold of the world of the dead. Nizam al-Mulk constructed *khanqah*s as well as *madrasa*s, showing the complementarity of the two as establishments for the study of the esoteric mystical and exoteric legalistic aspects of Islam respectively.

Most of the religious facilities in towns were for Muslims, but churches and synagogues remained part of the cityscape and many monasteries continued to operate in the countryside. In one area, however, that of shrines, there was not just coexistence but a genuine overlap in religious belief and practice. In Syria and Palestine many shrines endowed and supported by Muslims had Judaeo-Christian origins and were visited by

Fig. 22. Portal of the hospital of Nur al-Din in Damascus showing its re-used
Byzantine lintel. (Author's photograph)

pilgrims of all three faiths. The shrines on Mount Qasiyun outside Damascus described by Ibn Jubayr include the birthplace of Abraham, which was
also believed to be at Harran in Mesopotamia, the cave where Cain killed
Abel, the 'Grotto of Adam', the dwelling of Jesus and his mother Mary,
and the oratory of Elijah, all of which had attached mosques and apartments for pilgrims supported by 'endowments consisting of gardens, arable
lands and houses'.[51] Islam's status as the final revelation in the Abrahamic
tradition made it natural for such holy sites to become shrines visited by
adherents of all the Semitic faiths, but even in Iran and later India Muslims
often attended the same shrines as Zoroastrians and Hindus in a common
recognition of sanctity.

Although not explicitly religious, hospitals were also considered charitable institutions and were supported by pious endowments. A community of practising physicians, many of Nestorian Christian origin, emerged
in Baghdad under the aegis of the caliph al-Mansur, and hospitals using
Hellenic and Persian medicine became part of the infrastructure of the city
during the caliphate of Harun al-Rashid. There were at least five by the late
ninth century, as wealthy benefactors, including women, put up funds for
their establishment and upkeep. Although Muslims often attributed the
origin of the hospital to Hippocrates, hospitals were not a common feature
of the Graeco-Roman cityscape, and the inspiration was more likely to have
been the hospital in Sasanian Gundeshapur from which the first 'Abbasid
court physicians came. Many hospitals doubled up as medical schools where

successive generations of doctors – Muslim, Christian and Jewish – were trained, and it was in their courtyards and halls that the great advances in Arabic medicine were made.

From Baghdad, hospitals quickly became widespread, springing up in Rayy, Shiraz, Isfahan and Fustat in the course of the tenth century. In his account of Shiraz, al-Muqaddasi approvingly noted, 'Here too is a hospital like at Isfahan in its equipment, physicians, attendants, food, the like of which I have not seen in any [other] country'.[52] By the later 'Abbasid era, cities of note in the Islamic east usually had one or more hospitals, staffed by a team of specialist doctors. Ibn Jubayr mentions hospitals in Alexandria, Cairo, Mosul, Harran, Aleppo and Damascus as well as Baghdad. He describes Salah al-Din's Cairene hospital as 'a palace goodly for its beauty and spaciousness', made up of three separate establishments: a men's hospital, a women's hospital and a mental asylum. To run it:

> He [Salah al-Din] appointed as intendant a man of science with whom he placed a store of drugs and whom he empowered to use the potions and apply them in their various forms. In the rooms of this palace were placed beds, fully appointed, for lying patients. At the disposal of the intendant are servants whose duty it is, morning and evening, to examine the conditions of the sick, and to bring them the food and potions which befit them.[53]

The foundation of hospitals in North Africa coincided with Salah al-Din's activities in Egypt. The late twelfth-century Almohad caliph Ya'qub al-Mansur founded a famous hospital in Marrakesh which the historian al-Marrakushi, one of the city's native sons, believed unparalleled in the world. He reported that the caliph selected a choice spot in the city and commanded the builders to embellish the hospital with all manner of carving and decoration. He also ordered the planting of perfumed and fruit-bearing trees inside and the installation of flowing water to all the rooms in addition to four pools in the central courtyard. He then ordered rich furnishings of wool, cotton, silk and leather and allocated the hospital 30 dinars a day for food and expenses, excluding medical costs, stipulating that patients should be given appropriate night clothes depending on the season. Finally he appointed a pharmacist to make potions, creams and powders for the patients.[54] He may also have founded a hospital in Spain, although Ibn al-Khatib, a fourteenth-century scholar and courtier from Granada, insisted that the first hospital built in Islamic Spain was that commissioned by Muhammad V in Granada, which was completed in 1367.[55]

Cities naturally included places for burying the dead, who were either interred in communal cemeteries located on the perimeter of built-up areas or, in the case of rulers, within their palaces. Early Islamic funerary rites were very simple and involved washing and shrouding the corpse, placing it in a wooden coffin and then burying it as quickly as possible with the head facing Mecca. In keeping with pre-Islamic practice, graves were marked in a simple way without inscriptions, a practice still followed in rural communities in southern Morocco. This reflected the Prophet's own stated dislike for opulent graves, which smacked of pride and risked leading the faithful away from God into the grave sin of venerating the dead. However, Muslims soon came into contact with more elaborate approaches to burial and commemoration of the dead. Greater Syria was awash with shrines and tombs of Christian and pre-Christian provenance, from Roman mausoleums to the tower tombs of Palmyra which offered rich inspiration to Muslims. Although the Zoroastrians exposed corpses until the bones were picked clean on platforms known as 'towers of silence', these platforms and also small square-domed Zoroastrian fire temples offered indirect models to Muslim builders when they came to commemorate their own dead.

Prior to the 'Abbasid era, the most common form of grave marker was a simple stele which carried a few details about the person buried and perhaps some Qur'anic inscription and decoration. However, Muslims soon began to construct more elaborate tombs for important religious figures: the Prophet, the members of his family, his Companions, and then later Muslim luminaries. Although the great age of the Muslim necropolis was still to come, by the eleventh century simple graves had begun to share space with these grander tombs and even mausoleums which marked the burial places of important religious personages. The process was most fully developed in the Qarafa cemetery of Cairo, where members of the Prophet's clan, Companions of the Prophet and early scholars such as al-Shafi'i, eponymous founder of one of the Sunni law schools, were buried in tombs which had become the sites of shrines and other religious facilities. The tomb of al-Shafi'i, for instance, was the centre of a busy complex of buildings including 'a school, bath and other conveniences' by the twelfth century.[56] In the eastern Islamic world, the burial places of the Shi'i *imams* similarly developed into important religious sites with a mausoleum plus other facilities. Another category of people who merited more elaborate tombs were the holy warriors of the frontier who died in combat against the 'infidel' in areas like Nubia and Central Asia. Their small cuboid domed white mausoleums not only commemorated their sacrifice but also acted as a visual marker of the frontier between Islam and unbelief.

There was obviously some religious justification for celebrating the burial places of formative figures in the development of Islam and martyrs for the cause, but less for offering the same treatment to secular individuals. The powerful tended to be buried within their own palaces in private funerary vaults or walled gardens. These are often described as *rawdat*, gardens, but in the absence of physical remains it is not clear whether this should be taken as a literal description or an allusion to the garden of paradise. Even the caliphs did not immediately rush to construct mausoleums worthy of their station. Although the 'Abbasid caliphs had a sepulchre in the Baghdad suburb of Rusafa, site of their first palace outside the round city, many were also buried in their individual palaces in Baghdad and Samarra. The first generations of Umayyads in Cordoba were laid to rest in the old palace in the centre of the city, although by the late tenth century there were also Umayyad mausoleums in the Rabad cemetery across the Guadalquivir river from the palace. The Shi'i Fatimids, who claimed descent from the Prophet, were also buried within their palaces rather than in more public tombs.

This promenade through the cities of the 'Abbasid era, whether in the 'Abbasid heartlands or in independent regions influenced by 'Abbasid models, projects an image very different to that of the unpleasant, insanitary places described and denounced by Orientalists. Although the sober al-Muqaddasi does comment on filth, dirt, poor water and cramped conditions from time to time, and we can be certain that the homes of the poor were often hovels, these cities could also surprise and dazzle with their palaces, their cosmopolitan shopping districts, their many mosques, colleges and schools and their advanced water and sanitation systems. Although not everyone had running water, in many of these cities water was carried to public fountains and baths in every quarter and to many wealthier private dwellings as well. Although there was no social security or national health system as such, there was moral pressure on the wealthy to make endowments for the support of public facilities such as hospitals and asylums open to all. Courtyards and gardens, sometimes on rooftops, alleviated the inevitable oppressiveness of any large and bustling city. Rather than responding to later Orientalist stereotypes, these cities of the 'Abbasid age offered one way in which humans could live a sophisticated and pleasant urban life.

CHAPTER 3

Princes and Beggars: Life and Society in the 'Abbasid Age

Here are examples of problems of every region, and people dealing with them to the best of their capability, So the reader can thus see the marvels of creation and all the varied coloured ornamentation on the earth.[1]

The daily life of those who lived in the past is one of the hardest things to evoke, but the literature of 'Abbasid times can give us some inkling of the way people spent their lives and the society of which they were part. Historical chronicles, the copious biographies of scholars, mystics and other religious eminences, poetry, with its huge range of themes from romance to ribaldry, and *belles lettres*, with their salacious and edifying anecdotes of the lives of rich and poor alike, conjure up a world both familiar and exotic yet often far removed from the stereotypes of Muslim culture circulating today. Although men are much more ubiquitous than women in their pages, they still offer many a glimpse of the lives of the fairer sex, who frequently found ways to circumvent social constraints placed on them and to maximize the rights and opportunities which Islam granted them.

In rather the same way, Muslims dominate most of the narratives we have, even though 'Abbasid society was not just composed of Muslims. Important religious minorities of Christians, Jews and Zoroastrians of many varied sects lived within a larger Islamic society which showed toleration as well as occasional hostility and prejudice to those that were 'different'. In fact the majority of the population in Egypt, Syria and Iraq was Christian well into the 'Abbasid era: during his famous expedition against Byzantium in 830, the caliph al-Ma'mun was shocked to discover in northern Meso-potamia an Arab tribe, the Tanukh, who were still Christian and issued orders that they and the pagans of Harran in the same area should convert to Islam – the Tanukh because they were Arabs and should have converted to Islam like the majority of their people, and the Harranians because they were not Peoples of the Book. The latter avoided complying by arguing that they were Sabians, a mysterious community mentioned alongside Muslims, Jews and Christians in the Qur'an as those 'who believe in God, the Last Day and do good works'.[2] Al-Ma'mun's command to pagans and Christians alike reminds us that at the beginning of the 'Abbasid caliphate, Muslims were still a minority everywhere, but that was to change dramatically, and by the fall of the caliphate in 1258 the Middle East, North Africa, southern Spain and Central Asia were all Muslim areas with larger or smaller Christian and Jewish minorities. Zoroastrianism and its offshoots Manichaeism and Mazdakism fared less well but hung on in Iran and northern India, as they still do today. Throughout the era, however, 'Islamic' society was one which included Muslims, non-Muslims and converts whose lives were shaped by competing religious traditions and cultures.

Religion could not help being socially important in a world where it had gone hand in hand with empire since late Antiquity, but the 'Abbasids and their subjects did not understand society purely as a series of religious communities. The pre-Islamic Arabs had made a distinction between nomadic tribesmen – the bedouin (*badu*) – and settled populations known as the *hadar*. They considered the former to be truly free men and women (*ahrar*) primarily because they could evade taxation and fight for themselves, while the *hadar*, although not slaves, were rendered unfree by the fact they were tied to their land by custom and lack of opportunity to do anything but till the soil, and had to pay taxes to their overlords because they were unarmed or incompetent with weapons. They were, from the bedouin perspective, rather like medieval European serfs, although a feudal system as such did not exist in Islamic lands during the 'Abbasid caliphate. Such ideas were not exclusive to the Arabs but were also maintained in various forms by other freedom-loving tribal peoples such as the Berbers, the Turks and later the Mongols.

For nearly 100 years, 'Arab' and 'Muslim' were virtually synonymous terms and the virtues of the bedouin were those of the Muslims too. However, as Persians began to convert to Islam and play their role in shaping high culture, they countered Arab celebration of the independence, manliness and generosity of the bedouin with an assertion of the wealth, sophistication and civilization which the *hadar*, settled peoples such as themselves and the Byzantines, had contributed to the development of the new Islamic society. This movement, spearheaded by many of the Persian ministers and courtiers who served the early 'Abbasid caliphs in Baghdad, was called the Shu'ubiyya movement, from the Arabic word for 'peoples' (*shu'ub*) which appears in a Qur'anic verse celebrating diversity, and the implication of the movement's name was that many different peoples, with the Persians in the vanguard, had contributed to the contemporary efflorescence of Islamic culture.[3]

Authors claiming Arab origin meanwhile wrote their own epistles to remind everyone of the supremely important role played by the proud and virile Arab bedouin as recipients of the last Abrahamic revelation and the founders of the Islamic empire. Although this movement was centred in eighth- to ninth-century 'Abbasid Iraq, it echoed across the Islamic world, and in the eleventh century Ibn García, a Muslim of Hispanic Christian origin resident in Valencia, wrote his own Shu'ubi epistle as a reaction against long-standing Arab chauvinism in Spain, using language taken straight from the earlier Persian movement in Iraq. In it he criticizes Arabs, whom he characterizes as nomads as opposed to the urbane elite of Spain, while lauding Muslims of Hispanic origin as the descendants of Persia and Byzantium:

> Am I to suppose that you have maligned or despised this respected non-Arab nation, without realising that they are the blond, the fair-complexioned ones. They are not Arabs, possessors of mangy camels. They are skilled archers, descendants of Chosroes [a Sasanian emperor], of glorious ancestry ... a proud people who were descendants of Caesar ... of Roman origin and blond.[4]

As ethnic groups jostled for precedence and jousted with their pens, and the imperial elite ceased to be a solely Arab preserve, Muslims also began to survey society from the Aristotelian perspective, which had influenced the Greeks, Romans and Persians before them. According to this model, society was divided into four categories: men of the pen, men of the sword, merchants and peasants. Although numerous, slaves were not considered a separate social group but the possessions or dependants of their masters whose status they shared. The elite of Muslim society, known as the *khassa*, was drawn from the first two groups, the men of the sword and pen, which produced the scholars, bureaucrats and soldiers of a regime. The merchants – a category which included craftsmen and artisans and basically meant townsfolk – and the peasants made up the common people, the 'generality' or *'amma* of the population, respectable but usually anonymous. At the very bottom of society came those who had no formal place in the system at all: beggars, prostitutes and such like, unflatteringly described as 'riff-raff' or the 'rabble' in Arabic writing. Tribesmen, historically considered to be the 'barbarians' outside any empire, also had no place in this schema except when they used their military skills to become empire builders themselves and a proportion of them served as 'men of the sword' or, more accurately, the bow – a trajectory followed by the Arabs, Turks and Berbers in turn. Other tribesmen lived on the fringes of the empire, providing auxiliaries for military campaigns, protecting passing caravans for a price and herding their flocks to the livestock markets of nearby towns and cities.

Peasants and country folk

What was common to all these ways of categorizing society was that people were born to a particular station in life. For the peasant masses residing in the Fertile Crescent, the Nile valley, the North African littoral or the Spanish countryside there was relatively little chance of social mobility or travel far from their natal region, and the replacement of Sasanian, Byzantine or Visigothic overlords with Muslim masters made little appreciable difference to their daily lives. In much of Iran, the Persian landowners simply converted to Islam and a similar pattern is evident among Visigothic notables in Spain, leaving peasants in much the same situation as they had always been. Treaties of the conquest era confirmed the status of landholders such as the Coptic church in Egypt in return for payment of tribute, which local officials levied themselves in keeping with the tax levels customary under the ousted Byzantine and Sasanian regimes. The Umayyads and early 'Abbasids adjusted this devolved system in favour of more direct taxation levied by Muslim officials, a process which often entailed the re-categorization of land as conquered by 'violence' rather than 'negotiation' and thus liable to the relatively heavy *kharaj* tax. A lighter tithe was levied on the lands which the caliphs handed out to Muslims of the conquest era, but this was a perk for the landholder, not the peasants working the land. When non-Muslim landholders began to convert to Islam they hoped to improve their tax status as a consequence. The fact that they were not able to because it would have been too prejudicial to the treasury was another bone of contention between 'old' and 'new' Muslims, although again such changes had little relevance to farmers themselves, unless landlords intended to make the unlikely gesture of passing on the savings.

Major changes in rural land tenure and administration occurred as a result of the introduction of the new Turkish army of al-Mu'tasim in the ninth century. In order to remunerate Turkish commanders, the frequently cash-strapped 'Abbasid caliphs began to offer them land grants, known as *iqta'*, a word literally meaning a 'portion', when they could not find other forms of wages for them – a practice which became widespread under the Buyids and Saljuqs. These grants entitled the holder to a proportion of the usufruct, or produce, of the land he, or sometimes she, held. They were not inheritable but sons could receive their father's land grant in the form of a new gift from the caliph or sultan, if the latter so wished. Such grants, which continued to be made in some shape or form in the Middle East well into the Ottoman era, were a convenient way for caliphs and sultans to pay their troops, but grant holders usually preferred city life and had little concern for the well being of the peasants working the land, or its long-term productivity. As a result, in Iraq especially, the carefully maintained irrigation canals of Sasanian times began to fall into disrepair and crop yields to decrease. The difficult life of the peasants was further exacerbated by sporadic periods of political unrest and localized war which led to the ravaging of the land, the destruction of villages and attacks on the peasants themselves, many of whom fled from the land to swell the teeming ranks of paupers and vagabonds in the cities.

Although drought, famine and epidemic diseases could strike at any time, the problems of the fertile but high-maintenance plains of the Tigris and Euphrates were not representative of the entire empire. Soldiers and tribesmen could be disruptive, but most towns were enveloped by verdant gardens, prosperous farms and lush meadows. Al-Muqaddasi's laconic descriptions of the agricultural produce of various Muslim regions in the tenth century evoke an image of an empire of milk, wheat and honey, with thriving local agricultural economies filling the market stalls of provincial towns and, ultimately, the tables of the powerful *amir*s of Baghdad, Rayy and numerous other grand cities. North Africa was a bucolic idyll: 'the cities of this region are concealed from view by olive trees, the ground covered with fig trees and vineyards; streams make their way through it, trees fill the lowland valleys'.⁵ The picture was similar in the unrepentant outpost of al-Andalus, where the Umayyads spearheaded a rural revival by repairing and improving the battered irrigation system of the Iberian peninsula and introducing new plants from the Islamic east, of which 'Abd al-Rahman I's Syrian palms, planted at his agricultural estate of Rusafa outside Cordoba, are the most famous. From such small beginnings, Muslims in Spain took a particular interest in the land and constructed country villas which were not just for leisure but also experimental farms that helped to foster the prosperity of the countryside.

Like land tenure and taxation, religious affiliations in the countryside changed slowly and almost imperceptibly. Across Egypt, Syria and Iraq the monasteries of the different Christian sects continued to serve their local communities, offering education and welfare. Ancient sacred sites and rituals persisted and only gradually shed their Christian, Zoroastrian or pagan attributes for new Muslim ones. In many areas rural conversion only really got under way after the development of Islamic mysticism when some Muslim ascetics and mystics rejected the seductions and distractions of the city and chose to wander the countryside or settle in isolated areas to contemplate God. Although such mystics were not necessarily concerned to preach to the peasants and tribesmen they encountered, their behaviour corresponded to very old pre-Islamic notions of holy men and saints, and they were quickly accepted as such and became agents for the conversion of rural populations. People came to them for advice and help, mediation in local disputes and healing, and when such mystics died, people came to their tombs with their whispered requests and promises, hoping for their intercession with God from beyond the grave. The Shi'a attributed a similar role to the *imam*s and their close relatives, and in this way the conversion of the countryside to Islam and the development of a Muslim 'cult of saints' went hand in hand.

Religion and the seasons provided the festive cycles which country people enjoyed. The Muslim calendar is a lunar one and the Muslim year is 11 days shorter than the solar equivalent. Religious festivals therefore moved through the year following the waxing and waning of the moon. The two festivals of most importance were *'id al-kabir*, the great festival, which took place during the annual pilgrimage to Mecca and commemorated Abraham's near sacrifice of his son – Isma'il, progenitor of the Arabs in the Muslim tradition, rather than Isaac as in the Judaeo-Christian tradition – and *'id al-fitr*, the festival of fast-breaking, which celebrated the end of the holy fast month of Ramadan. To these should be added any number of local celebrations of pre-Islamic provenance such as the Persian new year festival of Nawruz and the Egyptian celebration of spring, Shamm al-Nasim. The celebration of Nawruz was customarily accompanied by bonfires or fireworks, parades of 'grotesque figures' and the throwing of water at passers-by. Although sometimes forbidden by the authorities, these practices persisted, and al-Tabari was scandalized to report that when the caliph kindly responded to the populace's remonstrances that they be allowed to celebrate Nawruz by throwing water, the crowd took the whole thing too far by throwing water all over the police at one of their guard posts – a disgracefully disrespectful act![6] By the end of the 'Abbasid era, Muslim festivals also included the Birthday of the Prophet on 12 Rabi' al-Awwal and numerous other 'saints' days, celebrated with the music of tambourines and lutes, dancing and singing.

The people of the city

Life in cities, about which we know much more, was more variegated and colourful than that of the countryside. All social strata could be found in the city, from swaggering Muslim *amir*s to beggars and mountebanks, but most of the population were respectable craftsmen, artisans and traders who worked in the market areas or in small shops in residential quarters, which they either rented or owned, in other words, the 'amma or common people. The rhythm of urban life was modulated by the Muslim prayer times. The work day began at first light after the dawn call to prayer, the noon prayer signalled a break and then work continued until the sunset or evening prayer. People worked hard, and even Friday, when Muslim men gathered for the communal prayer and sermon, was not a day of rest like the Jewish Sabbath. But the cities had their idlers too: the sons of the rich, wannabe scholars and a colourful assortment of characters who loitered in the mosque courtyards and marketplaces, whiling away the hours exchanging stories and boasting of their exploits.

As in most pre-modern societies, sons tended to follow the professions of their fathers, whether princes or beggars, but there were some opportunities for social mobility for those who showed scholarly talents or who made enough money to put their sons on the scholarly track. Book learning opened the door to a number of careers and 'men of the pen' – religious scholars and those whose talents lay more in literature or administration – came from all ranks of society, not just established scholarly lineages. The early 'Abbasid elite consisted of all kinds of new men of the most eclectic backgrounds who gave it its dynamic, creative and sometimes brash character. The famous Basran man of letters al-Jahiz was from a family of black slave origin which had become part of a prestigious Arab tribe, the Kinana, via the clientage system. The well-known 'Abbasid minister Muhammad b. 'Abd al-Malik b. al-Zayyat was the descendant of an oil merchant (zayyat), as his name reveals, a fact which encouraged Fadl b. Marwan, a secretary of Christian origin, to taunt him for wearing the black robes and sword of an aristocrat, saying, 'You are only a trader, what right do you have to wear black and carry a sword.'[7] In Spain, Berbers broke into the highest echelons of society using their religious scholarship to overcome Arab prejudice towards their 'barbarian' origins in Morocco, the 'Wild West' of the Islamic world.

A talent for poetry or Arabic *bons mots* was just as useful as religious learning: patrons paid high prices for the poetry of men who could eulogize them in a witty and effulgent way, or improvise poems at the drop of a hat, or even cast down their enemies with a vicious word. The celebrated 'Abbasid poet Abu Nuwas (d. 814), reckoned to be one of the makers of Islamic civilization, was the son of a south Arabian soldier and a Persian seamstress called Jullaban, who brought her son from Ahwaz in Iran to the bustling city of Basra to get a proper Arabic education after his father died. He found patrons in both Basra and Kufa before moving to Baghdad, where he enjoyed the support of the Nawbakht family of Persian courtiers and wrote poetry at the behest of the caliph Harun al-Rashid and his son al-Amin. Later in the ninth century, when Spain was rent by rebellions of all kinds, the Umayyads and their rivals hired poets to compose scornful lines which were catapulted into the enemy's camp. During a series of engagements between Arabs and Hispanic Muslims around the cities of Elvira and Granada, an Elviran poet, 'Abd al-Rahman b. Ahmad al-'Ibli, threw a paper with a poetic taunt at the besieging Arabs and a war of poetry followed.[8]

The life of a poet, rather like today's spin doctors, was one of highs and lows: one minute esteemed and showered with gold, the next incarcerated for a scurrilous ode. When al-'Ibli was eventually captured, he was killed and thrown into a deep well as punishment for his poetic insults.[9] The power of the word was such, however, that many a poet saved himself from imprisonment, exile or even death by quickly improvising a brilliant new verse or composing an elegantly worded plea for forgiveness which lightened the offended party's mood. When the famous poet Bashshar b. Burd mocked the caliph al-Mahdi in the following subversive couplet, 'A caliph who fornicates with his paternal aunts and who plays with a child's toys and polo mallets. May God give us another in his place', Yahya b. Dawud, whose brother had also been lampooned by the poet, reported him to the caliph and then sent thugs to kill him, fearful that if Bashshar had an audience with the caliph to explain himself he would be able to extricate himself with his golden tongue.[10]

Scholars, poets and secretaries were among those who broke into the urban elite, the *khassa*, those people who were known by name, whose 'word' or 'voice' carried weight in society and who had the likelihood of being remembered in poetry or in the voluminous biographical dictionaries which recorded the prestigious and illustrious men of every generation, the 'Abbasid equivalent of a *Who's Who*. It was an elite predicated on lineage, learning and power, with the caliph at its heart surrounded by a penumbra of chief ministers, advisors, army chiefs and an assortment of physicians, scholars and hangers on. In the provinces similar elites clustered around the governors who represented the caliph and emulated the court in Baghdad or Samarra. The elite also included those whose credentials potentially challenged the 'Abbasid establishment – eminent members of the House of 'Ali and the fallen House of Umayya, and renowned religious scholars who preferred not to be tainted by association with the political authorities. The *Fihrist* or *Catalogue* of al-Nadim, a tenth-century work which provides information on a huge number of authors and their books, gives a very good sense of the wider elite of the period. Al-Nadim's work is divided into ten chapters and begins with a list of those who wrote on Arabic language and the Qur'an – the cornerstones of cultural identity – as well as other scriptures, before going through grammarians, historians, courtiers and officials who wrote books, poets, writers on Muslim sects, the founders of the law schools and other legal authorities, and scientists, with a few final chapters on non-Muslim faiths and Muslim miscellanea. These were the 'movers and shakers' of 'Abbasid society who were considered to be members of the *khassa*.

Although the caliphs acted as the pivots of this social system, they were often distant figureheads. The Umayyad caliphs had been fairly accessible in the style of pre-Islamic Arab chiefs, but the 'Abbasid court developed a more elaborate protocol inspired by Sasanian models. The caliphs disappeared from public view and only emerged in full ceremonial regalia shaded by the caliphal parasol, previously a Persian symbol of kingship. They received petitions and visitors via their ministers and chamberlains, whose power was thus augmented by their ability to control access to the caliphal presence. In the heyday of the caliphate, the caliphs and their close male relatives escaped the sometimes stultifying life of their palaces in Baghdad by going on military campaigns to Byzantium to demonstrate their commitment to expanding the frontiers of the Islamic world. If the stories and anecdotes of the time are to be believed, many also roamed the streets in disguise to find out what was happening on the streets of Baghdad.

Much of the real work of governing lay with a succession of chief ministers such as the Barmakids who gained their positions through a combination of judicious advice, financial expertise and personal contacts. Talent was hugely important in this world, but one's survival also depended on backing the right political horse and ensuring that one never faced a coalition of enemies with access to the caliph's ear. Numerous ministers and army chiefs found their careers or even their lives cut short because of intrigue and accusations of malpractice which were not always true. Those most likely to gain the caliph's trust were often his slaves and those manumitted slaves who became clients. Among their slaves, the caliphs placed greatest confidence in their eunuchs, a group believed to be particularly trustworthy given their inability to have children and thus to develop family concerns counter to the interests of their masters. According to al-Muqaddasi, black eunuchs came from the Sudan and Abyssinia and entered Islamic lands via Egypt or the Yemen, while white eunuchs of Byzantine or Slavic origin were imported from Spain or gathered in raids against the Byzantine frontier. Some may have been castrated already, others were operated on once they had reached Islamic territory:

I asked a group of them about the process of castration and I learnt that the Byzantines castrate their youngsters intended for dedication to the church, and they confine them so that they do not preoccupy themselves with women or suffer carnal desires. When the Muslims raid, they attack the churches and take the youngsters away from them. The Slavs are taken to a town beyond Pechina [in Spain], where the people are Jews, and they castrate them.[11]

The black eunuchs of the 'Abbasid caliph were a well-known and powerful coterie of men. When a passer-by disparagingly called one of al-Mu'tadid's black eunuchs a 'slave', a brawl erupted. When called on to explain himself, the eunuch reported the insult he had received. The caliph then sent another eunuch with guards to arrest and flog anyone who insulted them. Fifteen people were arrested, whipped, paraded on camels and detained overnight.[12] Slavic eunuchs possessed similar influence at the Umayyad caliphal court when it was located at Madinat al-Zahra'.

City folk of all social backgrounds relaxed in several settings. Apart from chatting in the mosque after prayer or in the marketplace, they also met in the baths, like their Roman predecessors. However, in the absence of either restaurants or cafés – which only started to appear after the sixteenth century – private homes, gardens and country estates were the usual venues for social activities. All homes of substance had one or more reception rooms for the man of the house and his guests to gather, enjoy entertainment and share food. Ornately decorated with marble panels and columns, intricately carved plaster and inlaid wood, these chambers were further enhanced by rich tapestries and carpets, scented with burning musk or ambergris and lit by candles of every size. In winter, braziers provided warmth, while in the long hot summers of the Middle East men gathered in walled gardens where paths led between beds of fragrant herbs, rose and orange flower scented the air and stands of fruit trees provided shade and sustenance. Small pavilions and tents enhanced with rugs and cushions offered welcome extra shade.

Harun al-Rashid was said to have disliked the artifices for cooling the air in his pavilion, such as moistened canvas sheets, and instead built a double roof to protect the interior from the sun, inspired by the Sasanian practice of coating the outer walls with wet mud each day. On a more glamorous note, he had the air scented by a series of seven slave girls dressed in thin shifts dipped in 'fragrant perfume, saffron, aromatic substances, and rose water' who sat on a stool with a perforated seat under which aloes wood and amber were placed. As each girl's shift dried she ceded her place to the next until the air was heavy with the commingled fragrances.[13]

Musicians, singers and poets of both sexes attended such parties, although the women at male gatherings were highly educated slaves rather than freeborn women, who had their own parallel social life which might include male relatives and eunuchs but not other men, officially at least. Rich women had their own cohorts of female singers, poetesses and musicians, against whom they sometimes pitted their own talents. An 'Abbasid princess, 'Ulayya, and Wallada of the Umayyad house have both gone down in history as accomplished poetesses. One of the best schools for singing girls was located in Medina, which seems an unlikely place given its eminent past as home to Muhammad and the first Muslim community, but by the 'Abbasid period Medina had lost its political role. It had a thriving community of scholars, and pilgrims regularly visited the city to pay their respects at the tomb of the Prophet before or after performing the pilgrimage to Mecca, but its pleasant oasis, full of 'gardens, groves of palm trees and villages', was also a favoured retirement place for the rich, who were keen for entertainment of the highest quality.[14] Girls from every Islamic frontier came to Medina to perfect their musicianship, singing or dancing before finding placements in the city itself and in the courts which dotted the Middle East and North Africa.

Social gatherings could not take place without refreshments. Although syrupy mint tea and strong cardamom-scented coffee seem timeless Middle Eastern drinks, they are actually relatively modern imports. In the 'Abbasid age, people drank infusions, syrups and fruit juices of various kinds and *sharbat* (sherbet), sugared water scented with rose, violet or orange flower. Many cities also had wine shops and taverns run by non-Muslims where people purchased wines made of different fruits, mostly date or grape, to consume at home. Wine production was the preserve of Christian monks and Zoroastrians, who sold it alongside Jewish merchants, ostensibly but not exclusively for non-Muslim consumption. Although it is an uncomfortable fact for some Muslims who interpret the Qur'anic prohibition on drinking alcohol strictly, Islamic societies have upheld quite varied views on the appropriateness of drinking, and it is clear from our sources that 'Abbasid society was quite liberal – or lax, depending on one's perspective – in this respect, as a result of its multicultural character.

It is a well-known and incontrovertible fact that the Qur'an prohibits consumption of alcohol, but which specific drinks and in what specific circumstances was a matter of some ambiguity even from the perspective of jurists. Was it just the date wine of pre-Islamic Arabia, or grape wine and fermented drinks and liquors of other types as well? Were there times and places where the prohibition had particular weight – such as prayer times, religious festivals and the fast month of Ramadan – and could it be dispensed with at others? Physicians recommended drinking alcohol for some medical conditions, and many intellectuals such as Ibn Quzman in Spain felt that abstaining from wine during Ramadan was sufficient. As we shall see below, the famous philosopher Avicenna considered both prayer and wine essential to his intellectual life and he was as likely to quaff a goblet of wine as hurry to the mosque to pray when he had a mental block. While al-Muqaddasi expressed disapproval at the level of public drinking in tenth-century Shiraz, a city he clearly disliked in several ways,[15] al-Shayzari, author of a manual for market inspectors composed in Damascus in the twelfth century, discussed the appropriate ways to handle Muslims who either smelt of alcohol or were obviously blind drunk in the great mosque as a fairly routine matter:

> It is said that a drunken man should be beaten and forcibly expelled from the mosque. We disagree with this. Whenever he is rational he may stay in the mosque but be prevailed upon and ordered to stop drinking. As regards giving him a beating to stop him, this is not up to the ordinary people, but rather to the governor and then only upon the man's confession or the testimony of two witnesses. This is not the case when the man merely smells of alcohol. Certainly when a man is staggering in such a way that he is clearly drunk, then whether he is in the mosque or outside it he may be beaten to stop him showing the effects of his intoxication.[16]

Wine also flowed freely in the palaces of the caliphs, although particularly pious rulers did on occasion empty out the wine cellars to make a public show of their religiosity, and poets and scholars sometimes protested that they had never touched a drop and did not wish to. The tales surrounding the provocative poet Abu Nuwas give a taste of the ambiguities of wine. In one verse he irreverently proclaims:

> Do not reproach me over wine, my friend,
> Do not scorn me with a frown for drinking;
> Merciful God has decreed a love for her of me,
> And of those with whom I pass the time.[17]

Abu Nuwas's drinking companions included the 'Abbasid prince Muhammad al-Amin, but when he became caliph his brother 'Abd Allah al-Ma'mun, governor of Khurasan, used this 'dissolute' friendship to justify his opposition to al-Amin. The latter responded by imprisoning Abu Nuwas and only restoring him to favour when he promised not to drink publicly again, leading the poet to say, 'I will not taste aged wine except as a fragrance, I was reproved on account of it by an Imam,' a pious sentiment he probably did not maintain for long.[18] Similarly mixed mores pertained in Cordoba, where a servant caught by the judge carrying a wineskin full of vintage wine to the royal palace was severely punished in tacit recognition that if the judge allowed the wineskin to continue on its journey it would be a damaging public assertion that the Umayyad ruler drank.

As our tale from Cordoba and the advice of al-Shayzari about handling public drunkenness show, the guiding principle in classical Islamic society was that one could turn a blind eye to what went on behind closed doors but that in public a respect for religious law and the social order it represented was of utmost importance. To drink in private was one thing, to make a public spectacle of it was quite another. A *hadith* recorded by the tenth-century political theorist al-Mawardi expresses this principle very clearly:

> It is related that 'Umar [b. al-Khattab, the second caliph], may God approve of him, surprised a party of men drinking and lighting fire in shacks. Said he, 'I forbade you to drink but you drank, and I forbade you to light [fires] in the shacks but you did.' They said, 'O Prince of the Faithful, and so did God forbid you to spy but you spied, and He forbade you to enter [a building] without permission but you entered.' Said 'Umar, may God approve of him, 'Two for two,' and left without doing anything to them.[19]

For reformers, however, this kind of compromise was unacceptable, and one mark of a zealot such as Ibn Tumart, founder of the Almohad movement in North Africa in the early twelfth century, was his furious smashing and emptying of wine jars from Tunis to Marrakesh. Contradictions nonetheless remained even in the empire created by Ibn Tumart's followers, where, two generations on, the Almohad governor of Granada forced his secretary Ibn Jubayr to have a drink of wine, so traumatizing the latter that he went on pilgrimage in 1182 to expiate the sin. Conversely, a century later, when the Mongol ruler Ghazan Khan converted to Islam in 1295, his advisors assured him that he would not have to give up the hard drinking, which was so integral to Mongol culture, in order to be a Muslim.

The social life of the general public, who lacked the reception halls and leafy bowers of the rich, revolved as much around the great mosque, the marketplace and the cemeteries as their own homes. Something of the atmosphere of great markets like the Mirbad in Basra still survives in Cairo in the great plaza in front of the Husayn Mosque or in the famous Jama' al-Fana' in Marrakesh, where storytellers, conjurers, quack doctors and musicians ply their trade. Festivals brought crowds out on to the streets and sometimes aroused the criticism of strict religious scholars who despaired at the sight of Muslims, Christians and Jews indiscriminately enjoying the feast days of every faith, and men and women mingling together without any thought for propriety. In Cordoba, Christmas was celebrated by all and sundry and in Baghdad the fireworks and revelries accompanying Nawruz went on despite official disapproval of such Zoroastrian practices.

Sickness was also very much part and parcel of pre-modern life in the Islamic world as elsewhere. Epidemic diseases such as typhus, small-pox, cholera and plague sporadically ravaged society as a whole, but they did not usually evoke quite the same sense of divine punishment in the Islamic world, where there was no doctrine of original sin, as pestilence did in medieval Christendom. At the time of the Islamic conquests, the cycle of plague initiated by the infamous Plague of Justinian in 541–42 was still going on and at least five epidemics took place before the end of the Umayyad caliphate, mostly in Syria and southern Iraq. The second caliph, 'Umar, defined the normative Muslim position on plague by ordering the Arab army to withdraw from infected areas of Syria in 638–39, while also reassuring them that 'plague was a mercy and a martyrdom from God for the faithful Muslim and a punishment for the infidel'.[20] This rather contra-dicted the Prophet's denial of contagion and his insistence that Muslims should neither enter not leave plague areas, but at least it offered a practical response which may well have inspired the Umayyad caliphs to retreat from the pestilential cities of Syria to their desert palaces in summer, the season when plague generally struck.

The plague was not so prevalent in eastern Islamic lands and abated during the 'Abbasid caliphate, but epidemic diseases continued to be a problem which both physicians and religious scholars needed to respond to. While the *hadith* included religious directives on the appropriate social response to epidemics, which was basically to keep society functioning as normally as possible, physicians set to work translating the medical tracts of Hippocrates and Galen from Greek into Arabic in an attempt to understand the pathology of recurrent epidemic diseases. The outcome was a belief in the transmission of such diseases by a miasma and a policy of changing the air to avoid it, but also a strong sense, reminiscent of Thucydides' under-standing of the Athenian plague, that disease was part of the natural order ordained by an all-powerful God and should be borne with stoicism rather than hysteria.[21]

This combination of religious sayings and scientific medical knowledge constructed on the twin pillars of Greek expertise and the Arabs' own empirical observations conditioned social attitudes to and the treatment of other maladies as well as epidemic disease. In general Arabo-Islamic medicine advocated an extremely pragmatic clinical approach to the sick, the insane and the disabled. Religious justification lay in the Prophet's own lauded sympathy for the sick and his stress on the importance of offering charity to the afflicted. This sort of attitude also provided a starting point for al-Jahiz to write an entire tract against mockery of the disfigured and disabled, which stressed the ways in which such people could participate fully in Islamic society. Initially most medical practitioners were Christians and Jews, but by the tenth century Muslim doctors had begun to write tracts on various diseases and medical complaints, and a century later Muslims were entering the medical profession in significant numbers.

The predominant theoretical view, derived from Greek and Persian medicine, was that illness represented an imbalance in the four humours – choler, black bile, yellow bile and phlegm – present in every person's physical and psychological composition, and that treatment required an adjustment of the balance between them which could be most successfully affected by changes in diet or environment. In actual fact, most treatments were tried and tested, and physicians used them because of their proven efficacy, which was then rationalized and explained by humoral theory. Conventional medicine also employed some means that we would consider quite unconventional, such as astrology, to predict the best time for a treatment, although the use of horoscopes was much more common in the realm of popular medicine. Medical ethics also looked to Greek antecedents. According to al-Shayzari, one of the *muhtasib*'s responsibilities was to make physicians take the Hippocratic oath and 'swear not to administer harmful medicine to anyone, not to prepare poison for them, not to describe amulets to anyone from the general public, not to mention to women the medicine used for abortions and not to mention to men the medicine preventing the begetting of children'.[22]

When illness struck those of wealthy families, they summoned one of the many physicians available to treat them at home, and those with chronic conditions were similarly cared for. Physicians also treated out-patients at clinics in their homes. Those too poor to afford medical treatment and care within the home went to the hospitals founded in Baghdad and other cities from early 'Abbasid times, which served as charitable and teaching institutions. Treatments were derived from the extensive range of vegetal and mineral pharmaceuticals recognized and used by doctors which built on Greek, Persian and Indian foundations. The 'Abbasid apothecary stocked hundreds if not thousands of products, including distilled oils, creams, unguents and drugs such as opium, which physicians could prescribe for their patients. Muslims also used a range of clinical techniques ranging from bleeding and cupping to complex surgery and bone-setting of a very advanced nature. Al-Shayzari's complete list of medical instruments for a practising doctor included pincers for extracting teeth, tweezers to remove blood clots, syringes, a clamp to hold haemorrhoids prior to excision, an instrument to remove excess flesh from the nostril, a probe for fistulas, an instrument to lift the eyelid, lead for weighting, a key for the womb, an instrument to detect pregnancy, a poultice for the intestines and a vessel to remove air from the chest.[23]

The most dramatic chronic disease in 'Abbasid times was probably leprosy, a disease which carried an extreme social stigma in medieval European societies but elicited a less punitive response from Muslims. Although disfigurement caused some sufferers to lead reclusive lives, lepers were not automatically shunned or excluded and sometimes shared therapeutic springs with other categories of sick people. For instance, the famous well of Job outside Edessa used by all manner of the sick had a pre-Islamic refuge for lepers constructed by Bishop Nona in the sixth century CE which remained in use in Islamic times. Hospitals often had a section or ward for lepers, and where special institutions were established for lepers they were supported with pious endowments which provided revenue to feed and clothe the inmates, who were allowed to socialize and even marry among themselves. Although the social segregation of lepers appears to have occurred in the Islamic west – North Africa and Spain – in eastern Islamic lands it was more usual for lepers to remain within society and even to beg for their living from passers-by. The possible profits of such begging were such that professional beggars were not above maiming themselves to look like lepers to elicit sympathy and, of course, a few coins from the healthy. It has even been suggested that the Crusaders' acceptance of the leper king Baldwin III of Jerusalem (r. 1173–84) reflected the influence of more tolerant Muslim attitudes to leprosy and those suffering from it. Leprous Crusader knights were also allowed to continue fighting as long as they were fit enough, and among the ordinary Latin settler population the remarriage of a healthy person divorced from a leper was permissible, in keeping with Muslim practices, unlike in Latin Christendom.[24]

Hospitals also cared for the insane, a rather subjective category in any society. Like Byzantine Christianity, Islam accepted the notion of the holy fool, often known as a *bahlul* or *buhlul* after a particularly well-known Baghdadi character, Abu Wuhayb Bahlul b. 'Amr al-Kufi, who lived during the time of the caliph Harun al-Rashid. The harmless mutterings and foolish exploits of these so-called 'fools' were interpreted as indicative of their special link with God, and they were not only tolerated but offered charity as a normal part of life. More violent or disruptive behaviour was attributed by doctors to imbalances in the four humours and thus not qualitatively different to physical illness, and treatments sought to restore the patient's humoral balance by means of medication, by what we might call 'therapy' sessions and by music which calmed and improved the mood of the insane.

For many of the common people, however, violent behaviour was not indicative of a physical or psychological problem but of possession by the *junun* (genies), the spirits of smokeless fire described in the Qur'an as inhabiting the world alongside humankind. The remedy was thus to charm the genie or exorcise it from its unfortunate host by means of music, singing and medicaments of a symbolic or sympathetic nature. The common people also used these kind of popular remedies for physical illnesses, since they could not afford the services of a doctor and would go to hospital only as a last resort. People treated their own minor complaints such as headaches, stomach complaints, problems in childbirth or venomous bites with remedies from the market, where it was possible to buy all kinds of potions and unguents alongside amulets, papers with verses of the Qur'an written on them, magic squares and magic bowls which patients would drink particular brews from. These folk remedies, which were also stocked by the apothecaries of every town and city, worked alongside the more conventional medicines of the physicians. In many cases, popular healing methods overlapped with scientific medicine: prayers and amulets were combined with sometimes very effective plant remedies. It was also a branch of medicine in which female practitioners abounded alongside male cuppers and bone-setters, working in the Arabian 'prophetic medicine' tradition, and astrologers who forecast the best time to attempt healing.

Women and children

Since the nineteenth century the status of women in Islam and Islamic societies has been a source of heated disagreement and a yardstick used to measure 'progress' or the lack of it, often to the detriment of the countless women involved who have become pawns in a global political game. Nineteenth- and early twentieth-century Muslim modernizers, who had observed the situation in Europe and America, considered the education and empowerment of women crucial to development in the Islamic world, but consistent and often badly informed criticism from Westerners has made many Muslims defensive about their attitudes to women and critical of those of Western society. They argue that their religion protects the sanctity of women and respects them rather than treating them as sex objects in the Western manner, a view expressed by Muslim women as well as men. On the other hand, some frustrated feminists from the Islamic world have come to the conclusion that Islam and female liberation are mutually incompatible! All shades of opinion exist in between, with the veil frequently used as a symbol by all parties.

For Muslims of the classical age of Islam, the status of women was a less important issue and they felt no need to justify themselves before a critical world audience or uphold a single monolithic opinion. Modern concepts of human rights and equality did not exist anywhere, and the Muslim under-

standing of gender relations was formed in the same Middle Eastern cruci-
ble as that of the other monotheistic faiths with all their contradictions.
The status of women in pre-Islamic Arabia was ambivalent: on the one
hand, the Arabs worshipped goddesses as well as gods, including al-'Uzza
in Mecca, who is identified with Aphrodite and the evening star in some
sources. On the other hand, they sometimes left newborn girls out to die
because they were considered much less desirable than sons, a practice the
Qur'an forbade.[25] If we turn to early Islam, the gender segregation practised
in the Prophet's own day was limited and related first and foremost to his
own wives, after he was embarrassed by a male Muslim bursting in upon
him when he was with them. According to the exegetes of the Qur'an, early
Muslim women actually challenged the Prophet and asked him why the
revelation only referred to Muslims using the male plural, *muslimun*. Subsequently male and female Muslims were given equal status in the revelation
and the female plural, *muslimat*, began to appear alongside its male coun-
terpart in discussions of spiritual responsibilities and rewards.

In addition to this recognition of the spiritual equality of the sexes,
several women are described as playing forceful roles in early Islam, even
wielding weapons, and there is no evidence that men and women were
physically separated in the mosque. In the stories of the golden days of the
Prophet and the Rightly Guided Caliphs, recorded in the first 'Abbasid
centuries, several women emerge as powerful figures, from the Prophet's
own wives – the wealthy widow Khadija, who proposed marriage to him
rather than vice-versa, and 'Aysha, who led the political opposition against
'Ali – to Na'ila, the strong-willed wife of 'Uthman, who tried desperately to
fight off his killers. For the Shi'a, Muhammad's forthright daughter Fatima
and her daughter Zaynab, who stood up to Yazid, the caliph responsible for
the death of her brother Husayn, acted as similar role models, and this type
of assertive Arab woman continued to appear in literature well into 'Abbasid
times. In terms of inheritance, the Qur'anic stipulation that women should
inherit half as much as their brothers was considered an improvement on
earlier practices, according to which daughters had no obligatory share. It
was also seen as fair, given that a woman had no legal obligation to support
anyone other than herself, whilst a man was obliged to support his female
dependants and his children.

The relative social status of men and women and the rules of gender
mixing which developed in Islam's imperial age owed as much to Sasanian
and Byzantine norms of social interaction rooted in earlier Mediterranean
practices as to Islam or the Arabs. Anthropologists talk at length about
what is called the Mediterranean honour-shame complex which permeated not only Muslim society but also Mediterranean Christian society in

its Greek Orthodox and Catholic forms. All these societies were patriarchal and believed that a woman's primary purpose was procreation, but that
women were sensual rather than intellectual beings who could be driven or
tempted to contravene patriarchal rules by their desires. Men had the task
of guarding a family's 'honour', while women had to avoid bringing 'shame'
upon their family. If they did, they were to be harshly punished to restore
the family's honour – the rationale behind Muslim honour killings even
today. Men meanwhile were not judged at all harshly for either raping or
seducing girls, a scenario all too familiar in our own society, where women
are often described as 'asking for it' in the grey area of date rape.

Each Mediterranean society applied the notions of honour and shame
in its own way and developed its own strategies to prevent sexual misde-
meanours. Even within the world of Islam there was an enormous variety of
attitudes. Away from the bedouin camp fires in the socially stratified cities
of the Middle East with their 'civilized' notions of polite conduct, Muslim
jurists of varied Arab, Christian and Zoroastrian origin developed the classical Islamic position on gender. At its most idealized and extreme, the tradition advocated that freeborn men and women of marriageable age should
not mix together unless they were closely enough related for marriage to be
impossible or were married to each other. Even then they were assumed to
inhabit separate worlds which only intersected in the marriage bed unless
the marriage had fostered love and amicability as well as obligation. The
reasoning behind this was that men needed to be sure that no other man's
child would inherit their property, juxtaposed with Islam's recognition that
women as well as men had sexual urges which could only be legitimately
satisfied within the confines of marriage. In keeping with this view, Islam
did not advocate celibacy for either sex, although mystics often did take this
path, and one of the few grounds on which a woman could seek a divorce
was if her husband was impotent.

The perceived importance of guaranteeing the purity of male lineages
thus dictated women's theoretical place in society. Although the Qur'anic
punishments for adultery and fornication were the same for men and women
– stoning and flogging respectively – the burden of chastity lay much more
heavily on women, who were expected to be virgins at marriage unless they
were widows or divorcees, and monogamous, in contrast to men, who could
have up to four wives simultaneously and as many concubines as they could
afford. But this theoretical system was rarely upheld fully in practice. Islamic
law stated that charges of adultery or fornication had to be backed up by the
testimony of four adult males who had witnessed the act, a situation which
rarely arose. Moreover false accusations were subject to the same penalty
as the sexual crimes themselves. Theory was further skewed by marriages

in which the wife came from a more powerful family than the husband or simply had a stronger character. It was subverted by tribeswomen from the frontiers who rode alongside their men and sometimes led their people. It was cast to one side by families who lived in homes too small to bother with segregation, and in the parallel world of slaves who provided entertainment as well as sexual favours and bridged the gender gap in all kinds of ways.

As in Roman and Greek society, slavery was commonplace in the 'Abbasid Empire and female slaves were found in most affluent households, working as domestic servants, companions for freeborn women and entertainers and concubines for the men of the house. Both men and women owned slaves, but if a slave belonged to a man, he could sleep with her, and if the liaison produced a child it had the same legitimate status as the child of a freeborn wife. A man could manumit and marry a slave if he so wished, a path considered meritorious in the Qur'an if the woman in question was Muslim, and some jurists considered that when a slave produced a child she should be freed, whether marriage followed or not. This relative lack of a connection between marriage and legitimate children reflected the Islamic stress on paternity and the popular perception that women were little more than vessels which protected and nurtured a man's child rather than biological parents of the same rank. The key from the Islamic perspective was a father's recognition of a child as his own, not the marital status of the mother.

Despite the legal equality of children born to slaves and concubines, there was sometimes a social stigma attached to having a slave mother. Among the tales of pre-Islamic Arabia retold and embellished in 'Abbasid times and beyond, was the epic of the warrior 'Antar, initially forbidden to marry his cousin Abla because his mother was an Ethiopian slave, 'so 'Antar lost his heart to his cousin 'Abla who was yet so far above him that never could he aspire to marriage with her, being a slave although of noble blood'.[26] Although of less personal consequence, the Umayyad caliph Marwan II was disparaged for being the progeny of a Kurdish slave rather than an Arab woman. Women themselves could be very competitive about their offspring, and freeborn wives were not above despising concubines and their children for their servile origin, but in imperial and elite circles it really did not matter very much and the vast majority of Islam's caliphs, whether 'Abbasid, Fatimid or Umayyad, were born to concubines not wives.

It was as mothers – whether slave or free – that women made their often unrecognized but immensely important contribution to the synthesis which emerged between Arab, Byzantine and Sasanian cultures and created mature Islamic society. This important role is obscured by Arab genealogies, which only recognize the paternal line, except in the case of extremely prestigious women such as Fatima, the Prophet's daughter, who founded the line of the Shi'i *imam*s. However, even in this case there are indications that the male line represented by Fatima's husband 'Ali, the Prophet's cousin, had as much if not more weight than the female line. In 685 a rebellion was launched against the 'Abbasids in support of Muhammad b. al-Hanafiyya, 'Ali's son with 'the Hanafi woman' not Fatima. The amount of support secured by the rebel leader al-Mukhtar on behalf of Muhammad b. al-Hanafiyya indicated that 'Ali's status as a male cousin of the Prophet had in a sense trumped that of Fatima, who was a closer relation but a woman. In fact, the possibility of the inheritance of 'noble' status via female descendants of the Prophet remained a contested matter throughout the 'Abbasid period and well after.

In most cases, it went without saying that social status was derived exclusively from one's father and his lineage. The obvious effect of this was to create a quite false impression of the purity of Arab lineages over the centuries because biographical dictionaries usually present only the male halves of genealogies. This was what was socially important and placed people, predominantly men, in the broad sweep of Islamic history from its primordial Arab beginnings, but from a cultural and domestic perspective maternal origins were equally important. As we have seen, Muslim men were entitled to take any number of concubines at one time in addition to four wives, and any of these women might become mothers of legitimate children who were automatically Muslim members of their father's line but were also influenced by the culture and faith of their mothers.

Concubines usually entered Islamic lands as war captives, as tribute payment from conquered peoples or as slaves. They came from Ethiopia, Berber North Africa, the Basque country, the Caucasus, India and many other places and they had responsibility for the nurture and upkeep of their children until they went to Qur'an schools or were given home tutors. Although some concubines or wives of non-Muslim origin converted to Islam, Muslim men were legally permitted to marry or cohabit with Christian and Jewish women without conversion being a requirement, allowing a number of different faiths in the same household. Even when women did convert to Islam, they naturally spoke to their children in their own tongues, sang the nursery rhymes familiar to them from their own childhood and passed on the lore of their people. Nannies and wet nurses were equally likely to be of non-Muslim origin. In this potent way, much quieter but more influential than the Shu'ubiyya, cultures truly met in the world of Islam.

We know most about domestic politics from the annals of the royal houses of the 'Abbasids, Fatimids and Umayyads of Cordoba, which all demonstrate the cultural diversity of the female household, the *haram*, or harem as it is more commonly known in English. In the case of the 'Abbasids, marriages were sometimes contracted with women from the 'Abbasid clan and from other elite Arab families, but most caliphs from the ninth century onwards were the sons of concubines of Byzantine, Turkish or Armenian extraction and more often than not the caliph's mother rather than his sexual partners dominated the harem.[27] Al-Mansur married two Arab aristocrats, Arwa, a Yemeni princess, and Fatima, a descendant of Talha who fought 'Ali at the Battle of the Camel in 656. His son al-Mahdi married his cousin Rita, then, in a break with tradition, his beloved Yemeni concubine Khayzuran, raising some eyebrows in the process. He also married another cousin and, fourthly, an Arab noblewoman, Ruqayya, who was descended from the third caliph, 'Uthman.

His successor al-Hadi did not marry but Harun al-Rashid married his cousin Zubayda – a match based on love as well as propriety – and then four other women from the 'Abbasid household, including widows and a concubine of his dead brother. Finally, the last celebrated 'Abbasid marriage was that of al-Ma'mun to Buran, the daughter of one of his chief Persian political advisors. Al-Ma'mun was himself, however, the son of a Khurasani concubine called Marajil and in future generations the 'Abbasids mostly shied away from marriage in a manner similar to the Fatimids and Umayyads, and the Ottomans much later on. Marriages only resurfaced in the last centuries of the caliphate when caliphs needed the support which a marriage alliance could provide, and Turkish parvenus such as the Tulunids of Egypt and the Great Saljuqs were keen to improve their own credentials by linking their families to the politically enfeebled but prestigious 'Abbasid clan.

The path trodden by the Fatimids was a little different.[28] Their legitimacy depended upon an ancestress, Fatima, daughter of the Prophet and thus of impeccable Arab origin. In their propaganda the Fatimids contrasted this 'noble' maternal line with the 'Abbasids' ignominious descent from a slave woman, Nutayla, but in practice they were actually more reliant on concubines than their 'Abbasid rivals after they had established their Isma'ili Shi'i caliphate in Tunisia and Egypt. Whether they married them or not is a bit of a mystery given their casual use of the words *zawja*, 'wife' or 'consort', and the metaphorical *jiha*, literally meaning 'side' or 'flank', which denoted someone very close to the caliph. The first caliph, 'Ubayd Allah al-Mahdi, is said to have married his first cousin but no information about her exists. His son al-Qa'im took a Byzantine Greek slave and a woman called Karima as his partners. His grandson al-Mu'izz, however, took a distant cousin as his consort as well as having a number of concubines. The next caliph, al-'Aziz, made a Coptic woman from a prominent church family his chief consort, and she was mother to the most well-known of all Fatimid princesses, the fabulously wealthy and powerful Sitt al-Mulk, who often ran rings around her half-brother, the caliph al-Hakim. His consort, Amina, was a minor princess of the Fatimid house, while in the next generation the most prominent woman was Rasad, an Abyssinian slave purchased by the caliph al-Zahir and mother to his son and heir al-Mustansir. As the dynasty began to weaken in the eleventh century, chief ministers tried to marry their daughters to rather unwilling heirs to the caliphate, but this strategy was largely unsuccessful and concubines and princesses of the blood continued to be the caliphs' preferred partners.

In the far west, Umayyad practices mirrored those of the Fatimids with a strong inclination towards concubinage right from the outset.[29] The first Umayyad *amir*, 'Abd al-Rahman I, was the son of a Berber slave girl called Rah from the Nafza tribe, brought to Damascus as tribute. The mother of his successor was a dark-eyed girl called Halal, possibly a wife chosen from among his Berber relatives. From that time onwards, however, the important women in the harem and the majority of the royal mothers were of northern Christian origin from the Basque, Navarrese and Frankish territories beyond the Muslim frontier. Some were captives won in war, others were daughters of defeated kings and nobles who handed them over to make peace. The grandmother of 'Abd al-Rahman III, Iñiga, or Durr as she was known in Muslim circles, was the daughter of King García of Navarre. Subh, the infamous and powerful concubine of al-Hakam II, who became effective regent for her son Hisham II, was a Basque or Frankish slave who attracted the possibly homosexual caliph with her boyish ways.

In a sense it was utterly logical for caliphs to dispense with marriages which created bonds of equality and reciprocity between two families, given the perceived superiority of caliphal bloodlines to all others. In early 'Abbasid times, when it was important for the caliphs to make alliances and heal wounds, they took wives from the elite which had supported them and from families whose assistance was valuable – when al-Mu'tadid later married the daughter of Khumarawayh, his wayward governor of Egypt, the same dynamic was at play – but over time it became important to emphasize the uniqueness of their line and the utter impossibility of finding a wife of equal status except within their own clan. Concubines, either slave or free, had the advantage of coming into the harem without too many strings attached and had no automatic claim on their masters. Occasionally they had relatives who hoped to gain by their elevation but by and large they did not represent important families or political interests and were therefore ideal 'mothers of children', as those concubines who produced offspring were called in stark recognition of their childbearing function.

Although the practices of royal families are not necessarily very good mirrors of society as a whole, the cultural mixing which occurred in caliphal harems took place throughout society. Monogamy was undoubtedly the most common situation, but there was still much taking of 'foreign' women as wives or concubines, albeit on a much smaller scale than in royal households where women constantly arrived as gifts, tokens of goodwill and servants. While most people had neither the status nor resources for this and were satisfied with more modest households, they sometimes chose non-Muslim partners over Muslim ones. When he wrote his history of Spain and Morocco for a thirteenth-century 'Abbasid audience, al-Marrakushi, a native of Marrakesh as his name implies, thought fit to mention that during the regency of al-Mansur in the late tenth century not only the silver bells of the Church of Santiago de Compostela but countless Christian girls were captured and brought to Cordoba and Muslim fathers were forced to produce extremely large dowries to get their daughters married because everyone wanted one of the beautiful Christian girls flooding the market![30]

It would be pointless to deny that there was considerable misogyny and gender inequality in 'Abbasid society: polygamy was a male privilege, on occasion scholars expressed their disdain for the intellectual capacities of women, and it was a trope of advice literature that political affairs would go badly if entrusted to women. However, with the exception of polygamy, none of this was absent from the other religious traditions in the Middle East and North Africa and had deep regional roots, as the well-known ancient Greek disdain for women and their exclusion from the *demos* shows. Greek democracy, whatever its symbolic meaning for us, was a club for well-born men who had no time for women or slaves. Aristophanes, for instance, could write a whole comedy about the ludicrous spectacle of women demanding a public say by using the only weapon they had – their ability to deny their husbands sexual favours.

Moreover many of the concerns expressed by Muslim men at the pernicious effect of the governance of women naturally only arose when women had assumed a certain degree of power as the mothers, sisters and wives of caliphs, sultans or *amir*s. From Baghdad to Cordoba it is possible to identity hugely influential women of enormous wealth and status – since Islamic law allowed women to inherit and own assets – who put up buildings, paid armies and persuaded men to follow their directions. At the time that al-Tabari and other chroniclers were recording the daring exploits of early Islamic women, most 'Abbasid princesses had their own independent households in Baghdad, two sisters from Tunisia were busy founding what are now the two most important great mosques in the Moroccan city of Fes, and the wives and concubines of the Umayyads in Cordoba were establishing mosques in every suburb of that expanding city.

The Turks had a more egalitarian attitude towards women than the sedentary peoples of the Middle East, and the arrival of the Saljuqs in Baghdad in 1045 initiated regular appearances of women in the pages of Ibn al-Athir's *Complete History*, holding fiefs, threatening their male relatives with war when displeased and demanding marriage terms to their liking. When the caliph al-Muqtadi asked for the hand of Malikshah's daughter, 'she accepted his suit but stipulated that the settlement in advance should be 50,000 dinars, and that he would keep no concubine and no wife but this one, and that he would sleep with no-one else'.[31] The caliph accepted what were tough terms in Baghdad's high society but his Turkish wife later persuaded her father to dissolve the union in 1089 when she still found al-Muqtadi less attentive than she expected. Slightly later, in the 1140s, al-Marrakushi attributed the fall of the Almoravids of Morocco and Spain, Sanhaja Berbers from the Sahara, to their excessive reliance on the counsel of women and the fact that every thief or bandit had a female patron who protected him from justice![32] Put in a more positive light, the prominence of women reflected their important status in Almoravid circles where, according to the rules of the desert, inheritances passed to a man's sister's son, and women rode, fought and offered their patronage to men. According to legend it was a woman, Fannu, daughter of 'Umar, who defended the citadel of Marrakesh from the attacking Almohads in 1147 and it was only with her death that the Almoravid capital finally fell.

Outside aristocratic circles, gender segregation was rarely absolute and often more honoured in the breach than the practice. In reality social constraints on women were most assiduously upheld by the middle strata of society consisting of religious scholars, well-to-do merchants and minor officials. Among the poorer classes, the labour of women as well as men was required to sustain a family financially and in both towns and the countryside men and women rubbed shoulders in the course of the working day, buying and selling, tending to the animals or nurturing their crops. The substantial population of female slaves in any 'Abbasid city were often sent on errands to the market or carried messages from one home to another. They were not expected to adhere to the same rules as their mistresses owing to the diminished responsibilities which slave status carried in comparison to freedom, a situation which freeborn women on occasion lamented as they endured the irony of the seclusion forced upon them by their 'freedom' and reflected on the permissive lives of their slaves, highly prized concubines excepted.

The frequent repetition in manuals used by the *muhtasib*, the official responsible not only for the market but public morals, of the need to keep men and women separate shows the endless ways in which they did in fact meet in the normal course of life. In al-Shayzari's handbook for practising *muhtasib*s, the various improprieties the overworked *muhtasib* should prevent occur at regular intervals. In the section on managing the markets and roads he admonishes:

> It is not permissible to stare at the neighbours from rooftops and windows.
> Nor is it permissible for men to sit without good cause in the roads which
> women take, or for women to sit by their doors in the roads which men
> take. The *muhtasib* must chastise whoever does these things, especially if
> he sees an unrelated man and woman talking together in a secluded place,
> for this is even more suspicious.[33]

Later on he recommends that oven keepers' 'servants and hirelings should be immature boys because they enter the people's houses and meet their womenfolk' when collecting and delivering food for the public oven.[34] The cotton carders and flax spinners should not allow 'women to sit by their shop doors waiting for the carding to be completed' or chat with them.[35] In a final section on general matters, al-Shayzari lists the places where women gather, 'such as the yarn and flax market, on the banks of rivers, at the doors of women's baths and other places', and instructs, 'If he sees a young man alone with a woman or speaking to her about something other than a commercial transaction, and looking at her, the *muhtasib* should chastise him and forbid him from standing there.'[36] The *muhtasib* also had to monitor preachers' meetings to make sure that there was a screen between the men and women and that they left separately by different roads, and discourage women from drawing attention to themselves by wailing at funerals or visiting the cemeteries.

Last but not least, the *muhtasib* had to police the baths, where dangerous liaisons and improper behaviour were especially likely to occur. As had been the case in the Middle East for millennia, public baths were not only used for hygiene but also for recreation and ritual purification before prayer, and they were heavily used on a regular basis. Although the richest families had private baths, public baths were one of the most ubiquitous facilities in a Muslim city. Most catered for men and women on alternate days, while others were exclusively for the use of women. Staff of the appropriate gender were employed to service them at the requisite times but there was always the risk that someone would slip in, and peeping toms were to be apprehended and punished and customers in general were expected to wash discreetly rather than flaunting their nudity.[37] This seems to have been quite a common complaint across the Middle East, as one of al-Muqadda-si's many complaints about Shiraz was that he saw the people 'entering the bath naked without wraparounds'.[38]

One gets the impression of ordinary bustling town life, with men and women going about their business, indulging in mild flirtations and paying rather little heed to stuffy religious injunctions, not a society in a strait-jacket. When the caliph al-Muqtadi – in addition to taking pollution of the Tigris with dirty water from Baghdad's baths rather seriously – issued the following list of directives designed to clean the city's morals up, he seems to have been fighting a losing battle:

> He ordered the expulsion of singing girls and loose women from Baghdad and the sale of their establishments. He stopped people from entering any public bath without a waist wrapper, and he demolished reed shacks and towers built for pigeons. He banned any sport with them on account of women's quarters being overlooked ... and boatmen were prohibited from ferrying men and women together.[39]

Aristocratic men might also gate-crash the parties of ladies and meet women in unorthodox ways, as two very different stories from Baghdad and al-Andalus illustrate. In a popular tale, dismissed by Ibn Khaldun as unlikely to be true, the caliph al-Ma'mun met his future wife Buran, the daughter of the courtier Hasan b. Sahl, one night in Baghdad. He was wandering the streets, in much the same way as Harun al-Rashid, his father, in *The Thousand and One Nights*, when he stumbled on a large basket which had been let down from the roof of a mansion by a pulley and thick woven cords of silk. The mystified caliph hopped in and tugged the pulley which began to move upwards until it reached the roof. Servants then showed him into a magnificent chamber and a 'woman of uncommon seductive beauty' appeared and invited him to keep her company. They passed the night drinking wine together, after which the enchanted caliph returned to his companions who were beginning to worry about his absence. He subse-quently asked Hasan for Buran's hand in marriage.[40]

Similar tales of unsuspecting men being ensnared by the beautiful, wilful but officially secluded women of the elite abound, sometimes with more sinister undertones. An almost identical story is told of the Bagh-dad poet Ibrahim al-Mosuli, who was also whisked up into a mansion in a basket, although he was entertained by a cluster of beautiful women and had to explain his prolonged absence from court to the caliph, who then accompanied him to meet the mysterious beauties, who turned out to be slave girls of the caliph himself who had sent them to the mansion as a punishment for some misdemeanour. Luckily Ibrahim had warned the girls to sing to him and his guest from behind a curtain, despite their more open behaviour when he had been alone, for, as the caliph chillingly commented, since propriety had been maintained he would reward them and restore them to favour but would have had them killed had they revealed themselves to strangers.

Our second tale is the love story of Bayad and Riyad from thirteenth-century al-Andalus, the very end of the caliphal age when the Almoravids and Almohads ruled in the west. Riyad was a beautiful slave girl, the favourite of the unnamed 'chancellor', whom a young Damascene merchant's son, Bayad, had glimpsed and fallen in love with while taking the air on the banks of a river near the chancellor's home. An old woman acting as a go-between arranged for Bayad to 'drop in' while the chancellor's daughter and her female slave companions, including Riyad, relaxed in the garden on silken cushions, playing music and singing poetry. Bayad sang to the women and then admitted to the lady of the house that he had seen Riyad a few days before. The lady counselled him, 'by your merit, and the truth of your affection and the superiority of your origins and the acuteness of your intellect, keep secret all that you see here, and don't go making yourself all hoarse about it – do the right thing and the proper thing'.[41] It was Riyad, however, who spoilt the tryst by making her feelings towards Bayad obvious in a torrent of emotional poetry. Her mistress immediately halted the party and Bayad was sneaked out of the house by the old woman, after which both Riyad and Bayad languished from their unfulfilled love, impossible because the chancellor would never relinquish his favourite and Bayad could never even ask him to without admitting to his original illicit meeting with her.

It is in these anecdotes and love stories that we can sense the other side of the coin – the power women could exert over men, the thrill of breaking the rules for young men and women, the irritation which social norms could engender and the yearning which made unrequited love a complaint discussed in medical treatises and a powerful metaphor for the soul's yearning for God in mystical writing. Although very different from our own perception of gender relations, the 'Abbasid vision was also distinct from contemporary Islamic views on the subject of gender. It was multi-faceted and nuanced everywhere by local customs and social realities which modified the Qur'anic template and its juridical interpretations. While jurists despaired to see men and women mixing on a daily basis, and the *muhtasib* tried to prevent things going too far, the 'Abbasid court poet Abu Nuwas complained that a veiled girl was rather like an onion and just as annoying to peel!

The religious minorities

Muslim relations with non-Muslims were informed by their conception of the place of their new faith in relation to other religions and the social and political circumstances in which they found themselves, a small ruling elite in a multi-ethnic world with time-honoured methods of handling religious difference. The early Islamic milieu was permeated by Judaism and Christianity, and the new religion identified itself as the final message in the string of revelations sent by God, beginning with the Old Testament prophets – a claim naturally rejected by Jews and Christians. Muslims believed that their version of the eternal message revealed in the Qur'an was superior but that Jews and Christians, fellow Peoples of the Book, could be allowed to practise their religions in return for submission to Islamic rule and payment of a poll tax known as the *jizya*. In the conquest era, this rule was applied to almost everyone regardless of their faith – villages and towns were simply told the sum they needed to pay and expected to work out exactly who paid what among themselves. At this stage Muslims were not concerned to proselytize but to assert Islam's political dominion over the known world, and their actual knowledge of other religions was quite shaky.

During the Umayyad and early 'Abbasid caliphates, the conditions of the covenant of protection (*dhimma*) between the Muslim state and its non-Muslim subjects (*dhimmis*) were elaborated, drawing on both the Theodosian code current in Byzantium and on Sasanian regulations (see Chapter 1). In addition to their liability to pay the *jizya*, non-Muslims were sometimes obliged to wear distinctive garments or markers of their various faiths – coloured shoulder strips, shawls and belts were all stipulated at different times – and forbidden to build ostentatious places of worship, ring bells or sound clappers, sell wine and pork in Muslim areas, carry weapons or hold positions of power over Muslims. Such apparently discriminatory measures did not necessarily originate as such: early agreements between Christians and Muslims simply required members of each community to carry on wearing their usual clothes and allowed Christians to worship, sell wine and pork and possess crosses but not in such a manner as to offend or attract Muslims. In succeeding centuries the imposition of these 'rules' was very variable, they differed in detail from place to place and were often allowed to lapse. Churches, monasteries and synagogues were built in many places and non-Muslims soon blended into the population, despite the disquiet of elders on both sides of the confessional line.

Probably the most important disadvantage that non-Muslims endured was the *jizya* tax, although in some times and places their freedom from other taxes levied on Muslims brings the financially discriminatory character of the *jizya* into question. In the jurist Malik's *Muwatta'*, an early *hadith* collection which served as the legal basis for Maliki law, he certainly depicts the *jizya* as a marker of subjection of the Peoples of the Book and also Zoroastrians, but implies that Muslims and non-Muslims alike have a similar tax burden from the financial point of view:

> The *sunna* (custom) is that there is no *jizya* due from women and children of the people of the book, and that *jizya* is only taken from men who have reached puberty. The people of the *dhimma* and the Magians [i.e. Zoroastrians] do not have to pay any *zakat* (alms) on their palms or their vines or their crops or their livestock. [42]

He goes on to say that this is because alms are levied from Muslims to purify them and for the benefit of their poor, while the *jizya* is levied to humble non-Muslims. The distinction between the two was therefore not so much a matter of quantity but quality: Muslims paid taxes for the benefit of their own souls and the needy amongst them, while non-Muslims were obliged to pay their masters taxes of no particular benefit to themselves, except to guarantee their protected status. Taxation in general could be onerous, and even though the *jizya* was means-tested it could still evoke bitter laments from non-Muslims, as the following statement from a Jew in Fatimid Egypt shows:

> My present state is marked by illness, infirmity, want and excessive fear since I am sought by the controller of revenue, who is hard upon me and writes out warrants of arrest, sending 'runners' to track me down.[43]

The elaboration of the *dhimma* contract between the Muslim state and its non-Muslim subjects gave sectarian communities distinct identities as social units: Christians were subdivided into Nestorians, Jacobites, Melkites (Greek Orthodox), Armenians and Copts. The Jews retained a greater cohesion, but in the eighth century a split occurred between the Rabbinites and Karaites, creating two main sects in addition to smaller offshoots. The Samaritans who mostly lived around the Palestinian town of Nablus were another Judaic community recognized by the Muslims. They also acknowledged the pagan Sabians of Harran in Mesopotamia and the Zoroastrians or Magians who were dotted across eastern Islamic lands. It was the responsibility of the religious elders of all these communities to organize collection of the poll tax and ensure their flock's loyalty to the political authorities in return for their right to effectively govern their people according to their own religious law. All civil and personal matters therefore remained within the religious communities themselves, and when non-Muslims did approach Muslim judges because they saw it as personally advantageous to do so, the compact between the caliph and the

Christian patriarch or Jewish *gaon* enabled non-Muslim religious authorities to demand the return of their errant co-religionists to the appropriate judge.

Although the division of society into a series of religious communities functioning as separate social units is often considered distinctive of Islam, in Iraq and probably other places too this was a path that many communities were taking for themselves prior to the arrival of Islam. The Nestorian and Jacobite Christian authorities of sixth-century Iraq, for instance, had forbidden intermarriage between their two communities as well as between Christians and Jews or Zoroastrians. In their relations with the Sasanian state, Jewish, Nestorian and Jacobite religious leaders jealously guarded their right to administer their own congregations and maintain order in return for paying a poll tax. When the Muslims arrived on the scene, it was therefore often religious leaders themselves who approached their inexperienced new masters and sought to re-create the governmental recognition of their communities which they had previously enjoyed. The *dhimma* was therefore a negotiated compact between Muslim rulers and the religious leaders of various faith communities who had often maintained similar agreements with their pre-Islamic rulers, not an alien institution imposed by Muslims.

Muslims' willingness to recognize the validity of other religions made 'Abbasid society a pluralistic one, and Islam acquired its mature form as a result of the debates, discussions and polemics which took place between the practitioners of different religions. Several of the earliest recorded dialogues were between caliphs or Muslim governors on one side and Christian patriarchs or Byzantine emperors on the other. These exchanges included correspondence between the conqueror of Egypt, 'Amr b. al-'As, and the patriarch John I, the Umayyad caliph 'Umar II and the Byzantine emperor Leo III, and the 'Abbasid caliph al-Mahdi and the patriarch Timothy I. By the ninth century such debates had spawned a literary genre of which the *Apology* of the Christian 'Abd al-Masih b. Ishaq al-Kindi, dated to about 820 when al-Ma'mun was caliph, is a good example. In the *Apology* a Muslim asks his Nestorian Christian friend to convert but the latter demurs in a long refutation of Islam and celebration of Christianity, including a harsh description of Muhammad as 'a man who had no thought or caring save for beautiful women whom he might marry or men whom he might plunder, shedding their blood, taking their property and marrying their wives'.[44] The Christian's frankness correlates with his Muslim correspondent's description of his own intellectually open and tolerant engagement with Christians:

> I have conversed with [Nestorian] metropolitans and bishops famous for their scholarship and fine culture and not less for their Christian character

and the rigor of their abstinences. ... I have allowed them perfect freedom to make good their cause, and to speak out their minds without fear.[45]

As the last quote implies, Jews, Christians, Zoroastrians and other minorities were not segregated from the Muslim population – ghettos were a Venetian creation – nor were they excluded from certain professions. Although technically excluded by the *dhimma* regulations from the army and from sensitive areas of the civil service, most obviously those related to tax collection, this exclusion was not absolute. On the fairly rare occasions when popular Muslim hostility to religious minorities did erupt, it was often triggered by government laxity in maintaining these exclusions by using non-Muslims as guards or tax collectors. In early ninth-century Iraq, in particular, *dhimma* regulations were very loosely applied, triggering a reaction at mid-century led by the caliph al-Mutawakkil, who issued a decree which opened with the preamble:

> It has become known to the Commander of the Faithful that men without judgement and discernment are seeking the help of *dhimmi*s in their work, adopting them as confidants in preference to Muslims and giving them authority over Muslim subjects.[46]

He therefore issued orders that his officials in the cities and provinces of the empire should not employ *dhimmi*s anymore. At around the same time, he asked al-Jahiz to compose a tract against the Christians in which the latter sheds more light on the social interaction of Muslims and Christians in Baghdad and the high levels of assimilation between the two communities, albeit as something to criticize.

> As for the manifestations of the high social rank of the Christians. We know that they ride highly bred horses and dromedary camels, play polo ... wear fashionable silk garments and have attendants to serve them. They call themselves [Muslim names such as] Hasan, Husayn, 'Abbas, Fadl and 'Ali and employ also their forenames. There remains but that they call themselves Muhammad and employ [his] forename Abu'l-Qasim. For this very fact they are liked by the Muslims. Moreover many of the Christians failed to wear their belts, while others hid their girdles beneath their outer garments. Many of their nobles refrained from paying tribute. They returned to Muslims insult for insult, blow for blow.[47]

Al-Jahiz also lamented the admiration which the masses felt for wealthy and successful Christians and the appeal of Christianity to some Muslim youths. In a similar vein, clergy concerned about the appeal of Islam to their congregations could be just as keen as the Muslim authorities to see *dhimma* regulations enforced in order to insulate impressionable young people from the rival religion's seductions.

The rise of Islam and its consolidation as an elite religion across the Mediterranean basin and Middle East impacted on the existing religions of the region in different ways. The situation of the Christians and Zoroastrians was most changed by the arrival of Islam on the scene, while the Jews and other existing minorities fared better. This was not entirely a religious matter but reflected the challenge created by the loss of imperial status which some of these faiths had enjoyed for centuries. It is revealing that of all the Christian communities and sects in the Middle East and Mediterranean, those which suffered least from the establishment of an Islamic empire were those which were viewed as misguided if not downright heretical by the state Byzantine church – the Copts of Egypt, the Armenians, the Jacobites and the Nestorians, although the latter did have a bit of a struggle to regain the recognition they had been afforded by the Sasanian authorities in the new Islamic world order.

For sects which had enjoyed and expected considerable state patronage – the Melkites of Syria and the Catholics of Spain – the overthrow of their kings or emperors was traumatic and inexplicable. Surely it could not be God's plan to replace a Christian empire, and, if it was, Christians must have sinned very deeply to warrant such a reversal. Two generations after the fall of Damascus in 635, John of Damascus, a Christian official in the Umayyad administration who retreated to a Palestinian monastery to become a renowned Greek Orthodox theologian, was still writing as if the Muslim conquest was a temporary interlude and that the Byzantine Empire ruled Syria. This existential crisis was compounded by problems in maintaining an episcopacy without the benign interventions of emperors or kings. The caliphs were not antagonistic to Christianity and welcomed Christian poets and churchmen to court, but neither were they supportive of the church as an institution – the churches were expected to oversee their own affairs, elect their own bishops and clergy and manage the daily lives of their flock for themselves. Although that did not prevent factions seeking caliphal approval for their candidate, the Muslim authorities did not intervene as a matter of course.

In Spain the Visigothic church was equally disorientated by the Islamic conquest and the steady replacement of the peninsula's Latinate culture with a new Arabic one. In the capital Cordoba, the Christian population swiftly adopted Arabic and with it an Islamic cultural perspective which drew them ever closer to their Muslim fellows. Many were prepared to be circumcised, as that became a requirement for government service in order to acquire 'the abundant riches, jewels, perfumes and a wealth of clothes and things' which such service could bring.[48] By the ninth century young Christian men and women delighted in Arabic poetry and letters and mingled freely with their Muslim peers while their shaky command of Latin drove their elders to distraction. Paul Alvarus, a church elder of the period, sums up the situation in an oft-quoted paragraph:

> Do not all the Christian youths, handsome in appearance, fluent of tongue, conspicuous in their dress and action, distinguished for their knowledge of Gentile lore, highly regarded for their ability to speak Arabic, do they not all eagerly use the volumes of the Chaldeans [i.e. Arabs], read them with the greatest interest, discuss them ardently, and collecting them with great trouble, make them known with every praise of their tongue, while they are ignorant of the beauty of the Church and look with disgust upon the Church's rivers of paradise as something vile.[49]

Worse still, they began to view Christianity and Islam as equally legitimate religions in the Muslim manner, rather than maintaining the official Latin Christian view that Islam was a heresy, and from this position conversion was only one small step away. The crisis facing Christianity triggered one of the most extraordinary episodes in Christian–Muslim relations, the Cordoban Martyr Movement of the 850s, during which 38 men and 12 women publicly denounced Islam and refused all attempts by their own leaders and the flustered Muslim authorities to persuade them to retract their statements. Many came from mixed marriages or convert households and several were apostates from Islam according to the law, a crime which was punishable by death, and when persuasion failed they were executed. Eulogius, one of the last martyrs, fanned the flames of the movement by encouraging several young women to hold fast to Christianity and endure death in a manner which shows exactly why Cordobans in general so intensely disliked the martyrs. In 859 Leocritia, a girl of Muslim parentage with a Christian aunt, decided to become Christian and run away from her parents. Eulogius and his sister harboured the runaway in direct opposition to her parents' wishes and encouraged her to stand firm. Both were arrested and subsequently executed, Eulogius for proselytizing and assisting in the abduction of a Muslim girl and Leocritia for refusing to return to the faith of her parents.

The deaths of the martyrs provoked a furore: many of their co-religionists criticized them for destabilizing inter-communal relations and pointed to the many ways in which they were virtually suicides rather than martyrs in the established Christian sense of the word. Bishop Reccafred of Seville was most displeased, and Alvarus describes him descending upon 'churches and clergy like a violent whirlwind' and throwing as many priests as he could in jail.[50] Then the Muslim authorities began to clamp down on Christians, destroying churches and imposing the *dhimma* regulations strictly, and large numbers of Christians took that last small step and converted to Islam rather than be tarred with the same brush as the extremists. In this case the blood of the martyrs was not seed, and the Martyr Movement reduced the Christian majority in Cordoba to a small minority among a new Hispanic, Arab and Berber Muslim majority.

In North Africa indigenous Christianity struggled against state indifference and a gradual decrease in the number of bishops only to disappear completely by the late twelfth century, despite the strength of the African church in the days of St Augustine, a native of Hippo in modern-day Algeria. It fared better in Egypt, Palestine, Syria and Iraq, where conversions did occur but on an individual rather than a mass basis, except in extreme circumstances such as al-Hakim's forced conversion of Jews and Christians in Egypt in 1009. The enduring importance of Christianity in rural Egypt is best shown by the theoretical problem which it gave al-Muqaddasi, who was unwillingly forced to deny some thriving settlements in Egypt the status of 'towns' because they had such a predominance of Christians that they had not a single great mosque, one of his criteria for a city:

> Towns in Egypt are not numerous, because the majority of the people of the countryside are Copts; and in accordance with the terms of our science, a town is only so-designated if it has a *minbar* [a pulpit found only in great mosques].[51]

In his description of his beloved hometown of Jerusalem, he lists its beautiful buildings, abundant fruit and splendid climate, then rather ruefully adds, 'the Jews and Christians are predominant here, and the mosque devoid of congregations and assemblies'.[52] When the Crusaders arrived over a century later, Syria and Palestine were still very religiously mixed, with an endless number of holy sites shared by all faiths, much to the consternation of the Crusaders who had less liberal attitudes towards religions other than their own. Indigenous Christian communities flourished well past the end of the 'Abbasid caliphate, and it is only in the last century that the Christian communities of the region have truly begun to face extinction as a result of the pressures generated by colonialism, nationalism and the formation of the state of Israel, which has ironically proved much more hostile to Christians as members of the Palestinian Arab community than any earlier Muslim regime.

Iraq, the heartland of the caliphate, also had an important Christian population which, as we have already seen, engaged freely in the religious debates of the first 'Abbasid century. Al-Kindi's *Apology* was only one among several Christian tracts written in Arabic and designed for a general audience of Christians and Muslims which argued for the superiority of Christianity against Qur'anic arguments to the contrary. Even in that epitome of Islam itself, the city of Baghdad, Christianity sometimes seemed too influential for the liking of the Muslim mob. In 895 the eunuch of a Christian doctor was accused of slandering the Prophet and arrested but not punished, triggering an angry crowd to criticize the minister responsible, al-Qasim, a Muslim of distant Christian origin, in the following verse:

> Al-Qasim's concern for the eunuch,
> Shows the religion of the father of al-Qasim,
> If the person slandered had been Jesus, one would not have
> Been satisfied with anything but killing the slanderer.[53]

For the Zoroastrians or Magians, the overthrow of the Sasanians rent their religious system asunder. In contrast to Judaism and Christianity, which functioned as religions with lay congregations, Zoroastrianism was an imperial cult practised by the priests, the Magi, alone and had a lay congregation only in its Manichaean and Mazdaean forms. Its identification with the Sasanian state encouraged Muslims to confiscate many fire temples as symbols of Sasanian imperialism rather than religion, but individual Zoroastrian priestly families were not prevented from practising their ancient way of life as a religious community akin to those of the other Peoples of the Book. Nonetheless the demise of the Sasanian imperial structure and the extinguishing of the eternal fires which symbolized their faith were severe blows to the Zoroastrians and many elite Persians converted to Islam, the new faith of empire.

The followers of Mazdak, a late fifth-century reformer sometimes described as a communist who had tried to make Zoroastrianism relevant to ordinary people rather than just the Magi, clustered in Iran and Azerbayjan. They were known to Muslims as the Khurramiyya and, rather than standing apart from Islam, they quickly became involved in radical Muslim movements including the 'Abbasid revolution itself. Their loyalty to Abu Muslim, the movement's Khurasani chief, rather than the 'Abbasids themselves led to their secession after Abu Muslim's assassination in 754 and they quickly came to be viewed as rebels and heretics as often as they were classified as a separate religious minority entitled to protection. In the early ninth century their most famous leader, Babak, led a major rebellion against the 'Abbasids in Azerbayjan that triggered sister rebellions around Isfahan in Iran. After the slow but steady quelling of these various rebellions, mentions of the Khurramiyya become few and far between, with the last coming in the twelfth century in the caliphate's own twilight years. Zoroastrian or Mazdaean religious and cultural practices persisted longest in the province of Fars in southwest Iran, where al-Muqaddasi noted that 'the practices of the Magians are in the open'.[54] He added with some distaste that 'the customs of the Magi are widespread' in Shiraz where 'they celebrate with the Magians the festival of Nawruz', linking that to a comment about the prevalence of public brothels in the city in a very common conflation of Zoroastrianism with sexual degeneracy.[55]

For the Jews, the arrival of a new imperial power and religion was frequently a relief from their persecution by Visigothic, Byzantine or Sasanian authorities, and they were well used to living as minorities within a host society, making the adjustment to the new order less severe than for Christians and Zoroastrians. Moreover both the Jews and the Arabs were of Semitic origin and reckoned Abraham (Ibrahim in Arabic) their ancestor via his sons Isaac and Isma'il respectively, which created a different dynamic between Jews and Muslims to that which had existed between the Jews and their previous imperial masters. There was plenty of sibling rivalry between the two peoples but also some deep-seated affinities related to the ritual and doctrinal similarities between Judaism and Islam – which were stronger than those between Christianity and Islam – and the proximity of their sacred sister languages, Hebrew and Arabic.

The Muslim attitude to Judaism and the Jews was conditioned by the Prophet's own interactions with the Arabic-speaking Jews of the Hijaz, which began cordially but then soured after the Jews of Medina and the nearby oasis of Khaybar refused to recognize him as the Messiah. For early Muslims this constituted a serious betrayal which gained divine corroboration in the form of Qur'anic descriptions of the Jews as hypocrites who supported then rejected Muhammad. As a result hostility to the Jews existed and was more pointed than anti-Christian or anti-Zoroastrian feeling, but it did not translate into the kind of pervasive anti-Jewish feeling exhibited by medieval Christianity. Judaism remained an accepted religion of the book, and early Muslims were usually better informed about Jewish beliefs than those of the Christians or Zoroastrians with whom they had had less intimate interactions. In contrast to the negative relations between the Hijazi Jews and the Arabs, Jews were often portrayed by irate Christians as collaborating with the Muslim invaders in areas outside Arabia, suggesting the proximity between the two communities which others perceived.

Although accounts of collaboration are as likely to be Christian prejudice as fact, individual Jews quickly offered their services to their new masters. Jewish folk tales, the Isra'iliyyat, were popular with Muslims and, as Jewish communities adopted Arabic, their scholars used Arabic philology and grammar to revitalize Hebrew and extend its use from the synagogue to other arenas, a development most dramatically seen in the Golden Age Hebrew poetry of Spain, when Hebrew burst out of the liturgical into secular and even erotic channels. In the religious and intellectual spheres, Jews contributed to the inter-religious debates taking place, and their theology and philosophy developed in parallel with Islamic explorations in these fields. The Karaite sect which emerged in Iraq, for instance, upheld similar views to the Muslim Mu'tazilis with whom they mixed. Baghdad, Cairo and Cordoba were centres of Jewish as well as Muslim intellectual life, and just as Iraq was the vital pulsing heart of Muslim culture in the early 'Abbasid caliphate, so too Babylon, as the Jews called it, was central for Jews across the Islamic world. Up until the tenth century, the Jews of Spain referred religious questions to the authorities of Babylon, whose own approach to the Talmud was evolving in correspondence with developments in the Muslim legal sphere. When the Muslims of al-Andalus proclaimed their own caliphate, the Jews simultaneously declared the religious and cultural independence of Sefarad, their name for Spain, from the rabbis of Babylon.

The flowering of Jewish culture in an Islamic social setting was underpinned by the commercial opportunities provided by the establishment of a vast Islamic realm. The Jews, a close-knit and mostly urban minority, were well placed to exploit this situation and create an extensive and prosperous commercial network from one end of the Islamic world to the other. The letters preserved in the Cairo Geniza – a medieval Jewish depository for documents which needed to be disposed of respectfully because they contained the name of God – gives us a most intimate portrait of Jewish life from Iberia to India, with traders exchanging contracts, rabbis overseeing the moral welfare of their communities and travellers reporting on the political ups and downs faced by Jews in different places. It shows the tremendous interconnectedness of the Jews of Islam but also their close relations with Muslims in every area of life. They were not an isolated minority but one which was deeply embroiled in the life of the larger community. Jewish astrologers and physicians served at court, wealthy Jews lent money to the Fatimids, among others, and in al-Andalus Jews served as chief ministers and even generals in the turbulent world of the Ta'ifa kings who succeeded the Umayyads in the eleventh century.

However, there were limits, and in 1066, the same year as the Battle of Hastings, the swaggering – and tax collecting – of Yusuf b. Naghrila, the son of the most successful of the Andalusi Jewish ministers and generals, became too much for the Muslims of his hometown, Granada, who rose up in a furious orgy of violence, killing Yusuf and many of his Jewish fellows. It is worth noting, however, that he and his father Samuel b. Naghrila had together overseen, if not actually ruled, Granada for 30 years before the population reacted against this perceived breach in the *dhimma* conventions and that the actual trigger of the massacre was political rather than sectarian. The Sanhaja Berber ruler of Granada, Muzaffar, was ageing, and Yusuf was suspected of intriguing with Ibn Sumadih, the rival ruler of Almeria. According to the memoirs of a later ruler of Granada, a drunken slave ran out of a party at Yusuf's palace yelling,

> Hey folks! Have any of you heard about al-Muzaffar being betrayed by the Jew [Yusuf b. Naghrila] and that Ibn Sumadih is about to enter the city! ... The prince tried to calm the mob, but all in vain. It was too late. The Jew turned and fled for his life inside the palace pursued by the populace, who finally ran him down and did him to death. They then turned their swords on every Jew in the city and seized vast quantities of their goods and chattels.[56]

A Judaic community deeply affected by the changing political and religious profile of the Middle East were the Samaritans who lived in the vicinity of the town of Nablus in Palestine and whose experience after the Muslim conquests suggests some of the push rather than pull factors involved in mass conversions to Islam when they did take place. Having survived Rome and the hostility of mainstream Jews, the Samaritans were decimated when they unwisely rebelled several times against the Byzantines between 452 and 556. They thrived again under the Umayyads, but the community came under renewed pressure during the 'Abbasid caliphate. During the civil war in the east between al-Amin and al-Ma'mun in the second decade of the ninth century, order broke down in Syria and Palestine, and Muslim rebels forcibly converted Samaritans to Islam. Subsequently a famine during the reign of al-Mutawakkil three decades later pushed more Samaritans to convert in order to evade the onerous poll tax and use the money to buy food. Finally, when Palestine came under the authority of the 'Abbasid governor of Egypt, Ahmad b. Tulun, in the late ninth century, collective punishments and fines against the community triggered another wave of conversion.[57] These kinds of material pressure must have driven many people of other religions to convert at different times and places and join the seductions of Arabic and Islam which swayed the Christians of Cordoba, and explain how Islam was gradually transformed from the religion of a ruling class to the faith of the masses.

Despite the varied experiences of non-Muslims, there is a sense in which the classical age of Islam, the centuries of the 'Abbasid caliphate and its sibling caliphates in Egypt and Spain, did provide a noteworthy level of toleration and accommodation which began to falter as the caliphal age closed. This intermingling found its greatest expression in the development of a multi-faith bureaucracy and intellectual elite, whose members gathered at the 'Abbasid court and those of their representatives, rivals and imitators. Non-Muslims initially made their way into the administration and court circles because neither the Umayyads not the early 'Abbasids could have administered the vast territories under their control without the services of ex-Byzantine and Sasanian officials. The caliphs were also quick to recruit Zoroastrian and Jewish astrologers and Christian physicians into their entourages, and it was in the palaces of the caliphs and their close associates that Christians, Jews and Muslims began to exchange views on their faiths and argue over their respective merits in an atmosphere of toleration, however heated a particular discussion became. It was also the collaborations between Muslims and Christians conversant in Greek and Syriac, sponsored by the caliphs and their circle, that made possible the translation of a vast quantity of ancient science and knowledge into Arabic (see Chapter 5). From this perspective, at least, Islamic society was a joint effort which drew on the resources of its Christian, Jewish and Zoroastrian subjects, who reshaped their own cultures and religions in response to the spread of Arabic and Islam.

Beggars and tricksters

So many of our sources deal with the elites of Muslim society and those considered respectable. It is therefore refreshing to come across a few extant examples of a type of scurrilous and vulgar literature which was extremely popular in Baghdad and indeed the entire eastern Islamic world in the eighth to ninth centuries. This literature, described as *majin* (saucy, brazen), took as one of its themes the lives of the vagabonds and beggars collectively known as the Banu Sasan, the sons of Sasan. Although Banu Sasan-like characters existed across the Islamic world, the origin of the name is most likely Persian. Explanations of it tend to be variations on the theme of the fall of the proud Persians into beggary as a result of the Arab-Muslim conquest of their empire, with 'Sasan' either standing for the Sasanian monarchs as a group or an individual prince of that name ousted from the succession. Such romantic attributions of the term Banu Sasan were given weight by early stories of Persian highwaymen apparently from noble families who had fallen on hard times, the best known of whom was Musa b. Shakir, the father of the Banu Musa trio of scientists and courtiers, who mended his ways to become a boon companion of the caliph al-Ma'mun while the latter was governor of Merv.

The famous *risala* or epistle of Abu Dulaf, a self-proclaimed king among vagabonds and a hanger on at court, where his sordid but titillating knowledge of the underworld kept him in favour, celebrates the beggar's life in the following couplets near the start:

> For I am of the company of the beggar lords, the confraternity of the outstanding ones,
> One of the Banu Sasan, and a person who has stoutly defended the group's territory from the earliest times.
> Yet we have found it good to seize the fleeting moments, in harsh times and in periods of ease.
> We have never relented in our imbibings, nor do we relax in our copulations,
> And the sweetest way of life we have experienced is one spent in sexual indulgence and wine drinking,
> For we are the lads, the only lads who really matter, on land and sea.[58]

As in many other societies, beggars and vagabonds formed an under-class with their own slang, codes of honour and ways of doing things. Men, women and children were all involved and had numerous tricks, which Abu Dulaf enumerates in often grotesque detail, to enable them to extort money from the other inhabitants of a town. There were those 'who feigned madmen or madwomen, with metal chains strung from their neck' and those who maimed themselves or simulated disfigurements and diseases by applying various ointments and tourniquets to create pustules or simulate 'a festering internal wound'. Others, playing on religious sentiment, paraded 'in the garb of an ascetic', begged 'on the pretext [of being] a pilgrim' or purveyed 'objects of veneration'. Another group of tricksters pretended to be holy warriors, refugees from the Byzantine frontier, or gentlemen fallen on hard times, while others borrowed small children to beg with in order to induce greater sympathy among the crowds or brought them up 'as compan-ions of the beggars'. Faith healers, fortune-tellers and quack doctors were also a common feature of daily life, as were the truly impoverished who lived by collecting rags or wandered into the mosques, naked and emaci-ated, begging for a crust.

Some earned money as storytellers who could tell Christian, Jewish or Muslim tales depending on their audience, often aided by an assistant in the audience who would 'oh' and 'ah' at the right moments and collect contri-butions in return for a share of the profits. Others would sing laments for 'Ali and Abu Bakr, hoping to fleece both pious Shi'i and Sunni Muslims. Such storytellers and reciters could have quite a following, sometimes of a disorderly nature. When the ninth-century historian and exegete al-Tabari criticized one such character for misunderstanding the Qur'an, an angry crowd pelted his Baghdad home with stones! In the tenth century one ruling caliph felt compelled to issue a decree prohibiting storytellers and diviners from plying their trade on the streets of Baghdad on the grounds that they encouraged fraternization between men and women and wine drinking.

The manuals of the *muhtasib* add additional insights to the life of the footloose and fancy-free in 'Abbasid society. Inevitably such people congregated in public areas, of which the most central in Muslim cities were the marketplaces and mosques. For those hoping to beg, the mosque was the ideal venue to attract the attention of people while their minds were focused on higher things, and Islam's injunction to believers to be charitable might be expected to carry more weight on the mosque steps than elsewhere. Among the endless tasks entrusted to the *muhtasib* and his team of underlings were keeping the interior of mosques clear of beggars to prevent them from disturbing those at prayer and ensuring that vagrants only slept in the outer porticoes of the building and not within the sacred precinct itself. From Abu Dulaf we find out that beggars extracted money from people at prayer with such foul tactics as farting loudly or hawking incessantly until disgusted members of the congregation paid them to go away! Al-Jahiz also describes men simply loitering in the mosque, whiling away the hours discussing any topic which took their fancy and repeating anecdotes of a less than pious nature.

The Banu Sasan also included prostitutes, male and female, who worked the streets. They tended to congregate in the hostelries and inns located in the market areas of a city, where travellers from out of town slept and where alcohol was sometimes served. Street entertainers might well sell sexual favours as a sideline, giving the name of 'actress' rather the same connotation it had in Regency London. Although extra-marital sex was not condoned within Islamic society, it naturally occurred and, given the difficulties well-brought-up men had in meeting women, it is not surprising that some resorted to prostitutes. There was also a strong homoerotic strand within 'Abbasid society, as there had been in ancient Greece, with the difference that it was not as openly accepted owing to religious opposition to homosexuality derived from the Qur'anic version of the fate of Sodom and Gomorrah. On the other hand, the *ghulam*, a young attractive male slave, was a celebrated figure in court poetry from Baghdad to Cordoba, and often the object of the poet's yearning and desire. Male friendships were close and intimate, and in this environment there was a call for male as well as female prostitutes in the crowded cities of the Islamic world. In a universal description of how people end up as prostitutes, Abu Dulaf speaks of the beggars' indiscriminate sexual preferences and the sad fate of the 'wretched beardless youth' made drunk by the master of the young beggars, after which 'the penises of the beggar leaders go into him without his being aware of it'.[59]

Although the lives of the destitute living on the margins of society are shadowy and elusive, Abu Dulaf's *risala* and the *majin* poets capture the gypsy-like independence and pride of the vagabonds, their *esprit de corps* and their ability to gull the unsuspecting inhabitants of the towns and cities in which they lived. They also evoke the real hardship and desperation which existed in the glittering metropolises of classical Islam. Although they wrote to captivate caliphs and courtiers and earn a handful of gold coins for their acerbic wit and salacious revelations, they also remind us that 'Abbasid society too had an underworld where religion did not matter much except as a way to con people into parting with their cash, where honour among thieves was the order of the day and where men and women simply did what they had to do to survive.

CHAPTER 4

The Lifeblood of Empire: Trade and Traders in the 'Abbasid Age

Praise be to God, who made us to love what is in the hands of others, and others to love what is in our hands, so that trade is feasible, and with it mutual advantage and the possibility of communal life.[1]

O ne of the great inadvertent achievements of the Islamic empire was to join up the Byzantine and Persian trading zones and create a single new commercial area dominating the heart of the old world. Although this was not necessarily one of the Arabs' strategic aims, the Islamic empire had an ideal geographic location for intercontinental trade, and Muslims were culturally and religiously well disposed towards commerce. Most pre-Islamic Arabian civilizations of any distinction had flourished as a result of international commerce, and the tribes of the peninsula had long benefited from extracting a tariff for allowing caravans laden with goods to pass through their territory. The Yemeni kingdoms of Saba (Sheba), Himyar and Kinda had traded in frankincense and other aromatics which went either by sea or desert to the emporia of Rome and Persia. Meanwhile the Nabataean Arabs, who resided in the northern part of the Arabian peninsula where it imperceptibly fades into the Syrian steppe, had constructed their own commercial empire centred on the oasis city of Palmyra, which, according to Appian, channelled commodities from India and Arabia between the territory of the Persians and the lands of the Romans.[2] Even out-of-the-way Mecca was within reach of several regional fairs, including 'Ukaz and Medina, and supplemented the income generated by its pagan shrine with trade. Arabia also had a mining industry, copper in Oman, gold and silver in Yemen and the Hijaz, which expanded in the early Islamic era and filled the coffers of the Rightly Guided Caliphs.

Islam was thus not the product of an isolated desert outpost, but of a region with a long commercial history in addition to well-established cultural, political and military connections with the Fertile Crescent and the lands beyond. Muhammad's first exposure to the cultural and religious diversity of the Near East probably occurred as a result of the trading trips he undertook to Byzantine Syria as a boy and young man. Stories in his *Sira*, a collection of pious and miraculous biographical anecdotes compiled by Ibn Ishaq from oral accounts in the eighth century, shed light on the intimate relationship between religion, culture and trade apparent from Islam's inception, or at least imagined to be by 'Abbasid times. In the most famous such anecdote, a young Muhammad accompanied his uncle Abu Talib to Syria and:

> When the caravan reached Busra in Syria, there was a monk there in his cell by the name of Bahira who was well versed in the knowledge of the Christians. ... They had often passed him in the past and he never spoke to them or took any notice of them until this year, and when they stopped near his cell he made a great feast for them.[3]

He then sent word to them, 'I have prepared food for you, O men of Quraysh, and I should like you to come both great and small, bond and free.' The Arabs went to eat, leaving Muhammad in charge of the baggage, but Bahira noticed his absence and called for him. He then questioned him and 'saw the seal of prophethood between his shoulders' just as his sacred Christian books described. Although the point of this anecdote is Christian verification of Muhammad as a true prophet, it is telling that the connection between the Christian monk and his Arab visitors was made possible by trade.

Trade and Christianity similarly figured in Muhammad's relationship with Khadija, who later became his wife. Ibn Ishaq describes her as a 'merchant woman of dignity and wealth' who 'used to hire men to carry merchandise outside the country on a profit-sharing basis, for the Quraysh were a people given to commerce'. She suggested to Muhammad that he 'take her goods to Syria and trade with them' and on the journey a monk again identified him as a prophet, this time to Khadija's slave Maysara, who reported back to his mistress.[4]

Within the string of revelations which together make up the Qur'an, there are many allusions to trade, ranging from direct injunctions about how transactions should be carried out to imagery describing religion in commercial terms as a transaction between man and God. It is obvious from the Qur'an that some Arabs had an ambiguous attitude towards trade and saw little difference between legitimate profits from the sale of goods

Fig. 23. A caravan of pilgrims or merchants at rest near Asyut, Upper Egypt.
From David Roberts, *Egypt and Nubia* (London, 1846–49), vol. 1, plate 37, tab.b.19.
(Reproduced by kind permission of the Syndics of Cambridge University Library)

and illicit gains from interest charged on loans, known in medieval times as usury. But the overall thrust of the Qur'an was to dispel such apprehensions and offer religious approval for commerce, as long as it was conducted within certain moral boundaries. The second chapter of the Qur'an, Surat al-Baqara, states:

> Those who devour usury will not rise again except as one rises whom Satan has caused to stumble by his touch. That is because they say: trafficking is like usury but God has permitted trafficking and forbidden usury.[5]

The *hadith* collections also have lengthy sections full of sayings legitimizing commerce and handle the minutiae of exchange in loving detail. The *Sahih* of al-Bukhari, one of the canonical collections of *hadith*, places commerce immediately after the initial chapters on prayer and ritual before every other chapter dealing with human relations. This ideological stance gave the role of merchant a respectable status and enabled mercantile activity to thrive after the Islamic empire came into being, although banking, which brought Muslims dangerously close to usury, tended to remain in the hands of non-Muslims, primarily Jews.

The creation of an empire and a sympathetic religious atmosphere were only the first steps in restoring the Eurasian commercial routes, badly damaged by generations of war between the Byzantines and Sasanians and the depredations of plague, which abated only towards the end of the Umayyad caliphate. Just as important was the Muslims' preference for settling in towns, both new and old, which had the effect of stimulating the market and increasing demand for all kinds of commodities across the empire. The Muslim elite's wealth, derived from conquest booty and the taxation of their non-Muslim subjects, ensured that this demand did not just incorporate foodstuffs and other basic items but also quickly came to include luxuries – spices, precious metals, porcelain, rich silk textiles, perfumes and slaves – which not only galvanized trade but also the associated pursuit of the manufacturing crafts.

An additional incentive to and support for commerce was the pre-Islamic Arabian connection between trade and pilgrimage which metamorphosed into the tendency for Muslims to support themselves whilst on pilgrimage by buying and selling along the route, and for the annual pilgrimage to Mecca, the *hajj*, to be accompanied by a trade fair outside the city. As provincial pilgrimages to the tombs of the descendants of the Prophet and other holy personages developed, they too went hand in hand with markets and fairs. The fact that performance of the pilgrimage to Mecca was incumbent on all Muslims, male and female, at least once in their lifetimes if they had the means, created a steady stream of people moving across the Islamic empire which oiled the wheels of trade as well as testifying to their piety. Servicing the pilgrim caravans with food, water and lodging was something the 'Abbasid caliphs, their wives and concubines invested heavily in and it provided employment for numerous people along the many routes converging on Arabia from north, south, east and west. The facilities on these routes were equally useful for merchants passing the same way.

In the first instance, trade and manufacture were predominantly in the hands of non-Muslims who quickly moved to benefit from the new conditions. The Jews of the new Islamic world rapidly constructed an efficient and successful series of mercantile links which connected Spain to North Africa and the eastern Mediterranean littoral and reached on into Iraq, Iran and Central Asia. As the distinguished economic historian Eliyahu Ashtor says, '[the Jews'] legal status improved and the facilities which the vast new empire offered created unprecedented opportunities for traders'.[6] They were soon joined by Muslim merchants of varied ethnic origins who worked alongside them and ventured in new directions, pushing well beyond the frontiers of the Islamic world into the wilds of Europe, along the Silk Road to China and across the Indian Ocean to India. In Africa, Berbers pioneered the expansion of trans-Saharan trade, a development facilitated by the introduction of the camel to North Africa in the late Roman period, which made crossing the ever increasing sand wastes feasible again after the journey had become impossible for beasts of burden requiring regular water.

Routes and commodities

Although the incense and spices of Arabia were famous in the ancient world, sought after by Assyrians, Persians, Greeks and Romans alike, in the centuries immediately preceding the rise of Islam the Arabs probably did not trade extensively in such opulent products. Graeco-Roman demand for incense had faltered as Christianity replaced paganism, and Byzantium's more frugal needs could be satisfied by the purchase of various aromatic woods and resins from Christian East Africa. It is more likely that the Meccans and other Arab merchants in the Hijaz traded in rather more humble commodities such as leather and dried fruits, with some perfume thrown in, which they exchanged for the grain, wine and weapons produced by sedentary communities on the fringe of the desert. Pre-Islamic Arabian commerce travelled by sea as well as camel caravan. The Red Sea port of Jeddah already existed and, according to Ibn Ishaq, it was the scene of the shipwreck of a Byzantine ship whose wood was used to repair the Ka'ba shortly before Muhammad received his first revelation.[7] There were also numerous ports strung along the southern coast of Arabia and in the Persian Gulf. When commodities were carried along the long and laborious land routes of Arabia, it was most likely the will of rulers who hoped to profit from the tariffs rather than merchants who preferred cheaper and quicker sea transport up the Red Sea or Persian Gulf to plodding through the desert for months on end.

With the construction of the Islamic empire, Arabs quickly moved into the sale of booty and military equipment while local traders settled in the garrison towns to sell homegrown produce and other daily necessities to the tribal warriors. Early taxes on non-Muslim subjects were often paid in kind, ensuring a regular supply of grain, fruit, vegetables and meat to the cities where such products were purchased using the copper and silver coins of the old empires until coins of Islamic issue began to circulate under the Umayyads. Despite these humble beginnings, trade and industry soon began to flourish across the Islamic empire and a number of important routes developed to bring all kinds of commodities to the thriving cities of Iran, Iraq, Egypt, Syria, North Africa and Spain. Although our image of Middle Eastern trade is usually of cameleers wending their way through the desert, the caravan routes passed through a variety of terrains. While

camels did cross the sands of the Sahara and Arabia, other animals transported goods along the main arterial roads running along the North African coast from Gibraltar into Egypt, along the Nile valley, up through Syria
along the Orontes valley, across the stony Syrian desert to Iraq, through
the flood plains of the Tigris and Euphrates and into Iran, where routes
threaded across mountain and desert east to Afghanistan and India, south
to the Persian Gulf and north into Central Asia, the start of the ancient
Silk Road leading to China.

River and sea routes were equally important. The Arabs were already
sailing on the Red Sea and Persian Gulf in pre-Islamic times but they were
not greatly experienced seafarers in contrast to the Persians. This soon
changed as their struggle to conquer Byzantium turned into a naval contest
in the Mediterranean. Assisted by Persians and the Copts of Egypt, the
Arabs hastened to develop a navy which they used to defeat the Byzantines
at the Battle of the Masts in 655 and to besiege Constantinople shortly
afterwards. Although Constantinople's sea defences were too strong for the
Muslims, they rapidly evicted their Byzantine rivals from other Mediterranean ports and islands as they sailed ever further west.

Within a century or so, Muslims controlled the Mediterranean seaways,
a dominance they did not lose until the Italian city-states of Pisa, Genoa and
Venice began to develop their fleets many centuries later. While merchants
and pilgrims preferred land routes during the winter season, when Mediterranean storms made it perilous to sail, from March to October Muslim
and Jewish traders took to the sea. The usual method of sailing was island-
hopping rather than venturing into the open sea, which not only minimized
the risk of being wrecked in a storm but also maximized the opportunities for picking up passengers and cargo along the route. From Alexandria
ships sailed west, stopping off at Malta, Sicily, Majorca and Menorca, or a
series of North African ports, before reaching the great Spanish entrepots
of Almeria, Denia and Malaga. Ibn Jubayr, sailing in the other direction in
March 1182, describes one such route:

> Our course lay along the Andalusi coast, but this we left on Thursday 6
> Dhu'l-Qa'da when we were opposite Denia. The morning of Friday the
> seventh of the month we were off the island of Ibiza, on Saturday the
> island of Majorca, and on Sunday we were off Menorca. ... We left the
> coast of this island, and early on the night of Tuesday the eleventh of the
> month, being the eighth of March, the coast of the island of Sardinia,
> all at once appeared before us not a mile away. Between the islands of
> Sardinia and Menorca lie about four hundred miles. It had been a crossing
> remarkable for its speed.[8]

In addition to 'refashioning ... the Mediterranean economy of antiquity' in the west, Muslims also harnessed 'the productive resources of the lands around the Indian Ocean in the east'.[9] In Sasanian times, Persians had sailed the Indian Ocean from the port of Ubulla at the head of the Persian Gulf and Kish and Siraf further east along the coast. There were also numerous Arab ports dotted along the coast from Oman to Yemen and up the Red Sea, whose seafarers tended to handle local rather than oceanic trade. Soon after the establishment of the Islamic empire, however, Muslims of varied backgrounds and traders of other faiths began to negotiate the Indian Ocean and the seaways leading to China in their lateen-rigged dhows. By the ninth century the merchants of Siraf organized their fleet to make annual journeys to the coast of East Africa, Daybul in Sind, Calicut in India, and China, where a thriving Middle Eastern mercantile community existed in Canton, consisting of Muslims, Christians, Jews and Persians 'of the ancient faith'.[10] From the tenth century, however, the Chinese started to bring their products westwards in huge ocean-going junks, and ships from the Middle East began to stop at the Malabar coast in India rather than making the difficult and perilous journey all the way to China. Muslim merchants therefore concentrated on settling around the Indian Ocean from Zanzibar and Kilwa to Calicut, often alongside Jewish merchants of similar origins.

From coastal ports, ships sailed up and down the great waterways of the Middle East – the Tigris, Euphrates and Nile. As the historian al-Tabari and numerous Arab geographers noted, one of the great advantages of the location of Baghdad was its position close to the Tigris, from which the city could receive goods from China via the Persian Gulf while other commodities travelled south down the river from northern Iraq, Armenia and Azerbayjan. Fustat and later Cairo were similarly serviced by the Nile, which brought the agricultural produce of the Nile valley to feed the hungry city and all manner of commodities from the Mediterranean port of Alexandria. In Central Asia, the Oxus and Jaxartes played a similar role, and intrepid Muslims also ventured up the Volga and Don to establish trade connections with the Vikings. Ibn Fadlan's famous account of the strange Viking practices he witnessed in the ninth century not only became a Muslim classic but more recently inspired the Hollywood film *The Thirteenth Warrior*, which mixed the experiences of Ibn Fadlan with a dose of Beowulf! At the other end of the Islamic world in Spain, the great Guadalquivir river allowed the passage of Mediterranean shipping up from Cadiz to Seville and finally Cordoba, whose political troubles in the eleventh century were compounded by the silting of the Guadalquivir and the consequent decline in river-borne trade. In later times, Seville was as far as ships of any size could sail upriver, which was one reason the Almoravids and Almohads preferred it to Cordoba as a capital.

The commodities carried by the vast Islamic trade network varied enormously. The bread and butter of the trade was often bulk goods such as grain, rice and dates, which receive relatively little mention because of their mundane nature but were nonetheless crucial to the survival of Islam's teeming cities and more truly the lifeblood of empire than rarer and more costly items. These goods were carried alongside manufactures of all qualities, with cotton textiles, metal goods, porcelain and glass high on the list. At the top end of the scale came the expensive and prestigious commodities which the rich and powerful in Islamic lands, India and China coveted or which had ceremonial or religious significance: silk, incense, sandalwood, spices, ivory, cut gemstones and even thoroughbred horses. Most merchants did not specialize in a particular commodity but put together assorted cargoes or caravans to maximize their chances of profit along their chosen routes. A ship cargo generally contained a mixture of very expensive goods with a ballast of cheaper items, all of which were packed in an assortment of bales, baskets and earthenware vessels. Dates were popular ballast for ships sailing from Basra and other Gulf ports, while ships in the Red Sea carried grain from Egypt to Jeddah, where it was used to feed the pilgrims who arrived in Mecca each year to perform the *hajj*. Traders did not necessarily return empty handed, as the pilgrimage was also the occasion for a massive cloth fair which kept Mecca in the commercial loop.

It is impossible to understand the trade of the 'Abbasid empire in terms of imports and exports because the Islamic world was a huge market in and of itself. Commerce with China, India or the Franks in Europe was small-scale in comparison to the massive circulation of products within the frontiers of the *dar al-islam*. This was especially true with regard to the most important industry of all, the textile industry. While Muslim rulers eagerly purchased Chinese silk and Indian muslin, virtually every region of the Islamic world produced its own cloth and clothing from wool, flax, hemp, cotton or silk, with many areas specializing in luxury textiles, cotton brocades, silks, and other embroidered or finely woven cloth which the rich used for clothing and home furnishings – mattress covers, cushions, wall-hangings and curtains.

In the small commercial summaries at the end of his description of each Islamic province, al-Muqaddasi lists a bewildering range of fabrics and clothing: al-Andalus specialized in cloth production; Fustat produced a special cloth of three-ply yarn made from camel hair and goats' wool; Palestine produced towels; the northern province of Rihab, modern Azerbayjan and Armenia, made curtains and quilts; Damascus was famous for its silk brocade; Baghdad, Basra and Ubulla for silks and embroidered linens of various kinds; and the cities of Khuzistan in southern Iran offered 'fine silk brocade, howdah blankets, fine [cotton] cloth', silk veils and fabrics of hemp.[11] However, pride of place went to Khurasan and Transoxania, where the cities of Nishapur, Herat, Merv and Samarkand exceeded all others in the versatility of their weavers and the variety of their textiles, which included high-quality white clothing, turbans, shawls, scarves in cotton and wool, and silk veils.

The luxury textile industry was further stimulated by demand from the caliphs and other rulers who bestowed garments with bands of silk or gold embroidery as a mark of their favour. This practice had Byzantine, Roman and Sasanian precedents and, like these regimes, the Umayyads and 'Abbasids set up royal ateliers to produce garments with caliphal insignia. Although these workshops were occupied with producing caliphal *tiraz* textiles, as they were called, by 'Abbasid times they were also promoting standards of elegance and textile designs which were then copied and manufactured elsewhere. Seville, for instance, was home to a thriving industry which produced cheap versions of 'Abbasid silk textiles for sale in Spain and as far afield as Khurasan. Carpets, woven or embroidered in wool, cotton or silk, were another item produced for local consumption but also exported when their quality allowed. The palaces of Baghdad, Samarra, Cairo and Cordoba all offered excellent opportunities to merchants selling textiles and carpets, and royal women often purchased such items to hoard as treasure as well as to decorate their apartments.

Another extremely important category of commodity was that of spices and aromatics, which included not only food enhancers but also medicines of various plant and mineral origins, incense, perfumes and the dyes used in the textile industry. They had the advantage that they were light and easy to transport and could bring great profits to those who invested in them. Muslims were aware of thousands of such commodities, some from the Islamic world and some from other parts of Asia and Africa. Among the most popular and regularly traded were black pepper, cinnamon of various types, cloves, camphor, saffron, musk, ambergris, aloes, attar of roses, frankincense, myrrh and sandalwood. Many of these had culinary, aromatic and medicinal uses and some, like arsenic, were used as medicines and also poisons. Sweeteners were also important to a society with a sweet tooth, and the wealth of Khuzistan lay not only in its textile industry but also in its production of sugar from cane and beets. Honey from Mosul and other more northerly districts was more commonly used by the poor.

Gold, silver and gems were another staple of long-distance trade within and beyond Islamic lands. Precious metals circulated as bullion and coin.

Gold was mined in West Africa and was one of the most valuable items of the trans-Saharan trade. Silver moved in the opposite direction, from mines in Khurasan westwards to Iraq and Syria and then across the Mediterranean. The availability of good-quality gold and silver coin was no small advantage in Islam's trading empire. The value of Islamic coins was such that some ended up in hoards as far away as Scandinavia, tempting the Vikings to sail south and raid Spain several times in the ninth and tenth centuries. Gems and semi-precious stones were also mined in the mountains of Khurasan. Diamonds, rubies, sapphires and emeralds were all popular, and most merchants sought to acquire a few to sell to rich customers along the route, or use as capital for other purchases. These precious stones were unset, but on occasion valuable jewellery also circulated – sometimes by dubious routes – rather like antiques today. One probable example of the 'Abbasid black market at work is the supposed transfer of striking necklaces from the 'Abbasid court in Baghdad to the treasure chests of the wives and concubines of 'Abd al-Rahman II in Cordoba after the disruption of the civil war between al-Amin and al-Ma'mun in the early years of the ninth century.

The empire also offered a good market for slaves. Although the existence of slavery in Islamic societies has sometimes been downplayed, like the Romans, the Muslims were heavily dependent upon slaves in some sectors of the economy and society. The type of slavery most frequently described for the 'Abbasid era is Turkish military slavery but, as we have seen, domestic slavery and concubinage were widespread. In some areas slaves were used as agricultural labour, most notably in southern Iraq, where the Zanj, as they were called, launched a major revolt in the late ninth century which the caliphs took decades to quell. Cities like Kufa, Basra and Baghdad all had slave markets where the wealthy could purchase the men and women they wished to have in their households. Since it was unlawful to enslave Muslims, the majority of slaves originated from the peripheries of the Islamic world, sub-Saharan Africa, the Christian parts of Spain, Frankish territories, Caucasia and the Turkish steppe. Some were sold into slavery by their impoverished families, but many were captured in warfare, either among their own people or with Muslims. Those destined to become eunuchs were castrated at recognized entry points such as the Spanish coastal town of Pechina, mentioned by al-Muqaddasi, before their captors transported them to the slave markets of major cities where they were checked for illnesses or defects and then put on sale alongside their fellows. According to Islamic law, slave dealers had a responsibility to disclose any problems, and buyers could only physically examine slaves in a way which accorded with 'Abbasid society's understanding of decency:

Anyone who wants to buy a female slave may look at her face and palms, but if he asks to examine her in his house and be alone with her the trader must not allow it unless there are other women present. These may see her whole body. Whoever wants to buy a male slave may look at what is above the navel and below the knees. ... The trader must be absolutely sure that the slave is not a Muslim. Whenever the trader knows that a person for sale has a defect, he must reveal this to the buyer.[12]

These then were the main commodities and routes of the thriving trade of the Islamic empire. To some extent this commerce gave an often politically fragmented world its unity and justified the Arab geographers' understanding of it as a series of provinces within a single cultural and economic sphere, despite the many obvious permutations and variations from one place to the next. All those who followed the trade routes – merchants, pilgrims and scholars – found that they were never complete strangers and that there was a universal Islamic culture which enabled them to communicate and operate with colleagues from places as different as Seville and Samarkand, an experience not completely dissimilar to that of international business travellers in today's very different global world.

Merchants and pilgrims

The traders of the Muslim world fell into two categories: first, professional merchants, commercial agents and pedlars, and, second, travellers with other objectives, for whom trade was simply an incidental means of support. Professional traders came from all religious groups and all social classes. At the bottom end of the scale, pedlars took an assortment of urban wares out to the neighbouring countryside. In southern Morocco, indigenous Jewish pedlars travelled from tribe to tribe and village to village up until the twentieth century. The middle stratum of the mercantile class consisted of small urban tradesmen who often manufactured what they sold, and commercial agents who bought and sold on behalf of investors and the rich merchant elite. At the top end of the scale came the wealthy merchants able to command whole caravans and cargoes and send their staff from one end of the Islamic world to the other. These men sometimes travelled with their goods, especially if they were young and needed to learn the ropes of the trade, but most mature heads of trading families preferred to use agents and the extensive networks of connections they had built up during their lifetimes. Abu'l-Fadl Ja'far al-Dimashqi, who wrote a book called the *Beauties of Commerce* which is tentatively dated to the late ninth century, categorized merchants in the following way:

There are three kinds of merchants: he who travels, he who stocks, and he who exports. Their trade is carried out in three ways: cash sale with a time limit for delivery, purchase on credit with payment by instalments, and *muqarada* [a trading partnership].[13]

We know more about Jewish trading networks than their Muslim equivalents because of the mass of information provided by the documents discovered in the Cairo Geniza mentioned in the last chapter. Letters between merchants show that few of them travelled the length and breadth of the Islamic world but instead used family and friends to organize and monitor trade over vast areas. The Mediterranean basin, the Middle East and the Indian Ocean were distinct trading zones, but commercial connections nonetheless spanned them, with merchants from all regions meeting their colleagues in key emporia such as Baghdad or Fustat. Where face-to-face contact was not possible letters sent with caravans or contacts instructed agents on the imminent arrival of goods, the details of their delivery, and recommended what additional goods should be purchased depending on market conditions. They also advised how to deal with the political authorities in each place and warned of rapacious behaviour on the part of governors and other state representatives. By the eleventh century at least, such missives were carried by professional Muslim and Jewish couriers who operated along known land routes, while friends and acquaintances carried letters on behalf of other merchants by ship and caravan. Merchants usually sent their letters in multiple copies to ensure their safe arrival and it was often one of the courier's tasks to read the letter to its recipient, especially if the letter was addressed to the women of a family, many of whom were illiterate.[14]

Although not officially merchants, pilgrims and to a lesser extent scholars were also integral to commerce. Such travellers customarily carried a small quantity of merchandise from their home town or region which they sold or exchanged for other merchandise as they proceeded towards their destination. This enabled them to pay for food and shelter along the way and make sufficient profit to complete their journeys, which often took several years. Even the speediest pilgrim could expect to spend months making the journey to Mecca and back, and for travellers from far-flung regions such as Morocco, Transoxania or Sind the journey routinely took a couple of years. Moreover the arrival of a pilgrim caravan outside any city was a great opportunity for its traders to make a profit selling local fruits, cheeses, manufactures or services. On his arrival at the Red Sea port of 'Aydhab in Egypt, Ibn Jubayr noted that its people 'by reason of the pilgrims enjoy many benefits especially at the time of their passing through' and well-to-do inhabitants made extra profits by hiring their ships out to carry pilgrims across to Jeddah in Arabia.[15]

Nowhere are the commercial ramifications of pilgrimage better attested than in Mecca itself, a city which survived only by virtue of the pilgrim trade. Caliph after caliph embellished the city, improving its mosque and markets, its water supply and its pilgrim accommodation, to service this thriving annual celebration of religion and commerce. Although the primary purpose of the *hajj* was performance of the set of communal rituals which took place in the Great Mosque of Mecca and various other locations, Ibn Jubayr's description of the late twelfth-century pilgrimage also reveals its commercial aspects. One of the rituals of the pilgrimage was to walk or run seven times along a flood course between two hilltops, Safa and Marwa, but here also was 'a market full of all the fruits and other things like grain and the various foodstuffs. Those who are doing the [ritual run] can hardly free themselves from the great crowd.'[16] More significantly in terms of the impact of the pilgrims themselves on the Meccan economy, he says:

> Although there is no commerce in it save during the pilgrim period, nevertheless, since people gather in it from east and west, there will be sold in one day, apart from those that follow, precious objects such as pearls, sapphires and other stones, various kinds of perfume such as musk, camphor, amber, aloes, Indian drugs and other articles brought from India and Ethiopia, the products of the industries of Iraq and Yemen, as well as the merchandise of Khurasan, the goods of the Maghrib, and other wares such as it is impossible to enumerate or correctly assess. ... All this is within the eight days that follow the pilgrimage.[17]

Ibn Jubayr mentions two venues for this great trade fair: Mina, a village near Mecca where the sacrifice takes place at the end of the pilgrimage ceremonies, which had been the site of 'commercial houses and stores' since the days of al-Muqaddasi, and the Great Mosque of Mecca itself, the sanctuary containing the Ka'ba. He says with some disapproval that, although it was forbidden by divine law, during the festivities at the end of the pilgrimage the mosque 'became a great market in which were sold commodities ranging from flour to agates, and from wheat to pearls'.[18] In keeping with the humble origins of many of those coming into Mecca during the pilgrim season, much of the trade in less valuable commodities took place by barter. Victuallers bringing wheat, beans, raisins, butter and other provisions to Mecca from Yemen did not sell them for 'dinars and dirhams' but exchanged them for cloth, 'together with women's veils and strong quilts and similar things such as are worn by the bedouin'.[19] After the conclusion of the pilgrimage, Mecca returned to its normal quiet and sleepy existence, and the great travelling market of pilgrims dispersed in their caravans back along the roads to Yemen, Egypt, Syria, Iraq and beyond.

Although it is undoubtedly true that the majority of travellers and pilgrims were men, they sometimes took their families with them and arrangements then had to be made. In one short paragraph in the chapter of his *Ordinances of Government* on the market inspector's tasks, al-Mawardi says that in addition to ensuring that shippers do not overload ships or sail in storms:

> If they carry both men and women, he should install a partition between them and if the ships are large enough he should have separate toilets installed for women so that they are not exposed to view when they need to use them.[20]

Women also performed the pilgrimage in their own right and mixed with the men performing the rituals of the *hajj* and the lesser pilgrimage which occurs six months earlier in the year. During the lesser pilgrimage, the great mosque was reserved for women on one day; women gathered to drink at the Zamzam well, associated with the place where Hagar finally found water after being cast out by Sarah, while those 'who walked [between Safa and Marwa] in the hope of a heavenly reward were many, and they competed with the men on that blessed way'.[21] Ibn Jubayr talks of three *khatun*s, Turkish noblewomen, who made the pilgrimage at the same time as him, the daughter of Mas'ud, *amir* of Darub in Armenia, the sister-in-law of Nur al-Din Zangi, and the daughter of the *amir* of Isfahan, all three of whom came from Baghdad with the commander of the pilgrimage, a Turkish lord called Tashtikin. He gives a rather amusing account of Mas'ud's daughter, a haughty 25-year-old who paraded around Mecca and Medina with great aplomb and then left the caravan to spend two days in Mecca alone in a fit of pique against Tashtikin who was obliged to hold up the caravan until she returned. These Turkish ladies enhanced their reputations by dispensing charity as they went along, and even when they did not perform the pilgrimage they sent water-bearing camels to offer thirsty pilgrims refreshment, causing Ibn Jubayr to remark, 'in all three is this most strange admixture of pious works and regal pride', a description which rather nicely sums up the attitude of the Saljuq elite of which they were part.[22]

Trade facilities

This brisk trading environment demanded a range of efficient services and facilities which the caliphs, their governors and the elite were prepared to offer, given the financial benefits accruing to them from tariffs, customs and fees and their sporadic reliance on the hard cash which merchants were best placed to provide. These services fell into two main categories: the provision of physical amenities such as warehouses, markets and hostelries for merchant use and the maintenance of a system of market regulation and good practice based on Islamic law but implemented by a state official, the *muhtasib*, whom we have already met several times in his guise as the official responsible for public morality and urban cleanliness as well as the markets.

Early evidence for warehouses and inns is rather patchy but it is obvious that Muslims built on a variety of pre-Islamic precedents, including Aramaean wayside inns of the sort frequented by the Good Samaritan, Byzantine guesthouses, and the courier relay stations used by Persians since Archaemenid times, which also inspired the 'Abbasid postal system. As the story from the Prophet's *Sira* with which we began shows, hermits and monks might also offer hospitality to passing traders. However, the speedy growth of trade and pilgrim traffic under the Umayyads and early 'Abbasids necessitated the construction of many more inns in the countryside as well as in towns with guaranteed water and food supplies, storage areas and stables or enclosures for animals. There are a bewildering number of words for such facilities – caravanserai, *khan*, *funduq* and *manzil* being the most common – but their functions were broadly similar.

In the countryside, caravanserais were commonly constructed by the caliphs, their relatives, other rulers and members of the elite, and were a day's travel apart along major trade, pilgrimage and courier routes. Those best served usually had a well or cistern so that thirsty animals and travellers could drink, stables to pen the animals, a prayer room, shops selling basic items, an apartment for the warden of the facility, and individual rooms or communal galleries where people could sleep, arranged around a central courtyard, often on the second floor above the stables and store rooms. Their physical appearance and the materials used in their construction reflected local practices and climate. In desert areas and the plains of Iraq and Iran, they were constructed of rammed earth or brick with large open courtyards, while in colder mountain areas they were more likely to be built of stone with a fully roofed courtyard to keep out rain and snow. In many places, however, wayfarers had to make do with less comprehensive facilities. The desert road from Mecca to Medina and on to Kufa offered water in cisterns, tanks or underground canals wherever possible but only rarely the shelter of walls, and travellers were obliged to remain on their guard from marauding bedouin throughout the night, although the very same bedouin might also consider it more in their interests to sell the visitors meat, milk and cheese.

Hostelries and inns in cities were naturally of smaller dimensions than

along the highways, and there were many more of them. They also fulfilled
a greater diversity of functions and were sometimes suspected of being
houses of ill repute which encouraged prostitution and wine-drinking, as
well as offering warehousing and accommodation. For this reason jurists
generally felt that women should not be innkeepers. Certainly, Muslim and
indeed Mediterranean traditions of hospitality competed and conflicted
with the concerns aroused by the presence in cities of strangers of different ethnicities, religions and mores who were also beyond the gaze of their
own families and communities and therefore could not be relied upon to
behave with as much probity as at home. Hostelries therefore also helped
to allay the tensions created by having strangers in town by confining them
to specific buildings and areas, usually near the markets, ports or city gates
and certainly not in residential quarters. For instance, in Alexandria, Ibn
Jubayr stayed in the Inn of the Coppersmiths located near the soap-works.[23]
Although some such inns catered primarily for merchants of a particular
region, religion or commodity, there is no indication that they refused the
trade of other people. The only exception to this were the *funduq*s established for European Christian merchants at the very end of our era, which
included chapels, taverns and sometimes pig pens to provide for the religious and dietary needs of their residents, and were thus not considered
suitable by Muslims and Jews.

Some urban hostelries were pious endowments in the sense that they
offered charity to pilgrims, the sick and other indigent wayfarers. Others
were designed to make a profit like modern hotels and charged a daily fee
for a room and storage space and any other services the customer used, but
their deeds specified that a share of the profit be used to support mosques,
hospitals or other good causes. Others again were constructed by the state
as a useful way of gathering merchants and merchandise in one place for
the purposes of levying customs and fees. In this capacity, some hostelries
also functioned as private retail houses, closed to the general public, where
merchants could meet and sell either high-quality products such as silk
or staple commodities such as grain without the trouble of going to the
marketplace.

Most merchants or commercial agents, however, sold their merchandise and stocked up on other commodities for their return in the bustling
public markets. It was at this point that they would benefit from the market
regulation practised in most cities of the Islamic world. Trade cannot flourish without shared rules and expectations, and good market practices were
highly valued by merchants and rulers alike. When rulers did seek to make
a quick buck out of merchants, or allowed commercial malpractices in the
markets under their jurisdiction, they risked those markets gaining a bad

reputation and being abandoned by traders. The universal importance of maintaining a town's commercial credibility meant that the position of market inspector had existed in some form or other across the Middle East for centuries, if not millennia, before the rise of Islam. The Arabs themselves seem to have been familiar with the concept, since the Prophet and the Rightly Guided Caliphs appointed officials to oversee the markets in Mecca and Medina. The title used for such officials was *'amil al-suq*, which may be loosely translated as 'overseer of the market'. According to tradition at least two of these individuals were women who probably had responsibility for the section of the Medinese market occupied by female traders, a feature that does not seem to have been retained later on.

In the Umayyad period, a similar official appeared in the garrison towns of Iraq and the Islamic west, where he was known as the *sahib al-suq*, the 'master of the market'. With the 'Abbasids, however, the role of market inspector expanded to include general oversight of public order, cleanliness and morality not just in the markets but in all the public areas of a city, including the great mosque and the thoroughfares. At this point the secular title of *sahib al-suq* gave way to the more religiously charged title *muhtasib*, which was derived from the noun *hisba*, denoting every Muslim's obligation to 'command the good and forbid wrong'. The office of *muhtasib* represented an institutionalization of this amorphous religious responsibility and consequently he not only worked closely with the municipal political authorities but also with the judge. The Islamization of the role of market inspector probably reflected the early 'Abbasid caliphs' impulse to centralize the administration and make it more distinctively Islamic as a larger proportion of their subjects became Muslim. It also implied that managing the market well was a religious duty and that commercial malpractices were not only reprehensible but also irreligious, thus decisively tying good market practice to Islam.

An intriguing aspect of the development of this office is whether or not it was related to the ancient Greek position of *agoranomos*, also translated as market inspector. The *agoranomos* was, however, quite a different office in that it was an elective post held by a team of men in large cities and was related directly to the *agora* zone of temples and markets, while the *muhtasib*'s duties ranged more widely across the city, more in the manner of a Roman *aedile*. Moreover the evidence for the perpetuation of either office into the Byzantine period is quite weak, although other officials did manage the markets and other municipal requirements. The consensus is now that the *muhtasib*'s office developed to meet similar needs to those that had in the past been addressed by various different Hellenistic and Roman officials rather than there being a direct connection between the *agoranomos* and *muhtasib*.[24]

The market inspector was sometimes a humble official and sometimes a grandee of the state, but in either case the incumbent had to do the job or make sure his delegates did. His primary obligation for most of the 'Abbasid era was to ensure the use of sound weights and measures, and prevent the fraudulent goings on associated with them. In al-Shayzari's words:

> As [weights and measures] are the bases of commercial dealing and an integral part of sales, the *muhtasib* has to be acquainted with them and verify their size so that transactions can take place without fraud and according to Islamic law.[25]

Although the Qur'an explicitly advocates such good practice, in reality it was extremely difficult to monitor, given the lack of standardization in weights and measures from one place to another and the numerous different measures used simultaneously for different commodities. Al-Muqaddasi felt it necessary to list the measures used in each locality in his summary of information about each region, as well as the different values of measures of the same name. In Fatimid Cairo, a special office was set up next to the *muhtasib*'s headquarters with equipment to check weights and measures, and merchants were obliged to take their scales and weights there to be checked and stamped before they could use them. It was not just the weights and measures themselves which needed checking but also how they were used or abused. Al-Shayzari gives a detailed list of the kind of tricks which a *muhtasib* must be aware of:

> The *muhtasib* must order those who use scales to wipe and clean them hourly of any oil or dirt, as a drop of oil may congeal on them and affect the weight. The merchant must settle the scales before he begins to weigh and should place the merchandise on them gently, not dropping it into the pan from his raised hand, nor moving the edge of the pan with his thumb, as all of this is fraudulent. Among the hidden swindles used with scales for weighing gold is for the merchant to put his hand in front of his face and to blow gently onto the pan containing the merchandise thus making it descend. ... The merchants also have ruses by which they give short weight when they hold the attachment for the scales. They also sometimes stick a piece of wax on the bottom of one of the pans and put the silver on it, then they put the weights on the other pan.[26]

In addition to keeping an eye on weights and measures, the *muhtasib* had to patrol the markets ensuring that goods were properly made and fairly priced. On occasion he also had responsibility for preventing the hoarding of foodstuffs, especially grain, during shortages. Clearly all these tasks were too much for one person, so the *muhtasib* had a team of assistants, men of good character with knowledge of the areas placed under their jurisdiction.

Muslim markets functioned on the principle of grouping manufacturers and sellers of particular goods in the same area or street, a pattern still visible in many cities in the Middle East today. This was believed to facilitate commerce by making it clear to purchasers where a particular commodity was to be found and to keep prices reasonable by encouraging sellers to offer a better price than their neighbours within reasonable limits. It was therefore usual for a *muhtasib* of a major city to have several assistants, each with expertise in a different area of manufacture and sale, as well as a team responsible for more general matters of public order and cleanliness, including refuse removal and monitoring of the sewers. Sellers could, of course, decide to band together to inflate prices, but in so doing they ran the risk of falling foul of the *muhtasib*'s assistant who could be expected to know what the acceptable price for a commodity was in the prevailing conditions, although in this market-driven atmosphere the *muhtasib*'s office was not supposed to set prices.

Market infractions were punished in a variety of ways. When there was no doubt about an infringement of good practice, the *muhtasib* could beat, fine or humiliate an offender by parading him through the streets sitting backwards on a donkey. He could confiscate goods and even prohibit people from making or selling their products. In less clear-cut cases where recourse to legal specialists was necessary, jurisdiction passed to a judge. The police, known as the *shurta*, could also be called in by the *muhtasib* to assist in punishing or intimidating offenders. On the other hand, if a *muhtasib* made a poor judgement on an important matter such as the management of the grain supplies essential to keep the city's population supplied with bread, he could face summary dismissal. Although the sources tend to present this as a reflection of rulers' concern that their flock should not go hungry, it also showed their deep-seated fear of riots should the people be deprived of their daily bread, the stable food across the region.

The other great support for Islamic commerce, especially long-distance trade, was an impressive range of financial partnerships and credit arrangements which seem to have grown out of Byzantine and Persian precedents and pre-Islamic Arabian market practices. Although the Qur'an firmly denounced usury, it was rather vague about what constituted an illicit gain and what types of exchange should be subjected to prohibitions on such gains – coin or bullion and foodstuffs usually topped the list. This vagueness enabled Muslim and non-Muslim businessmen to make money through investments, arrange credit and effect all kinds of money transfers and exchanges in ways which the schools of Islamic law recognized, even if they did not always quite approve of them. In general, contracts and partnerships were much less problematic than credit facilities, and Islamic jurists gave their approval to a variety of contracts and partnerships which allowed people to cooperate in commercial activities as investors, agents or partners.

The basic term for a partnership was *sharika*, which was widely used in legal literature for all kinds of asset-sharing, including shared inheritances, that entailed partnership between two individuals who agreed to pool their capital, labour or goods and then share whatever risks and profits resulted from the venture in agreed proportions. The *mudaraba*, *qirad* or *muqarada* was a more specialized partnership in which a wealthy merchant or individual or group of individuals provided all the investment in the form of currency with which an agent purchased goods, traded with them and paid his business costs. The investor(s) carried the entire risk of the venture but, as a result, also had the right to a larger share of the profits than the agent who did the actual work but did not risk any financial loss. The investor or group of investors trusted the agent to manage their funds appropriately and, at the stipulated end of the contract, return the capital plus a share of the profits. Such *mudaraba* or *qirad* arrangements were very useful in long-distance trade and also provided a mechanism by which money could be lent for profit without contravening usury prohibitions – here the profit officially came from trade rather than the lending of capital *per se*. Although there is disagreement on this point, these arrangements used by Muslim and Jewish merchants may have been the inspiration for the *commenda* agreements later adopted by the Italian city-states. They have also provided the basis for the development of modern Islamic banking.

Islamic jurists also reluctantly acknowledged that money transfers and credit notes which crept closer to usury were not forbidden but merely reprehensible. By the late eighth century, merchants routinely employed credit arrangements for numerous purposes. A merchant temporarily lacking in capital or goods could acquire them on credit, thereby enabling him to carry on trading. Credit also facilitated long-distance transactions by making it less necessary for merchants or their factors to carry large and heavy amounts of coin. It was even possible for a person in a market such as that of Basra to get a credit note at the beginning of his shopping trip which he could show to merchants throughout the market and then pay later in a manner rather like that of modern credit cards. Canny traders could also get around the prohibition on usury by offering lower prices for goods sold for cash than on credit – the higher price paid when goods were bought on credit was, in effect, a form of concealed interest.

Another common financial instrument was the *sakk*, from which the word 'cheque' comes, which was basically very similar to our own cheque, 'an order of payment made through a banker with whom the drawer has an account' which was used by the authorities from a very early date. According to Ibn 'Abd al-Hakam, the second caliph 'Umar paid for grain in Syria with just such a 'cheque', and they were similarly utilized by 'Abbasid ministers and other members of the Baghdad elite.[27] Another important tool for merchants was the *suftaja*, or money transfer, by which a trader or businessman or traveller in one city could pay a banker a sum of money for which he received his *suftaja*, a document stating that he could retrieve the stated sum from a named banker or merchant in another city. Not only did merchants and other travellers use *suftaja*s to avoid carrying large amounts of coin with them, provincial authorities also used them as a means to pay provincial taxes in Baghdad.[28]

With this array of financial instruments, hostelries and state management of the markets, commerce flourished throughout the 'Abbasid caliphate. Political insecurity and the rise and fall of governors and even caliphs forced merchants to move, to avoid trouble and sometimes to cancel their trips, but trade itself never ceased. Fustat and Cairo replaced Baghdad, Seville took over from Cordoba, but the vast Eurasian trade network enabled by the rise of Islam lived on. It was ultimately challenged by the rise of the Italian city-states and Barcelona in the Mediterranean, which severed its western arm, then by the rise of Portugal and Spain as global competitors, but for many centuries the merchants of Islam dominated the global economy of their day.

꯾ꙮꙮ

CHAPTER 5

Baghdad's 'Golden Age': Islam's Scientific Renaissance

The human things through which nations and citizens of cities attain earthly happiness in this life and supreme happiness in the life beyond are of four kinds, theoretical virtues, deliberate virtues, moral virtues and practical arts.[1]

It was a commonplace of the European imperial age that the Islamic world was intellectually backward and that Muslims not only could not have produced the Enlightenment and Industrial Revolution but also required European tutelage to cope with the package labelled 'modernity', which contained a colourful assortment of concepts: rationalism, secularism, nationalism, democracy and evolutionary progress. Although this was a gross over-simplification of a complex situation, many Muslim thinkers of the nineteenth and early twentieth centuries agreed with them but asked themselves how this could have happened to a civilization which had produced some of the world's greatest mathematicians, astronomers, physicians and philosophers 1,000 years before. Although it was easy for those of a secular bent to blame Islam for nineteenth-century problems using a European mindset originally generated by Enlightenment intellectuals' feelings about Christianity then transposed to Islam, it was not so straightforward to explain how that same religion had fostered such a cultural and scientific efflorescence in the first place.

The answers to such questions lie in the 'Abbasid era which began with what is often called Baghdad's 'Golden Age', during which Muslims built on the Arabo-Islamic intellectual foundations laid by the Umayyads to develop numerous branches of learning and practical expertise. The religious sciences became more sophisticated, literature and the arts moved in new directions inspired by Sasanian political theory, and the sciences of the Greek curriculum – mathematics, philosophy, astrology, astronomy and medicine – were translated, interrogated and improved upon by Arabic-speaking Christians and Muslims. In the realm of applied science, engineering, hydraulics and agricultural science all flourished and made possible the construction of the fine palaces, baths and mosques with running water and sewage systems described in Chapter 2, as well as rural irrigation systems such as the canals and underground channels of Iraq and Iran and the waterwheels of Syria and Spain. Although now considered a pseudo-science, the 'Abbasids were also fascinated by alchemy and the chimera of transforming base metals into gold for their treasury.

The centrality of the Qur'an and Arabic to Islam ensured that the Islamic intellectual tapestry was woven of many strands in which the warp was always Arabic – prose and the oral poetic tradition of pre-Islamic Arabia, which found its apogee in the Qur'an – while the weft incorporated Hellenic science, Persian literature, Indian and Jewish folk tales and much else besides. Although Arabic literature may seem far from jurisprudence, philosophy or engineering, educated Muslims of the 'Abbasid age prided themselves on being polymaths, and in an era where one's point needed to be eloquently proven, a mastery of Arabic grammar, rhetoric and poetics was essential to conveying one's understanding of any other discipline. In an inversion of the Greek and Roman categorization of those who spoke neither Greek nor Latin as barbarians, one group of so-called barbarians now asserted the cultural hegemony of their language and relegated the fine old tongues of Antique civilization to the category of meaningless babble. The biographical dictionaries noted with approval when someone was *fasih*, meaning fully able to handle literary Arabic, as opposed to merely speaking a colloquial form of it or any of the other myriad vernacular languages of the empire.

The mystique of Arabic among the Arabs was such that it not only played its natural role as the language of religion but also became the language of government across the Islamic world under the Umayyads and of scientific culture too during the 'Abbasid caliphate. Although many other languages retained domestic significance, and some – Persian and Urdu, for instance – were destined to enjoy a new literary flourishing using Arabic script, Arabic was the undisputed *lingua franca* from Spain to India and it is for that reason that one can speak of Arabo-Islamic knowledge even though many, if not most, scholars and scientists of the era were not of Arab ancestry and some were not even Muslim. By the ninth century, even tracts against Islam or the Arabs such as the *Apology* of the Christian al-Kindi or Shu'ubiyya literature, discussed in Chapter 3, had to be written in Arabic to be taken seriously.

Within this new Arabized intellectual sphere, the concept of knowledge was expressed by a variety of different terms. The basic word was *'ilm*, which could mean religious knowledge but also denoted acquired or learnt knowledge in a more generic sense. The plural, *'ulum*, conveyed the sense of 'disciplines' or 'sciences', a meaning it still has in contemporary Arabic. This type of knowledge came to be contrasted with *ma'rifa*, knowledge which was not learnt but intuited, a gift from God, the most perfect example of which was prophecy followed by mystic gnosis. The relationship between *'ilm* and *ma'rifa* emerged as an important philosophical and theological question but few educated Muslims doubted the general principle that knowledge was inherently desirable whatever its origin. Another term for knowledge favoured during the early 'Abbasid centuries, when learning of non-Arab or non-Muslim derivation began to enter the Islamic domain, was *hikma*, a term used in the Qur'an as a complement to scripture, which came to mean wisdom, science or philosophy, and implied a search for truth and the true meanings of things, an enterprise which lay at the heart of Muslim learning as it came of age.

Within such broad categories as *hikma* and *'ilm* there were many possible taxonomies and subdivisions which sometimes placed the religious and non-religious sciences in separate categories and sometimes combined them for methodological reasons, or placed them in a hierarchy based on their intellectual rigour. The general view for men of all faiths was that revelation was the highest form of knowledge. Working from a different perspective, philosophers often placed philosophy at the summit with revelation, below which they placed dialectic theology, and below which again they placed the religious beliefs of the masses. They believed that each type of knowledge was a manifestation of the same ultimate truth presented in different ways to satisfy different audiences. What is most important to note is that the frequent Western post-Enlightenment juxtaposition of faith in opposition to reason, which is too often employed to 'explain' Islamic civilization, was emphatically not applicable to 'Abbasid intellectual life. As Erwin Rosenthal stated as far back as 1953 in an article about the Spanish Muslim philosopher Ibn Rushd (d. 1198), known in Latin as Averroes:

> We shall never understand Islam, Judaism, and their religious philosophers unless we recognise that an all-embracing, comprehensive, perfect 'law' is the core and pivot of both religious ways of life, binding upon elect and masses alike. ... But there is an important difference between the elect philosophers and the masses of varying degrees of intellectual receptiveness ... the philosophers must attempt a rational interpretation of these beliefs and convictions. ... The masses on the other hand must accept these beliefs and convictions in their external sense.[2]

Although not everyone liked the so-called 'foreign sciences', as the secular sciences of Greek derivation were sometimes called, many people

accepted them and considered it a mark of a civilized society to cultivate
and apply knowledge of all different types, without that compromising religious faith. In some areas like mathematics and engineering it was hardly
an issue at all. Moreover the religious sciences came to rely heavily on ways
of thinking and reasoning derived from other disciplines such as logic and
philosophy. According to a famous *hadith*, the Prophet Muhammad had
said, 'Seek knowledge even to China', a statement which expressed an attitude as much as historical fact. Particularly revealing in this respect is the
example of Abu'l-Faraj Muhammad al-Nadim, a tenth-century courtier
who inherited a passion for books from his bookseller father and composed
his renowned *Fihrist* or *Catalogue*, an encyclopedic list of authors and
their books which starts with the religious sciences, Arabic grammar and
literature and then continues through to philosophy, medicine and other
sciences. What is most fascinating is that in every section – even religion
– pre-Islamic and non-Islamic sources of knowledge are acknowledged and
enumerated as equally valid. Al-Nadim and other scholars like him most
definitely viewed their own learning – that of the 'latecomers' – as existing
on a continuum with that of 'those who preceded them', whether they were
Greek, Persian or Indian, Christian, Jewish or Zoroastrian.

Confidence in the political power of Muslims in the global arena created
cultural confidence which in turn permitted and even encouraged unfet-
tered speech and a spirit of enquiry. However, the traces of this in our
sources, indicated by the preservation of polemics and debates about the
merits of different religions and sciences, have tended to be interpreted in a
negative way as signs of an innate religious conservatism which triumphed
and destroyed independent thought and scientific endeavour in Muslim
societies, rather than as a positive indication of intellectual discussion. We
need, however, to recognize both trends, since a confident spirit of enquiry
has been just as normative within Islamic societies as the moments of
political and social crisis which have engendered more defensive cultural
attitudes. Moreover the various classes in 'Abbasid society exhibited different attitudes in any given period, and apparent clashes between 'science'
and 'religion' sometimes expressed tensions within society rather than the
outlook of society as a whole.

The foundations of Islamic learning

From the outset the Arabs exhibited an openness to other cultures combined
with a strong sense of self-identity. Although those who conquered the
Byzantine and Persian empires in the name of Islam were not the bear-
ers of a great tradition of learning in a conventional sense, and were often

described as 'barbarians' by shocked Byzantine clergymen, it is a mistake to exaggerate the cultural poverty of the Arabian peninsula, given its own civilizational tradition and centuries of interaction with neighbouring empires and religions, which were vying for Arab hearts and minds in Yemen and the northern marches of Arabia. On the one hand, the Arabs possessed a thriving poetic tradition, knowledge of the stars – essential for navigating in the desert – a corpus of medical lore mainly based on plant remedies which survived into Islamic times under the title of 'prophetic medicine' (*al-tibb al-nabawi*), and distinctive artistic and architectural forms. On the other hand, several regions of Arabia were aware of Judaism, Christianity and Zoroastrianism, and the genesis of the new world of Islam was dependent on an intimate, albeit sometimes ill-informed, engagement with the established monotheisms of the Middle East and emulation of Byzantine and Sasanian cultures.

The Arabs approached their mission with supreme confidence. By means of the agency of Muhammad, Semitic monotheism was expressed in an authentic Arab voice which asserted its superiority to its Semitic forerunners – Judaism and Christianity – and Arabian paganism alike. As Muhammad said when challenged by rival Arab prophets and prophetesses, 'If you can equal me in a single *sura* [chapter of the Qur'an], my claims will be false and you will be entitled to call me a liar.'[3] This self-assertiveness and ability to reformulate ideas in an Arabic idiom helped prepare the first generations of Muslims for the diverse intellectual world which they began to encounter as they conquered Byzantine and Sasanian territories. They were, of course, ill prepared to run an empire and, as we have seen, relied heavily on local non-Muslim officials, tax collectors and craftsmen who fortuitously played the dual role of introducing their new masters to a wide range of skills and knowledge whilst also allowing them to focus their energies on those areas which were crucial to the survival of Islam – the prosecution of the wars of conquest and the elaboration of the new faith in a distinct Arabic form.

The first major intellectual exercise performed by the early Muslims was thus to define and refine their own beliefs, understand their application in the humdrum daily life of settlements established amongst a sea of Christians, Jews and Zoroastrians with mature, well-developed belief systems, and assert the linguistic hegemony of Arabic. For most of the first century of Islam, therefore, the types of knowledge most favoured among the small Muslim ruling elite of Arabs and their clients were the religious sciences, Arabic linguistics and poetry. Circulating and understanding the Qur'an, promoting Arabic and offering rudimentary legal rulings in keeping with Qur'anic or prophetic precedent were the aims of the first generations of Muslim scholars, who took a keen interest not only in what we might call higher education but also in the primary curriculum. In the early schools of Medina, Kufa and Basra, aspects of Arabic language, including philology, poetry and grammar, were studied alongside the Qur'an, and although the profession of school teacher, a function often performed by slaves in the classical world, was sometimes despised, eminent early specialists in the Qur'an and Arabic grammar such as Dahhak b. Muzahim (d. 723) considered the basic education of children crucial. His school in Kufa was said to have had 3,000 pupils, amongst whom Dahhak circulated on a mule.[4]

A century later, al-Jahiz described his own attendance at a local school in the Kinana quarter of Basra alongside children from all walks of life, including the butcher's son, showing the widespread social commitment to giving children at least a smattering of Arabic learning which had emerged by the early 'Abbasid era.[5] Such schools, known as *katatib* (sing. *kuttab*), were usually located in the neighbourhood mosque or an adjacent building and may have drawn their inspiration from Byzantine primary schools. The normal length of time children spent in a *kuttab* varied but most entered school at about four years old and left between seven and nine. Meanwhile rich families would often set up school rooms within their own homes, an arrangement which enabled daughters to gain some education alongside their brothers, or with their own tutors, if their parents were willing. It was certainly known for religious scholars to teach both their daughters and their female slaves, although some less enlightened scholars considered this tantamount to giving a snake venom!

The primary educational text used to teach children to read and write Arabic was the Qur'an, not only because it was a virtuoso Arabic composition but also because it gave them access to Islam's basic religious text and an important stock of quotes to help them progress in polite society. This moral and literary education formed the bedrock upon which educated Muslims stood, even if their later interests were not in the religious sciences or even scholarship *per se*. Other subjects, from arithmetic to sports, music and chess, were studied with private tutors, although al-Jahiz questioned the pedagogical soundness of letting grammarians and jurists monopolize education and applauded teachers who provided at least basic arithmetic alongside Arabic writing skills:

> Fine points of grammar are the last sort of problem likely to arise in polite society, and there is no need to bother with them. It may be wise to start your pupil on the study of simple reckoning, excluding Indian arithmetic, geometry and complex surveying problems; here you should limit yourself to the amount of knowledge needed in government employees and office scribes ... a thorough knowledge of arithmetic, which is the key to every kind of work ... is more valuable than a mastery of the craft of editing and

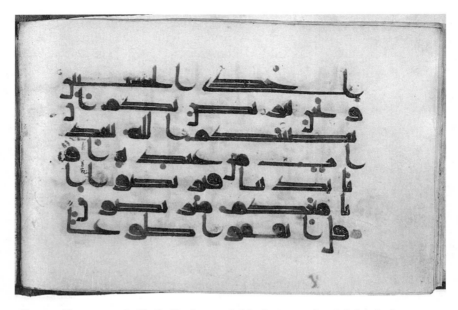

Fig. 24. Fragment of a Kufic Qur'an, probably dating to the eighth–ninth century CE. (Manuscript Add 1124, p 48 verso. Reproduced by kind permission of the Syndics of Cambridge University Library)

penmanship; for the worst handwriting will pass muster if the spelling is correct, which is more than can be said of arithmetic.[6]

Many children received only a smattering of education before becoming apprentices with their fathers or other craftsmen, but if their circumstances allowed, children who showed aptitute and managed to memorize the Qur'an could proceed to study the nascent religious sciences and associated disciplines such as literature and history with the scholars who could be found teaching in the great mosque of their home town. The calibre of such scholars varied from city to city and the best tended to move to recognized centres of learning such as Medina, Kufa and Basra, and subsequently Baghdad, Fustat and Qayrawan. In the east, Nishapur, Bukhara and Samarkand played a similar role. The peregrinations of scholars encouraged students to travel too, and as they progressed they began to support their own search for knowledge by teaching religious texts or subjects which they had already mastered.

During the Umayyad caliphate, the religious subjects taught to such advanced students were still in the first phase of development. These subjects – sometimes called the 'transmitted sciences' (*al-'ulum al-naqliyya*) – included Qur'anic exegesis, which entailed the explanation of each verse, its context and meaning; study of the *sunna* or practice of the Prophet; and auxiliary sciences such as Arabic grammar, without which one could not fully understand or explain the Qur'an. At this point the *sunna* was an oral body of information derived for the most part from the customs of the Muslims living in Medina, many of whom were the Companions of the Prophet or their immediate descendants. It was therefore supposed that the Medinese were more likely to be aware of the Prophet's practice than any other community and that Medinese custom (*'amal*) might be considered synonymous with it. Of course, Arabs from Medina had settled all over the Umayyad empire, but early Muslims considered the consensus of the Medinese community more weighty than the recollections of scattered individuals in other regions on the grounds that collective memory was sounder than that of the individual.

The most important function of the Qur'an and *sunna* was to tell Muslims how they should worship and behave in daily life, in other words to provide the regulations collectively known as the Shari'a, a word actually meaning 'way' or 'path' rather than 'law' as we understand the term. One of the most pressing responsibilities of the first Muslim scholars was therefore to collate information about the *sunna*, to derive legal precedents from it and to teach aspiring scholars how to do the same. Two influential scholars who preserved the Prophet's practice in Medina and extrapolated law from it were Ja'far al-Sadiq (d. 765), revered by the Shi'a as the sixth *imam* and founder of an important Shi'i law school, and Malik b. Anas (d. 795), founder of the Maliki law school which became one of the four acknowledged schools of Sunni law. Meanwhile in Kufa, Abu Hanifa (d. 767), a silk trader of Persian client origin, developed an alternative approach to law which relied on opinions (*ra'y*) made on the basis of individual reasoning and examples from the past to formulate legal principles which were the basis for the development of another Sunni law school, the Hanafi school.

The development of a legal framework within which Muslims could live was vital but rather dry, and it was not long before a new ascetic and mystical approach to Islam emerged to offer personal spiritual and emotional satisfaction. Although Muhammad had discouraged Muslims from adopting monasticism and devotional celibacy from Christianity, the conquest of Syria, Iraq and Egypt brought them into close contact with many monastic, ascetic and Gnostic communities whose ideas had an impact. Asceticism emerged most clearly in Basra, a city located in an area steeped in Nestorian Christian and Gnostic traditions, where its two most famous exponents were Hasan of Basra and Rabi'a al-'Adawiya, both of whom were of non-Arab origin and thus products in part of the pre-Islamic religious milieu.

Hasan of Basra (d. 728) was the son of a Persian who had been enslaved during the conquests and brought to Medina, where he was manumitted. He married and Hasan was the product of the union. After some years in the army, Hasan settled in Basra where he became both a renowned teacher who commented on the Qur'an and collected traditions of the Prophet and an ascetic who encouraged his fellow Muslims to pray, fast and maintain a distance from the riches of this world. He put his own teachings into practice by inveighing against the oppressive behaviour of the Umayyad governors of Iraq, creating what became a paradigmatic link between religious scholarship, piety and an aversion to political authority as inherently corrupt and corrupting. Rabi'a al-'Adawiyya (d. 801) was a very different character. She began her life as a slave but her Arab master freed her as a result of her outstanding piety. Although offered the chance of marriage, she declined and chose to spend the rest of her life as an ascetic in the Basra area, offering her love to God alone but giving spiritual guidance to the crowds who gathered outside her simple hut. Although it is difficult to separate fact from fiction in the many stories about Rabi'a's piety, humility and miraculous acts, she personifies the development of an important mystical strain – the pursuit of divine love and intimate knowledge of God – which was to be very influential in later Islamic mysticism, commonly known as Sufism.

By the end of the Umayyad period, then, the main strands in Muslim knowledge were Arabic grammar and poetics, exegesis of the Qur'an, the collection of oral information about the *sunna* of the Prophet and the early community, the extrapolation of rulings to ensure that Muslims understood their ritual obligations and the way they should live in the world, and a moral, ascetic mysticism. The extent to which Muslims of this era moved beyond the Arabic and Islamic domains is a debated point. The conversion to Islam of clients naturally brought their knowledge into the Islamic sphere, and the Umayyad caliph 'Abd al-Malik's introduction of Arabic as the language of government, administration and state symbolism began to extend its reach far beyond the original Arabs. Several of the religious figures mentioned above, for example, were of client or slave origin and brought Christian or Gnostic ideas into the new religion. Moreover there are hints in the *Fihrist* of al-Nadim that translation of varied materials of either administrative use or a literary nature were under way by the time the 'Abbasids took power. For instance, Ibn al-Muqaffa' (d. 756), an administrator and man of letters, translated the *Kalila wa Dimna* fables of Indian origin and various Sasanian chronicles from Persian into Arabic either in the late Umayyad period or the first years of the 'Abbasid caliphate. Nonetheless it was only during the 'Abbasid caliphate that these tender saplings matured and bore fruit.

The flowering of knowledge under the 'Abbasids

As we have seen, the establishment of the 'Abbasid caliphate entailed a geographical shift away from Syria, with its strongly Byzantine associations, and an ideological reorientation away from the Umayyads' Arab-centrism towards a more universal Muslim sense of identity. In the religious sphere, the ranks of non-Arab scholars began to grow, while in the domain of secular knowledge and culture, translations from Greek, Syriac, Pahlavi Persian and even Sanskrit nurtured the development of areas of scientific enquiry neglected for centuries. Although it is tempting to consider religion and science separately, in the 'Abbasid case it makes more sense to see them as existing on a social and intellectual continuum with a distinct overlap between theology and philosophy, where friction sometimes occurred. Moreover the limited numbers of scientists or philosophers should not automatically be taken as a sign of disparagement for their professions. Professional philosophers are hardly a large group in any society, nor were scientists before the modern age, and the fact that Ibn al-Qifti (1172–1248), author of a biographical dictionary of scientists, could find 414 names to mention is therefore rather impressive. The question is the degree to which their learning penetrated society as a whole, and in the 'Abbasid case one can see scientific and philosophical influences at work in many domains, despite the concern some religious scholars later felt about engagement with knowledge of non-Muslim provenance.

In the realm of religion, there was no dramatic break between the Umayyad and 'Abbasid caliphates but rather a diversification and formalization of earlier trends, and a great deal of cross-fertilization from other religions and bodies of knowledge. During the early 'Abbasid caliphate, the scholars of religion came to be collectively known as the *'ulama'* (those who sought and disseminated *'ilm*), an amorphous group subdivided into numerous categories of varying prestige of whom some of the most influential were the collectors of *hadith* who, as we discovered in Chapter 1, became vocal critics of the caliphs' wish to determine doctrine, a right and duty which they believed was their own. The scholars of *hadith*, often called traditionists, were the successors of those who had attempted to guide the community using the custom of Medina as an indicator of the *sunna* of the Prophet, with the difference that they preferred to write down previously oral testimonies and trace them back to the Prophet himself rather than to Medinese practice.

Oral reports were replaced by a new written corpus of information, the *hadith* or traditions of the Prophet, in a move which coincided with a rise in conversion to Islam, Arabic literacy and paper production. 'Abbasid culture was becoming a book culture and the early Islamic oral tradition could only maintain its credibility in that format. A written *hadith* consisted of two parts: an actual saying, known as the 'content' (*matn*), and a list of people who had conveyed the content through the generations from the time of the Prophet, known as a 'chain' (*isnad*). A typical *hadith* ran as follows:

> 'Abd Allah b. Yusuf reported to me that Malik reported on the authority of Nafi' on the authority of 'Abd Allah b. 'Umar – may God be satisfied with them both – that the Messenger of God – peace and blessings be upon him – forbade the *muzabana* which was the purchase of date palms with a dry measure of dates and the sale of vines for a dry measure of raisins.[7]

Or in a more political vein:

> 'Ali b. 'Abd Allah reported that Yahya b. Sa'id reported that Sufyan said Mansur reported from Mujahid from Ta'us from Ibn 'Abbas – may God be satisfied with them both – that the Messenger of God – peace and blessings be upon him – said: There is no migrating after the conquest [has begun], only *jihad* and the intention [to wage it] and when you go to war, hasten forward.[8]

By the early ninth century huge numbers of *hadith* were circulating on every imaginable topic, some of very dubious veracity, and it was the self-appointed task of *hadith* scholars not only to collect them but to examine them and weed out obvious fabrications. This process led to the compilation of several canonical collections of *hadith* still widely used by Muslims today, of which the most renowned are the two *Sahih*s of al-Bukhari (d. 870) and Muslim (d. 875). The first function of the *hadith* was to enable scholars to formulate the legal opinions which directed people's everyday lives, but command of the Qur'an and *hadith* also enabled the 'Abbasid *'ulama'* to pronounce on religion more generally, sometimes at the caliph's expense, and to develop the text-based approach to higher truth which became characteristic of Sunnism.

While the traditionists concentrated upon gathering *hadith* and verifying them, jurists (*fuqaha'*) specialized in theoretical law and its methodology, applied that law in real cases as judges and legal advisors, and trained younger generations of jurists. It thus fell to them to develop more systematic approaches to law than simply using the Qur'an or early Muslim practices as examples to be applied elsewhere. This was partly necessitated by the fact that neither the Qur'an nor the *sunna* covered every eventuality, but it also reflected the maturing of Islamic law in an imperial context where it was no longer feasible to consult a pious Muslim from Medina every time a query arose. The scholar credited with effecting the systematization of Islamic law is Muhammad al-Shafi'i (d. 820), who studied with Malik b.

Anas of Medina and the followers of Abu Hanifa of Kufa before producing his definitive methodology for Islamic law in his famous *Risala* or *Epistle*.

Although some of al-Shafi'i's ideas were rejected by later jurists, his *Risala* attempted to bring together conflicting views about the law, smooth over the contradictions evident in the Qur'an and *hadith* and produce a theoretical method for deriving legal norms from sacred texts. At the heart of his theory lay his concept of *bayan*, which he defined as a statement from God in the juridical context. It was the jurists' task to identify such statements using four main sources or tools in combination with each other. Naturally the Qur'an was the primary source, followed by the Qur'an and *hadith* when they expressed the same rule. Then came situations in which the *hadith* explained a Qur'anic statement, followed by statements which appeared in the *hadith* alone. This was the area where contradictions abounded, a problem al-Shafi'i resolved with a number of methods, including scholarly consensus (*ijma'*). Finally, in situations without precedent in either the Qur'an or *hadith*, jurists should use their rational faculty (*ijtihad*) to draw analogies (*qiyas*).[9] In other words, the primary source of law was the Qur'an, but in cases where the Qur'an was vague or silent, authenticated *hadith* should be used to clarify Qur'anic statements and supplement them, with the preferred solution being one on which a reasonable number of jurists were able to agree.

One of al-Shafi'i's students, Ahmad b. Hanbal (d. 855), whom we have already encountered vigorously opposing al-Ma'mun's efforts to impose the doctrine of the createdness of the Qur'an in Baghdad, became the father of the fourth canonical Sunni school of law, the Hanbali school, famous for its devotion to the *hadith* and their literal application. In this era, however, there were also countless other legal specialists, many of whom founded shorter-lived schools which had more or less disappeared by the end of the 'Abbasid caliphate in 1258, such as the Jaririyya school associated with the historian al-Tabari, and the Zahiriyya school, one of whose champions was Ibn Hazm in Spain. Although it has become common amongst modern Muslims and non-Muslims to see the Shari'a as a code, in actual fact it developed as a common law system in which numerous different opinions and interpretations offered great flexibility and adaptability to the varied circumstances of individuals and communities. Consensus was never absolute, and diversity of opinion (*ikhtilaf*) was as much a part of legal life as agreement, especially in its more theoretical dimensions where jurists indulged in highly intellectual problem solving using logical tools of Greek origin, which translators and scholars were rapidly making available to an Arabic-speaking audience.

The pre-eminence of the Islamic east at this time drew students from as far away as Spain to Fustat and Alexandria in Egypt, Medina, and then the cities of Iraq to study with such luminaries as al-Shafiʻi, al-Bukhari and Muslim. As a result, the study of *hadith* arrived in Spain at almost the same time as the great *hadith* collections were being compiled in Iraq. Baqi b. Makhlad (d. 889), a Cordoban scholar educated in the east, produced the first known Andalusi *hadith* compilation in the hopes of weaning his Maliki compatriots off their reliance on a narrow range of books explaining the works of Malik to a more flexible source-based approach. This was something of a reversal of the situation in Iraq, where the *hadith* scholars appeared as radical conservatives opposed to juridical rationalism and theology. Baqi b. Makhlad's hopes were dashed when he fell foul of the Maliki scholars who resented the sidelining of Medinese custom which acceptance of the new science of *hadith* entailed because of the close association between Malik, the founder of their law school, and his hometown, Medina. Another Cordoban scholar who studied abroad, Ibn al-Waddah (d. 900), solved the problem by making Malik's own collection of traditions, the *Muwatta'*, a canonical *hadith* text alongside the eastern ones, and retaining the enduringly popular *Mudawwana* of Sahnun, a legal work based on Medinese custom, as a compromise. The *hadith* as a scriptural version of the *sunna* thus came to stay across the Islamic world.

While the *hadith* and related materials provided Muslims with a dense quasi-historical account of the origins of their community, the challenges to Islam that arose in the early ninth century, from sophisticated Christians of a Neoplatonic persuasion in particular, obliged Muslims to engage with theology and develop a more philosophical understanding of their core beliefs in God's eternal oneness, the prophetic mission of Muhammad and the relationship between the 'religions of the book'. Muslims called theology *kalam*, literally 'speech', and its practitioners defined it as 'the science which is concerned with firmly establishing religious beliefs by adducing proofs and banishing doubts'.[10] It was also sometimes called the science of *tawhid*, the Arabic term for oneness, unity and, by extension, monotheistic belief, of which Islam was seen to be the perfect example, a designation which hints at *kalam*'s function to assert Islam's place against Christianity and Judaism.

This naturally took Islamic learning into abstract areas such as the nature of man and God, the status of the Qur'an, prophecy, predestination and human responsibility. For theologians these questions had to be addressed using *'aql*, human reason, to provide answers in harmony with the Qur'an, but they could not be answered by reference to the Qur'an and *sunna* alone as the *hadith* scholars would have it. The masters of *kalam* justified their approach as a response to the Qur'an's own injunctions that man should seek to understand creation and thus should be both scientist and theologian at the same time.

Theology had existed in embryonic form during the Umayyad era, but its focus at that time was the issue of religio-political leadership – who should be caliph or *imam* – and, by extension, who should mediate man's relationship with God and ensure the community's well being not only on earth but also after death? However, theologians as a professional group adhering to a number of different schools only became a phenomenon in the 'Abbasid era, which also, as a consequence, witnessed the steady crystallization of sectarian tendencies and the divergence of the Sunni and Shi'i paths as their initial disagreements over leadership gained more detailed theological elaboration and religious depth. Soon the frequent Muslim taunt that Christianity's division into endless sects showed how Christians had strayed from the path could be thrown in the opposite direction too.

The most renowned theological schools were the Mu'tazili school, which flourished during the ninth and tenth centuries, and the Ash'ari school, established in the tenth century and influential well into the nineteenth. Although necessarily Islamic, both drew on ideas and intellectual tools which the translation of Greek and Syriac materials (examined below) had brought within the Muslim purview. The amorphous Mu'tazili school flourished in Basra, Baghdad and Samarra and had adherents across the Islamic world who upheld a wide variety of different beliefs, making it perhaps more appropriate to call Mu'tazilism an 'approach' rather than a 'school'. Sometimes called the 'people of justice and unity', Mu'tazilis rejected predestination as unjust and asserted that people were responsible for their negative acts, which could not belong to God because of his absolute goodness and transcendence, and would be rewarded or punished as appropriate. They, like many other ninth-century Muslims, believed in the createdness of the Qur'an, again on the grounds of God's transcendence, which made it a nonsense to suppose that there could be anything of the same eternal, uncreated quality as God. For the same reason they also denied that God possessed such patently animal attributes as speech or sight which were co-eternal with him. The caliphs al-Ma'mun and al-Mu'tasim patronized Mu'tazili theologians because they were in favour of their rational and discursive approach to religion, but in later generations they did not find such overt favour. In a society where sons followed their fathers, however, Mu'tazilism continued on through the generations. There were also Mu'tazili preachers who spread the movement beyond the cities into the countryside, preaching the message of God's ineffable goodness. As a result, Mu'tazilism as a worldview and a theological school existed until the end of the 'Abbasid caliphate and, despite its own demise, influenced Shi'ism, Sufism and some branches of Judaism. Interestingly, there is currently a revival of liberal Muslim interest in Mu'tazilism as a form of indigenous Islamic rationalism which has much to offer Muslims in today's world.

While Mu'tazilism gradually decreased in popularity over the centuries, its offshoot and rival Ash'arism became the mainstream theology of Sunnis across Islamic lands. Named after its founding father, Abu'l-Hasan 'Ali al-Ash'ari (d. 935), who was originally a Mu'tazili, Ash'arism asserted that God did have certain eternal attributes, such as knowledge, power, sight and speech, in contradiction to the Mu'tazili position that God's transcendence prevented him from possessing any such attributes. In a similar vein, Ash'ari theologians believed that the Qur'an, God's speech, was eternal and uncreated. They also believed that God willed all human acts, good and bad, by empowering men to commit them, thereby moving much closer to predestination than the Mu'tazilis without completely sacrificing the notion of human responsibility. Ash'ari theology appealed to the Sunni scholars of the Qur'an and *hadith* and became the orthodox Sunni theological position. It achieved this in part by side-stepping awkward issues by 'not asking how' on matters that should be accepted on faith alone because it was beyond the capacity of the human mind to grasp the truth of them.

Alongside the Mu'tazilis and Ash'aris, various groups of Shi'i Muslims also elaborated their theology, concentrating on the central status of the *imam*s and then the challenging matter of their disappearance from earth. As we saw in Chapter 1, early Shi'ism grew out of what some Muslims perceived as the usurpation of the religious and political rights of the Prophet's family, particularly 'Ali and his descendants. Most Shi'i Muslims doubted the legitimacy of the three Rightly Guided Caliphs who preceded 'Ali, and all considered the Umayyads to be completely abominable owing to Mu'awiya's opposition to 'Ali and Yazid's culpability in the massacre of Husayn and his relatives at Karbala. Several failed rebellions later, the fifth *imam*, Muhammad al-Baqir (d. 733), began to develop a specifically Shi'i law and theology by asserting that the *imam*s were recipients of divinely inspired knowledge, albeit of a lesser degree than prophecy. His position was taken up and elaborated by his son, the sixth *imam*, Ja'far al-Sadiq (d. 765), who asserted that the *imam*s were infallible guides and that one would rise up in the future as the *mahdi*, a term often translated as messiah.

Prior to the occultation or disappearance of the *imam*s from earth they remained the living guides for the community in law, doctrine and the pursuit of inner truth. However, after the occultation of the Isma'ili and Twelver *imam*s in the ninth century, these duties were gradually delegated to their representatives on earth, the Shi'i religious scholars. Although the Qur'an and those *hadith* acknowledged by the Shi'is were important sources of law, Shi'i clerics retained the right to exercise their own judgement. Moreover Shi'ism absorbed a great deal from Islamic philosophy, Mu'tazili theology and Sufism, making it intellectual heir to many of the trends apparent in the 'Abbasid age, which is somewhat ironic given the Sunni character of the caliphate itself. The Buyids and Fatimids, for example, were great patrons of all the sciences and the latter made Cairo a vital centre for the study of philosophy and mysticism after Baghdad had lost that role.

The early 'Abbasid caliphate also witnessed the start of Sufism's long development from its ascetic beginnings in Basra into a meditation on the mystery of man's relationship with God and the soul's aspiration to return to its source, influenced by Zoroastrianism and Christian Neoplatonism. Unlike law with its communal focus or theology with its abstract metaphysical deliberations, Sufism became a highly individualistic enterprise which eschewed Islam's increasingly powerful public edifice in favour of a personalized approach in which men and women sought God by following the example of Muhammad and other exemplary characters. At this stage, Sufism was pietistic and easy to understand in its call for Muslims to live in simplicity, do good works and contemplate God, and there was little difference between those later labelled 'Sufis' or 'scholars' beyond the former's otherworldliness.

In Iraq the ascetics of Basra were succeeded by such retiring characters as Harith b. Asad al-Muhasibi (d. 857), a pietistic *hadith* scholar who was perhaps unfairly said to have been the son of a Zoroastrian by those keen to suggest that his religious approach was tainted by un-Islamic influences. Although a native of Basra, like so many others of his generation al-Muhasibi migrated to Baghdad, where he taught Junayd, one of the most famous of the so-called sober mystics who combined their personal search for God with respect for the outward rituals of Islam propagated by the legal scholars. Nonetheless al-Muhasibi fell foul of Ahmad b. Hanbal, who disliked his pietistic ways intensely, probably because he saw him as a rival for the support of the Baghdad crowd.

In many areas, especially Iran and Khurasan, early Sufism mediated the transition ordinary people made when they converted from Zoroastrianism or Christianity to Islam. In many of these cases it took quite another form from the sober, self-mortifying approach of Rabi'a or al-Muhasibi, gaining it the label of 'ecstatic' or 'drunken' Sufism. The experience of Abu Yazid Bayazid al-Bistami (d. *c.* 874), son of a Zoroastrian Persian, instructed in the mystical way by a mystic to whom he taught the Qur'an in return, is representative. Al-Bistami became notorious for claiming to have achieved union with the divine and for uttering blasphemous statements such as 'glory to Me' which implied that he and God were indistinguishable. His ecstatic approach to mysticism, however, bore some resemblance to Zoroastrian ritual, in which the priest would drink sacred mead to become one with the deity, and thus he made sense to converts from Zoroastrianism and their children, among whom memories of the old faith persisted.

Another famous Sufi of this ilk was Abu'l-Mughith al-Husayn al-Hallaj (d. 922), known as the 'carder of consciences', a Persian who grew up in Iraq where his father had moved in search of work. (This is a pun on al-Hallaj's name since *hallaj* is the Arabic term for a wool or cotton carder who combs the fibres to remove impurities, just as al-Hallaj was believed to cleanse the consciences of his adherents.) He was a devout man but only became a fully fledged mystical preacher after performing the pilgrimage and spending a year praying and fasting in the Meccan sanctuary. He then returned to southern Iran and began to preach to growing crowds how they could find God in their own hearts. He attracted some followers in high places and was able to move his family to Baghdad where he gathered the same mass following as in Iran, arousing great consternation among government officials and scholars alike. Al-Hallaj increasingly presented himself as ready to die for the sake of his fellow Muslims while also entering into trances in which he asserted, 'I am the Truth'. The parallels with the passion of Christ are unmistakable, and when al-Hallaj was eventually arrested and a warrant for his execution issued, it is said that he prepared for martyrdom sure of his resurrection.

For the common people, the *'amma*, ecstatics like al-Hallaj and pious scholars busy compiling *hadith* collections provided more satisfying guidance and leadership than the theologians whose subtleties meant little to them. That is not to say that the rich corpus of knowledge circulating among the elite had no impact at a popular level, since the ways in which traditionists and early Sufis thought were shaped by the intellectual trends current in Islam's great centres of learning, but there was nonetheless an intellectual hierarchy. The theologians, although not men of the people, stood on the cusp between the teeming population of Baghdad and other cities and the cultural elite surrounding the caliphs and those who emulated them. While they addressed some of the same matters as the traditionists, they also adopted rational methods of proof similar to those used in philosophy, and were among the assortment of intellectuals, scholars and scientists patronized by the caliphs and their courtiers who constituted the vanguard of the 'Abbasid intelligentsia. It is to this eclectic intellectual elite, whose hallmark effort was the translation movement which so signally shaped the 'Abbasid cultural matrix, that we now turn.

The 'Abbasid translation movement

In addition to the importance of religious learning and the sway of the *'ulama'* and mystics over the hearts and minds of the populace, Muslims of the elite showed a firm appreciation for the knowledge of the older cultures of the Mediterranean, Middle East and India, which were described as the 'rational sciences' (*al-'ulum al-'aqliyya*), the 'philosophical sciences' (*al-'ulum al-falsafiyya*) or the 'natural sciences' (*al-'ulum al-tabi'iyya*). Interest in this body of knowledge stimulated the translation movement, two centuries of feverish intellectual activity during which Muslims and non-Muslims worked together to seek out ancient sciences, make them accessible in Arabic, elaborate on them, apply them and circulate the resulting knowledge across the Islamic world. These sciences included mathematics, physics, metaphysics and philosophy, medicine, astronomy and what are now considered pseudo-scientific pursuits such as astrology, alchemy and magic.

Astrological works written in Pahlavi Persian were the first to be translated, along with a few Sanskrit texts, but the Greek heritage was the most significant in proportion and included almost all the works of Aristotle as understood by Greek commentators such as Alexander of Aphrodisias and Themistius, and the sixth-century Christian philosopher John Philoponus; digests of Plato's works, for the most part via the great Neoplatonists, Plotinus, his disciple, Porphyry, and Proclus and maybe a few Platonic political works in close to their original form; the complete works of the physician and philosopher Galen, which included much from Hippocrates; mathematical works by Euclid; in addition to Ptolemaic astronomy and an array of other materials. Some works were readily available in Christian monasteries and academic libraries now in Islamic lands, others had to be sought in the storerooms and archives of Byzantium, and a fair proportion were not in common circulation by the eighth century. Their retrieval and translation was therefore a directed effort promoted by Muslim society over a period of 200 years.

As well as being of inestimable value within the Islamic milieu, this corpus of knowledge was of universal significance in two intertwined ways. Firstly, by seeking out Greek, Persian and Indian learning, Islamic civilization acted as a vital link in the developmental trajectory of human civilization as a whole. Secondly, by engaging with earlier traditions and taking them in new directions, Muslims simultaneously made their own unique contribution to the sum of human knowledge. Although the process by which Hellenic knowledge passed to medieval Europe is often described as transmission via the Arabs, this downplays the innovative and path-breaking additions made to the body of knowledge which eventually passed on to other civilizations and peoples, and the extent to which factors in early 'Abbasid culture and society drove scholars to seek out and translate more and more arcane scientific materials which were by no means easy to find in either Byzantium or the Sasanian Empire prior to the Islamic conquest. It is a fact that some works or versions of them would have been totally lost if it were not for their survival in the Arabo-Islamic environment. This process, commonly known by the rather humble title of the translation movement, ranks with other major cultural movements in our shared history in terms of its impact.

When translation began in earnest in the mid-eighth century, three general categories of knowledge or science were most prominent. On the one hand, the young 'Abbasid administrative service which had to levy revenue from agriculture, among many other tasks, needed a range of mathematical and astronomical skills to apply in land surveying, revenue assessment, the calculation of harvests and the maintenance of irrigation systems. On the other hand, the 'Abbasid caliphs themselves showed a keen interest in astrology, which served state purposes by providing auspicious dates for important public undertakings, and medicine, which was necessary for their personal well being. Dialectical and philosophical texts joined them as Muslims found it necessary to develop arguments to support Islamic beliefs against non-Muslim ridicule or attack. As we shall see, the order in which works were translated was not haphazard and works of sustained utility and application in 'Abbasid high society were re-translated several times as research agendas matured and shifted.

Two questions have exercised scholars of the translation movement: first, whether the movement was a top-down process initiated by the caliphs themselves or a bottom-up one triggered by a combination of governmental utility and an intensification of competition between administrators; second, the related question of who should take the credit – the Arabs or those of Persian and Christian origin? Such questions are not without their agendas and the answers are sometimes politically motivated. Even at the time of the translation movement, its coincidence with the Shu'ubiyya encouraged the Persians to vaunt their contributions in contrast to the paltry cultural capital the Arab bedouin brought to Islamic civilization. Persian prominence at this time, and their claim to be possessors of a much greater level of civilization than the uncouth Arabs of the desert, has encouraged the assumption that most aspects of 'Abbasid culture, including the translation movement, can be attributed to Persian influence.

Early studies of the movement such as De Lacy O'Leary's *How Greek Science Passed to the Arabs*, published in 1948, pay astonishingly little attention to the translation movement at all and see the Arabs as lucky and chance recipients of other people's knowledge, mostly that of the Christian communities who had preserved Greek learning in their libraries and monasteries in Alexandria, Antioch, Edessa and Gundeshapur. More recent books by Dimitri Gutas and George Saliba, in contrast, celebrate the active and creative way in which Muslims sought, translated and interrogated knowledge from other civilizations. They, however, differ in their depiction of the motivating forces behind the movement. On the one hand, Dimitri Gutas sees the caliphs themselves as heavily involved in directing the movement, encouraging the court to follow their lead and personally commissioning translations, in emulation of the Sasanian monarchs who preceded them as rulers of Iraq and Iran.[11] On the other hand, George Saliba sees translation as being triggered by social change and competition among officials and administrators. He therefore attributes a much more passive role to the caliphs themselves, whom he sees as supporting a more purely Arab movement already under way in the Umayyad caliphate.[12]

At a distance of 1,000 years, it is hard to assess the relative roles of the different players in the translation movement and to perceive whether it was a top-down initiative promoted by the 'Abbasid caliphs as individuals or a more amorphous bottom-up process triggered by the specific social and cultural environment in 'Abbasid Iraq, where both Baghdad and the Islamic intellectual centres of Kufa and Basra were situated, in addition to older centres of Nestorian and pagan learning such as Nisibis, Edessa and Harran. It was perhaps natural for historians of the day to personalize the phenomenon by linking it to various caliphs, most notably al-Ma'mun, but their actions did not take place in a vacuum and depended on a certain social and cultural environment which, even if it was not the original catalyst of the movement, certainly perpetuated it long after the caliphs had lost power to their Turkish commanders and the Buyids. Whoever takes the credit, the great achievement of the 'Abbasids and the regimes which emerged in their shadow was to synthesize and build on the intellectual traditions which the early Islamic conquests had brought under their sway by not simply allowing converts to rediscover their heritage in an Arabo-Islamic idiom but also by creating an elite culture in which scientific knowledge and philosophy were actively sought out to be rigorously analysed and criticized in a new Arabo-Islamic environment.

Two essential factors in creating the context for the translation movement were the Arabization of the administration of the empire by the Umayyad caliph 'Abd al-Malik in the last decades of the seventh century, which initiated the process by which Arabic became the Muslim *lingua franca*, and the steady conversion of non-Arabs to Islam. Once the administration had shifted from local languages to Arabic, the participation of Persian, Greek and Aramaic-speaking groups in government service naturally entailed their application of their knowledge in Arabic. To some degree, then, the act of translating was incidental to the continuity which naturally resulted from the adoption of Arabic by non-Arabs. As the ranks of Muslims increased, however, Arabized non-Muslims in government service began to fear that their positions were no longer secure. Many such employees, or their children, therefore converted to Islam to maintain their positions, thus recasting their knowledge in the light of their new religion as well as their new language. In the first decades of the 'Abbasid caliphate, Christians, Zoroastrians and Jews were all to be found in the imperial service working in administrative, scholarly, scientific and medical capacities, but many of their descendants converted to Islam. For instance, the descendants of at least two of al-Mansur's Zoroastrian Persian astrologers became Muslim, as did members of the originally Christian Bakhtishu' family of physicians, and the descendants of Hunayn b. Ishaq, the most celebrated ninth-century Christian translator of texts.

It is George Saliba's contention that these social changes created such a competitive environment that officials and state employees began to seek out texts which they could translate or have translated in order to keep ahead of the game by acquiring skills and knowledge superior to those of their colleagues. Texts on mathematics, astronomy, astrology and medicine all fell into this category, and the knowledge gained was not for the greater good of mankind but for the advancement of individuals or individual families.[13] This rather Machiavellian reading of the situation probably has some truth to it but it was very hard to keep new knowledge under wraps, and the participation of courtiers, ministers, military commanders and some caliphs themselves in the translation movement ensured that no branch of learning could be monopolized by individuals or lineages in the long term. A coterie of highly talented and meticulous Christian and Muslim scholars, many bilingual or trilingual in combinations of Arabic, Pahlavi Persian, Syriac and Greek, made numerous manuscripts available in Arabic and, as a larger body of scholars, scientists and translators formed, scholars themselves made or sought out additional translations to comment on and criticize.

A close analysis of the way these scholars worked indicates that they were actually operating in a research environment that strikes a modern note even at the distance of a millennium. Christian and Muslim researchers developed projects related to the specific needs of the early 'Abbasid governing class for astronomy and astrology, mathematics, philosophy and medicine, and then identified the Greek texts which could be relevant. Once translated such texts were used to enhance or develop ideas already being tested by 'Abbasid scientists and scholars. Some scholars worked as individuals but there were also numerous research teams working in different areas such as medicine, optics and astronomy. This research culture explains the mutual interest of bureaucrats and caliphs in translation, the fact that many texts were re-translated for new purposes and the fact that translation ultimately became redundant in the late tenth century as Arabo-Islamic science outstripped its forerunners and translations from Greek ceased to be of scientific as opposed to antiquarian value.[14]

Before looking at the translations and the translators themselves we should briefly consider the institutional and technological framework that facilitated translation and other scholarly activities. An institution often considered integral to the translation movement was the famous but shadowy *bayt al-hikma*, the 'house of wisdom', founded by the 'Abbasid caliphs in Baghdad. Although very little is known about its practical functioning, the *bayt al-hikma* has been variously described as a royal archive, a library and the nerve centre of the translation movement. Traditionally its foundation has been attributed to al-Ma'mun, the golden boy of the translation movement, but some chance references suggest that it was established at least 50 years earlier by al-Mansur or his Persian ministers who were actually following the Sasanian practice of maintaining royal archives of dynastic chronicles and translated materials.[15] This may well have been part of al-Mansur's larger project to portray the 'Abbasids as the legitimate successors of the Sasanians in Iraq, Iran, Khurasan and Transoxania, a project equally evident in the design of Baghdad itself, discussed in Chapter 2, and al-Mansur's public reliance on Jewish and Zoroastrian astrologers from previously Sasanian territories.

By the reign of al-Ma'mun, the *bayt al-hikma* is said to have had a staff of translators – mainly Persians interested in astrology – copyists and book binders who assisted in the task of creating and maintaining the collection, but mention of it ceases a few decades later in the reign of al-Mutawakkil. Although al-Mutawakkil is often seen as a conservative who did not wish to promote 'foreign' sciences, it is equally evident that some important translations were made during his reign. It is more likely that the apparent demise of the *bayt al-hikma* actually reflected a diminution in the state role which it could play after the caliphs moved to Samarra. Nonetheless, in creating an academic institute modelled on pre-Islamic libraries and academies of learning from Gundeshapur to Alexandria, the 'Abbasids set a precedent rapidly adopted by the Muslim elite around them. Even if the *bayt al-hikma* had a relatively short life as an institution in its own right, the concept of a library with a reading room for scholars to meet and study outside the confines of the mosques had come to stay. Wealthy private individuals began to set up their own libraries, and rulers in Iraq and elsewhere competed to maintain the most splendid and varied collections, which complemented the more narrowly legal and religious titles held in mosque libraries.

This sudden efflorescence of libraries was made possible by the Muslim acquisition of paper-making technology from China by way of Transoxania, which made book production cheaper and easier than in the days of parchment. It also enabled authors and copyists to work more quickly, leading to a dramatic increase in the availability of works and copies of them, alongside older, rarer and more expensive parchment manuscripts. This in turn contributed to an important shift from the oral culture of earlier times, in which memorization was valued as more sound than written and possibly altered materials, to a new 'Abbasid written culture that cherished books as the repositories of true knowledge, a process we have already encountered in the religious realm with the committing of the *hadith* to paper.

In the environs of Baghdad itself, a courtly lineage, the Banu Munajjim, established their own library, the *khizanat al-hikma*, 'the treasury of wisdom', which was open to scholars who were not only allowed to read the books but also offered free board and lodging in deference to their commitment to the pursuit of knowledge. In the tenth century the Samanids established a fine library in Bukhara where the philosopher and physician Ibn Sina, known in the Latin West as Avicenna, acquired his knowledge of Greek science. He described the library as:

> a building with many rooms in each of which were chests of books opposite each other. In one room there were books on Arabic language and poetry, in another jurisprudence and each room was similarly [dedicated] to a single science.[16]

He adds that there was a catalogue for each subject, including the books of the ancient Greeks, and staff who brought the books to him when he requested them. In Mosul the governor Ja'far b. Muhammad (d. 935) founded a library which provided free paper for readers to make notes on, and Basra, Hurmuz and Rayy possessed similar facilities. The Buyid ruler of Fars, 'Adud al-Dawla (d. 977), set up a splendid library for persons of distinction in an upper storey of his palace in Shiraz, described in detail by al-Muqaddasi:

> There is a manager, a librarian and a supervisor from among the people of good repute in the town, and there was not a book written up to that time, of all the various sciences, but happened to be there. It consists of a long oblong gallery in a large hall with rooms on every side. He attached to all the walls of the gallery and rooms bookcases six feet in height and three cubits long, made of wood and decorated. ... For every subject there are bookcases, and catalogues in which are the names of the books.[17]

Meanwhile in al-Andalus the Umayyad caliphs 'Abd al-Rahman III (d. 961) and his son al-Hakam II (d. 976) built up their own royal library to rival those of Baghdad. To such major collections must be added countless small private libraries which sometimes held unique works. Avicenna mentions that an otherwise unknown jurist of Khwarazmian origin, Abu Bakr al-Baraqi, commissioned two books on philosophy from him for his personal library but that these were not commonly available because Abu Bakr never lent them out for copying.[18] He was an exception, however, and Cordoba alone was reputed to have 70 libraries and a thriving trade in book copying and selling which enabled wealthy collectors to acquire all the bestsellers of their day, including the translated Greek classics.

Such libraries reached their apogee in Egypt, where the Fatimid caliphs established a vast library and study centre in their palace with 40 rooms containing as many as 2 million volumes, including 18,000 on the knowledge of the Greeks. It was only surpassed by the caliph al-Hakim's great *dar al-hikma* or *dar al-'ilm* founded in 1005. As in Baghdad, 'state' libraries were accompanied by private foundations, an example of which was the academy of the minister Ibn Killis. In the case of the Fatimids and their courtiers, the great Hellenic academies in Alexandria, which had not been destroyed by Muslims despite the myth to that effect, provided as much of a model as the 'Abbasid libraries further east. Sadly the Fatimid *dar al-hikma* suffered many vicissitudes in the turbulent last century of the Fatimid caliphate and was finally closed by Salah al-Din after he assumed power in Egypt in 1171, its books sold, destroyed and dispersed forever.

The other institution which underpinned Baghdad's Golden Age was the salon or *majlis*, a word which denoted both a place and the gathering which took place within it. The idea of gathering together scholars, intellectuals, poets and other interesting types on a regular basis for a session of stimulating conversation and witty repartee was hardly new to Islam but it came to take very diverse forms under the 'Abbasids, from ribald poetic recitations with slave girls to extremely intellectual debates about religion and reason. While the Umayyad caliphs had patronized poets and cultivated an interest in the religious sciences, intellectual salon culture was the product of the 'Abbasid court in Baghdad, and temporarily Samarra, in the ninth to tenth centuries. The caliphs themselves presided over some salons, but soon the number multiplied as chief ministers and other court personnel competed to hold their own such gatherings.

It was understood that people of differing views would attend a *majlis* and that debates and even polemics might ensue. Christians, Muslims and Jews mixed at such gatherings and it is a measure of the academic freedom of the time that individuals of very different backgrounds felt able to express themselves. The Christian scholar and translator Matta b. Yunus was apparently attacked fiercely for his belief in logic at the salon of the minister Ibn al-Furat by Abu Sa'id al-Sirafi, who was opposed to the infiltration of philosophical ideas into Islam, while Matta's Christian student Yahya b. 'Adi criticized the logical premises of Islamic theology in a different salon.[19] The tenets of Mu'tazilism too were debated in the salons. Attendance at a *majlis* resulted in patronage and was the consequence of it. Newcomers who entertained the host with their acuity could expect remuneration while those who already enjoyed the favours of the patron would be required to attend. It was therefore not simply a social and intellectual institution but also a way in which aspiring intellectuals and scholars made their mark and found patrons willing to pay them, offer them board and lodging or help them secure access to more permanent employment as ministers, physicians, librarians and 'royal' scholars.

Translations, translators and scientists

It is generally although not universally accepted that the first tranche of 'Abbasid translations related to astrology and astronomy. Near Eastern society was saturated by astrology, which was used to write horoscopes and determine auspicious and inauspicious days for activities, and, although not condoned by Islam, such practices soon entered Islamic culture. It is related that in choosing the site of Baghdad and the date for the commencement of construction, al-Mansur consulted a team of Persian astrologers. Nawbakht, a Zoroastrian astrologer, assisted by the Jewish astrologer Masha'allah and other members of the astrological team, provided him with an auspicious date. In the ensuing years, astrology took pride of place among the sciences patronized by the caliph, and several Persian astrological works, some translations of Greek originals, were duly translated into Arabic. Astrologers soon began to author new works, the best known of which is the *Great Introduction [to Astrology]* of Abu Ma'shar (d. 886), a native of Balkh in Khurasan, which soon found its way to Spain, where the Umayyads had cultivated local astrology of Roman or Byzantine derivation from the early ninth century but eagerly added Arab-Greek works to that corpus.

Although a pseudo-science, astrology depended on a firm astronomical understanding of the positions of the sun, moon and planets. Astronomical manuals, known as *zij*, provided this information for particular locations in the form of tables and explanation, and the 'Abbasids eagerly sought out manuals such as the Sasanian *Zik-i Shariyar* and *Zik-i Arkand* and Ptolemy's *Almagest*. Manuals of Indian origin may have been added in the early 770s when a scholar accompanying an embassy from Sind supposedly brought

Sanskrit astronomical manuals with him which were then translated by two scholars called al-Fazari and Ibn Tariq. The translation and al-Fazari's subsequent compilation of Persian, Greek and Indian astronomical knowledge in a single manual are known as the *Zij al-Sindhind* and the *Great Zij al-Sindhind* respectively. There are also allusions to an Indian astrologer called Kanaka, who spent some time at the court of Harun al-Rashid. The latter's son and second successor al-Ma'mun founded observatories in Baghdad and Damascus where Muslim astronomers prepared new tables which amended those of Ptolemy, using the information they had gained from India and their own observations. Like astrology, astronomical manuals soon percolated west far beyond the formal boundaries of 'Abbasid territory to al-Andalus, either in the baggage of the Iraqi musician and courtier Ziryab or a Cordoban scholar called 'Abbas b. Nasih, who went to Baghdad to collect scientific works for the Umayyad *amir*.

In addition to bulking up the scientific component in astrology, astronomical knowledge also had more directly utilitarian purposes, since it was used to determine the correct times of prayer, the direction of Mecca for the proper alignment of mosques, and various agricultural dates. It was also useful in map-making and it was therefore not coincidental that al-Ma'mun also commissioned a world map. Mathematics was closely linked to astronomy and was therefore another focus of early translation activity. It is even possible that Euclid's *Elements* had already been translated in the late Umayyad period because of the importance of mathematics to administrators involved in land surveying and revenue assessment. Mathematics was also integral to the successful use of burning mirrors – lenses which refracted the sun's rays to meet at a certain point where their heat would cause combustion. Such mirrors could be used as weapons and as instruments for the cauterization of wounds. From this practical and applied base, mathematics became one of the most innovative areas of Islamic science, and several mathematicians made breakthroughs of continued relevance in modern mathematics.

Another science of immediate interest and utility to the 'Abbasids was medicine. The foremost medical tradition in the 'Abbasid heartlands in the second half of the eighth century was that of the Greeks, preserved and perpetuated by Nestorian Christian physicians working primarily in areas which had belonged to the Sasanian Empire. These physicians often combined their medical knowledge with some philosophy ever since the two had become part of a single curriculum first promulgated in Alexandria and then disseminated eastwards to Antioch, Edessa and Gundeshapur, the Persian city from which the most important medical families of the era came. Ironically these proponents of Hellenic medicine had found the

Sasanian Empire a more convivial environment to practise their craft than contemporary Byzantium, where pagan learning and the Nestorian sect had been outlawed by the Orthodox Church.

In 765 al-Mansur summoned Georgios b. Gabriel of the Bakhtishu' family to Baghdad to heal a stomach complaint from which he was suffering. Although Georgios returned home to Gundeshapur after offering the caliph a cure, a connection had been established and his son moved permanently to Baghdad where generations of the Bakhtishu' family served as caliphal physicians, treating not only the men but also the women of the royal house. They were joined by the Masawayh, Tayfuri and Serapion families who together formed an influential social clique in Baghdad able to dominate the medical establishment and promote what is quite likely a myth of the superiority of the Gundeshapur medical academy to other Nestorian centres on the eve of Islam.[20] Galenic and Hippocratic medicine thus combined with Arabian 'prophetic medicine' to produce the rich Arabo-Islamic medical tradition with its vast range of pharmaceuticals, surgical procedures and specialities.

More abstract sciences such as logic and metaphysics soon joined the list in response to the new exigencies of the late eighth century, most notably the need to develop *kalam* in response to religious challenges from Christianity and Manichaeism, a religion dating to the third century CE founded by a prophet called Mani who brought together elements from Christianity, Zoroastrianism and even Buddhism. Polemic was already well developed in Christian circles and, after the initial shock of the Islamic conquest had worn off, Christians of all sects responded to the conversion of fellow believers by arguing against Islam's tenets. They did this by presenting and arguing a particular point using dialectical logic of Greek derivation or by offering questions and answers or a series of points which brought one to the desired conclusion. This was the format of al-Kindi's *Apology*, discussed in Chapter 3. It was with some relief then that Muslims sought and found the intellectual tools to argue and develop their understanding of their own faith and criticize others in a logical and convincing way.

Translation of Greek works of logic may have begun with al-Mansur, since Ibn al-Muqaffa's son Muhammad, who served as one of al-Mansur's secretaries, is said to have translated such works from Greek or Syriac. During the reign of al-Mansur's son al-Mahdi, who came to power in 775, Aristotle's *Topics* was translated from Syriac into Arabic and the translation verified against the Greek text, a task entrusted to the Nestorian patriarch Timothy.[21] The *Topics* was a systematic explanation of the correct way to argue a case, in other words a manual of dialectic which scholars of religion could use to argue the Muslim position against that of other faiths, especially Christianity, just as al-Mahdi and Timothy did in a famous exchange of views. The *Topics* was re-translated twice in the ensuing 150 years and the techniques it provided came to play as great a role in debates between Muslim sects and schools of thought as they had originally played in inter-confessional ones.

Aristotle's *Physics*, translated a decade or so later during the reign of Harun al-Rashid, played a similar, more directed role by sharpening Muslim understanding of the nature of the universe and enabling scholars to counter the rise of popular religious movements in Iran and Khurasan, collectively known as *zandaqa*, which meant both 'heresy' and Manichaeism, a religion considered a heresy by the Sasanians. Many of these movements stood between Islam and Manichaeism or Zoroastrianism and promoted dualistic beliefs in the eternal struggle between good and evil, light and darkness, truth and the lie, which were characteristic of the latter faiths. As such they challenged Muslims to argue for their own vision of an essentially good universe in which evil was incidental rather than equal, as well as forcing the caliphal armies to quell the Khurramiyya insurrections in Azerbayjan and Iran.

By the reign of al-Ma'mun (r. 813–33) a wide range of materials were undergoing translation from philosophy to pneumatics, and the caliph himself is portrayed as a keen intellectual, a patron of translations and the *bayt al-hikma*, and host of regular salon sessions at court. Growing Muslim demand impelled scholars to hunt high and low in Syria, Palestine and Iraq for Syriac and Greek manuscripts. They knocked on the doors of monasteries and sent requests to the patriarchs in the hope of finding an ever expanding list of Hellenic works, many of which were no longer in common circulation in Christian circles either in the Islamic lands or Byzantium. The best scholars scrupulously compared manuscripts and then made the most accurate translations they could. Some whose Greek was rusty or too limited made strenuous efforts to improve their command of the language as well as working to develop an appropriate and systematic Arabic technical vocabulary for commonly used scientific or philosophical terms. In return for their efforts, they received very high salaries. Although it is very difficult to compare wages across 1,000 years, a good translator might receive 500 gold dinars, roughly equivalent to $24,000, per month for his labours, a princely sum which is a significant indicator of the appetite for translations among the early 'Abbasid elite and their respect for knowledge.[22] Moreover al-Nadim, writing in the last decades of the tenth century, gives a list of nearly 70 known, and by that we may assume prestigious, translators.[23]

Those who commissioned translations included a succession of caliphs, chief ministers and courtiers mostly of Persian background, Turkish military commanders and Christian administrators. The translators and scholars they supported included the cohort of Nestorian physicians from Gunde-shapur mentioned above, lineages of Zoroastrian origin and a variety of other Christian and Muslim translator-scholars working in all the scientific fields. On occasion, successful scholars also commissioned translations of texts which they wished to consult, or simply to expand the available materials on a particular subject. In fact the line between patron and scholar was often vague, with many patrons making their own contributions in the areas of interest to them in a manner similar to Italian gentlemen of the Renaissance. Their diverse backgrounds clearly convey the dynamism of the period, the intellectual ferment, the opportunity for advancement and political power which scholarship could provide, and the gradual shift taking place in the identity of individuals and their scholarship from varied starting points to a final hegemonic Arabo-Islamic profile around 1000.

One famous Persian lineage involved in Baghdad's intellectual life was the Banu Munajjim, a family of astrologers and astronomers descended from Aban, a Zoroastrian who served as one of al-Mansur's court astrologers. According to some sources, Aban was a descendant of one of the ministers of the Sasanian ruler Ardashir (d. 241). Although he remained Zoroastrian, his grandson Yahya converted to Islam before al-Ma'mun in 817, after which he went on to play an important role in the astronomical and astrological sciences alongside Abu Ja'far Muhammad al-Khwarazmi (d. *c.* 847) who was responsible for the compilation of a most influential set of astronomical tables and the development of algebra. Yahya assisted in the foundation of the Baghdad and Damascus observatories and used his observations of the sky at night to amend Ptolemy's *Almagest* and produce the *Zij al-Mumta-han*, the first known Muslim-authored astronomical manual.

Henceforth his descendants were known as the 'Sons of the Astrono-mer' (Banu Munajjim) and were frequent attendees at court, although the interests of subsequent generations were not always in astronomy or astrol-ogy. Yahya's son 'Ali and his grandson and namesake Yahya (d. 912) were both men of the sciences who also excelled in poetry and music. They were true courtiers, who acted as companions to many ninth-century caliphs and patronized the arts by building libraries and holding salons where the issues of the day were discussed. Yahya the Younger's work on Arab poets comple-mented that of his brother Harun, who wrote an important anthology of poems. Their combined works were invaluable to al-Isfahani in his writing of the *Book of Songs*, a very influential and important compilation of pre-Islamic and early Islamic Arabic literature. Several members of the family espoused Mu'tazilism and they remained part of Baghdad and Samarran high society well into the Buyid period.

Another important Persian lineage descended from an astronomer were the three Banu Musa brothers, Muhammad, Ahmad and Hasan, who hailed from the northeastern province of Khurasan. According to Ibn al-Qifti, their father Musa b. Shakir was a highwayman who used to say the evening prayer with his neighbours before nipping off to hold up travellers on the Khurasan road with great bravado, after which he would return, change his clothes and perform the morning prayer at the mosque.[24] He was also said to be skilled in astrology and geometry, talents which enabled him to become a companion of al-Ma'mun during his governorship of Merv. When he died al-Ma'mun became guardian of his three orphan sons and saw to their education, as a result of which they eventually became integral to his scientific projects.

Although Muhammad, the oldest, was the best scientist, the middle brother Ahmad, who had access to Philo's *Pneumatics* and Hero's *Pneumatics* and *Mechanics*, wrote the trio's most famous work, the *Kitab al-Hiyal*, or *Book of Ingenious Devices*, which describes how to construct 100 machines, mostly pouring vessels, self-filling basins, fountains and lamps. A large number of the vessels were designed to measure, pour and mix or separate water from wine and were clearly meant to delight and puzzle guests at parties. The frivolity aside, the mechanics underlying the construction of such rich men's playthings were sophisticated and applicable in more useful ways. The *Book of Ingenious Devices* also gives a list of the Banu Musa's other works, the majority lost, from which the brothers gained a reputation as geometricians, astronomers and engineers. Among their achievements was to verify the Greek estimate of the circumference of the earth – 24,000 miles – by measuring the altitude of the pole star from different points in Iraq. Needless to say, Muslims knew full well that the earth was round rather than flat.

The Banu Musa also acted as patrons and promoters of science in their own right. Al-Nadim describes them as 'men who took extreme pains to study the ancient sciences, for the sake of which they gave generously what was required, taxing themselves with fatigue', adding by way of explanation that they sent missions to Byzantium to gather manuscripts for translation and 'caused translators from the districts and localities to be in attendance for many years'.[25] One such translator and scientist was Thabit b. Qurra (*c.* 826–901), a pagan moneychanger from Harran 'discovered' by Muhammad, who became the greatest mathematician of the era after studying at the Banu Musa family home with Hasan, a talented geometrician himself. Thabit's maternal language was Syriac, but he knew Greek and composed his own works in Arabic. He translated Archimedes' *Cylinder and Sphere* and Nichomachus of Gerasa's *Introduction to Arithmetic* and also

Fig. 25. A page from a thirteenth-century copy of the version of Euclid composed
by the 'Abbasid mathematician Thabit b. Qurra. (Manuscript Add 1075, p 43.
Reproduced by kind permission of the Syndics of Cambridge University Library)

improved earlier translations of Euclid's *Elements* and Ptolemy's *Almagest*. He composed at least 30 works of mathematics and astronomy, in which he took a highly mathematical approach to astronomy as well as making advances in pure mathematics.

The field of medicine and medical translation established by the physicians of Gundeshapur continued to be dominated by Nestorian Christians and their Muslim descendants. One of the best-known doctors and medical translators was Hunayn b. Ishaq, a Nestorian Christian Arab from Hira, the old capital of the Christian Lakhmids, who was born around 808. Hunayn was probably bilingual in Syriac and Arabic and learnt Greek to a high standard during the course of his education. His father was a pharmacist and he went to study medicine with Yuhanna b. Masawayh, the foremost physician from the reigns of Harun al-Rashid and al-Ma'mun, and a prolific translator himself. According to popular legend, Hunayn was a rather inquisitive student whom Yuhanna b. Masawayh threw out of his classes for constantly interrupting, commenting sarcastically, 'What have the people of Hira to do with medicine, your metier is exchanging pennies in the street.'[26] However, it is equally likely that he left Baghdad to acquire a better knowledge of Greek in Byzantium before continuing with his studies while, as Ibn al-Qifti points out, Yuhanna's attitude also reflected the perception of the Christian physicians of Gundeshapur that medicine was their field and should not be disseminated beyond the charmed circle of their own children and community. Al-Nadim suggests that Hunayn was actually sent to Byzantium to collect scientific books by the Banu Musa brothers.[27]

On his return some years later, Hunayn was re-integrated into the Baghdad circle of doctors, translators and scholars, founded his own atelier of translators and became the caliph al-Mutawakkil's chief physician, after the latter assured himself that this talented Christian with Byzantine connections was not going to use his medical skills to poison him! Foremost among Hunayn's contributions to medicine were his popular translations of Hippocrates and Galen and his own medical works, which he designed as a series of questions and answers in a manner which evoked Nestorian Christian biblical exegesis, the techniques of *kalam* and legal instruction. According to Ibn al-Qifti, 'it was he who clarified the meaning of the books of Hippocrates and Galen and made the best summary of them', as well as writing several important and original works of ophthalmology, including his famous *Ten Treatises on the Eye*.[28] He also translated the Old Testament into Arabic for the benefit of the growing number of Arabized Christians in the Middle East.

His son Ishaq, who converted to Islam, was a companion of the caliph al-Muktafi (r. 902–08) and perhaps his astrologer, as well as being a qualified physician, author of many medical treatises and translator of philosophical works by Aristotle, Plato and other Greek philosophers. His linguistic talents were such that he also improved upon earlier translations by Thabit b. Qurra, a task facilitated by the steady development of a new scientific vocabulary which made it easier to render technical terms from Greek and Syriac into Arabic. Another Christian translator with a focus on medicine was Qusta b. Luqa from Ba'lbak, who was trilingual but specialized in translating from Greek rather than Syriac into Arabic. Although he was a physician, Qusta was also interested in astronomy, mathematics, philosophy, politics, music and theology and could be quite polemical in defence of Christianity on occasion. Eventually he accepted an invitation to go to the Armenian court – with many of his translations – where he died and was given a celebrity's burial around 912.[29] Medical translations also made their way west to Spain in the hands of men such as Yunus al-Harrani, a doctor who left Iraq for the court of the Umayyad *amir* Muhammad in the mid-ninth century.[30]

In the realm of philosophy, the translation of Greek texts and the development of Muslim philosophy (*falsafa*) went hand in hand. We do not have details of when exactly philosophical texts were first translated or by whom, but the first recognized Islamic philosopher, Abu Yusuf Ya'qub al-Kindi (*c.* 800–70), a descendant of the Arab kings of Kinda and of a Companion of the Prophet, is said to have had a solid education in Greek, Persian and Indian learning as well as Islamic law.[31] Although he did not know Greek himself, he had a team of translators who provided him with Arabic versions of works by Aristotle, Aristotelian commentators including Alexander of Aphrodisias and Porphyry, Neoplatonists such as Plotinus and Proclus, and the Christian philosopher John Philoponus. However, he did not have access to much work by Plato. In addition to his famous philosophical treatise *On First Philosophy*, he also wrote on the works of Archimedes and Ptolemy, on Euclid's theory of perspective, the astrolabe and Hippocratic medicine, as well as more mundane scientific and technical topics such as glass manufacture, swords and music. Although he authored as many as 250 works, only a mere 40 are extant, of which the best known is *On First Philosophy*, which confirmed his later reputation as a philosopher, although he clearly had eclectic intellectual interests and was as much a mathematician and astrologer as a philosopher in his own lifetime. Al-Nadim describes him simply as 'the distinguished man of his time and unique during his period because of his knowledge of the ancient sciences as a whole'.[32]

Al-Kindi was part of the glittering intellectual circle which surrounded the caliphs al-Ma'mun and al-Mu'tasim. He was tutor to the latter's son Ahmad, and dedicated *On First Philosophy* to him or to Ahmad, to whom he also dedicated several other works. Another biographer of scientists, Ibn Abi Usaybi'a (d. 1270), reports that in the reign of al-Mutawakkil the jealous Banu Musa brothers intrigued against al-Kindi and persuaded the caliph to beat him and confiscate his library. He only regained it when the Banu Musa appointed an engineer who made a gross miscalculation when constructing a canal. In order to salvage the situation the Banu Musa were forced to recall Sind b. 'Ali, an engineer whom they had sent away from Samarra to Baghdad, who made his assistance conditional on the return of al-Kindi's books to their rightful owner.[33] It has been suggested that the Banu Musa had used al-Kindi's leaning towards the Mu'tazili school of theology, which was not well regarded by al-Mutawakkil, to discredit him but this is by no means certain.

In contrast to later Muslim philosophers, al-Kindi lived at a time when the battlelines between Greek and Arabic ways of thought had not yet been drawn. His larger intellectual project was to present Greek philosophy as a coherent body of knowledge with a distinct methodology for approaching Truth, which could be put to the service of Arab-Muslim theology. For him, Greek metaphysics and Muslim theology had the same objective and, although he was a supporter of the emerging discipline of *kalam* against its Christian critics and *hadith* scholars who preferred to ascertain the nature of God through scripture rather than by logical proofs, he was deeply opposed to those theologians who failed to appreciate the value of Greek ideas for Arabic intellectual discourse.[34] Al-Kindi saw the difference between revelation and philosophical truth as one of process rather than essence. On the one hand, philosophical knowledge is knowledge based on the exercise of human reasoning and observation which can only be acquired by years of laborious study and reflection; on the other hand, the revelations granted to prophets are gifts from God. Nonetheless, the content of philosophy, 'the science of things and their true nature', is identical to that of the message of the prophets, 'the science of divine sovereignty and divine unity [and] the science of morality and ethics'.[35]

Al-Kindi's intellectual perspective placed him firmly in the group of rational thinkers around al-Ma'mun and al-Mu'tasim who wished to encourage the rational discursive approach to religion that the *hadith* scholars so disliked. For the latter, it was anathema to suggest that there were many paths to God, and their antipathy was probably only deepened by the inter-confessional character of philosophy. Although al-Kindi was Muslim, many of the philosophers of the following century were Christian, and the flourishing Aristotelian school of Baghdad engaged some of the most eminent Christian as well as Muslim thinkers of the age. Although the Christian and Muslim strands of this philosophical school are sometimes viewed as distinct, Muslims studied with Christians and vice versa, and Islamic philosophy benefited from solutions already found by Christians to reconcile pagan philosophy and Semitic monotheism.

One of the best-known Aristotelian scholars of this era was Matta b. Yunus (d. 940), a Nestorian Christian from Dayr Qunna, a monastic settlement in southern Iraq, who came north to Baghdad in the 930s. He himself had studied with both Syrian Christians and Muslims and was versed in Islamic theology (*kalam*) as well as Christian Aristotelianism. He made copious translations of philosophical texts from Syriac into Arabic, which greatly improved the access of Arabic-speakers to commentaries on Aristotle by Alexander of Aphrodisias and Themistius, and was regarded by his peers as a skilled logician and founder of the Aristotelian school of Baghdad. One of those who studied with Matta was Muhammad al-Farabi (d. 950), a Muslim philosopher whose father was a Turkish military man who perhaps served in the caliphal army. He was born at Wasij, a town on the Jaxartes river in Transoxania, but spent his adult years in Baghdad where he appears to have pursued his scholarly interests outside 'Abbasid court circles in order to assert his intellectual independence from political pressure – a gesture reminiscent of the aversion to the political authorities exhibited by many religious scholars. Towards the end of his life, however, he did accept the patronage of Sayf al-Dawla, one of the Hamdanid lineage who controlled northern Iraq and Syria in the tenth century, and moved to their chief city, Aleppo. This may have been due to Sayf al-Dawla's inclination towards Twelver Shi'ism, which also appealed to al-Farabi.

Al-Farabi acquired his knowledge of the Greek philosophical tradition from the Christian Aristotelians of Baghdad, but he also had access to a variety of philosophical texts including summaries of Plato's *Republic* and *Laws*. Although he wrote teaching manuals and erudite commentaries on some Aristotelian works, his most famous work is a tract entitled *The Principles of the Views of the People of the Virtuous City*, a piece of theoretical and political philosophy for people who were educated but not necessarily practising philosophers, written in the 940s. In this book, which is something of a commentary on Plato's *Republic*, al-Farabi leads the reader through an analysis of the universe and man's position within it, to an explication of the ideal state, 'the virtuous city' headed by a philosopher-king in which the justice and balance evident in nature are transferred to human society. Although he recognized that this ideal was generally not attained, al-Farabi nonetheless felt that government did require some kind of a philosophical underpinning:

When it happens, at a given time, that philosophy has no share in government, though every other condition may be present in it, the excellent city will remain without a king. The ruler actually in charge will not be a king and the city will be on the verge of destruction; and if it happens that no philosopher can be found, then, after a certain interval, this city will undoubtedly perish. [36]

One of Matta b. Yunus and Muhammad al-Farabi's students was Yahya b. 'Adi (d. 974), a Jacobite Christian Arab philosopher, theologian and translator from Takrit in Iraq, who earned a living as a copyist and bookseller in Baghdad. He translated the *Organon* and other Aristotelian works from Syriac into Arabic. In his own diverse writings, he showed a preference for logic and epistemology. He also helped popularize Platonic ideas about the three-way division of the soul into appetitive, spiritual and rational aspects, and engaged in polemics about the relative merits of Christianity and Islam in a series of theological treatises which explored the ideas emerging in Islamic *kalam* and undermined them using demonstrative logic. On the other hand, as a Christian he attempted to address the main Muslim criticism of Christianity – its association of others with God in the Trinity – to argue that God was of one substance but had three characteristics or attributes. This cleverly created a parallel with Ash'ari theology, which also credited God with eternal attributes, thereby closing the gap between the faiths and undermining the Muslim accusation that Christians were polytheists while Muslims were true monotheists.

The 'Abbasid court's interest in scholarship and the willingness of patrons to dedicate money and resources to it in the form of generous financial support to scholars, the commissioning of translations and the establishment of libraries reflected a number of different imperatives. Many of the caliphs were amateur scholars themselves with an interest in the sciences they supported, but they were also keenly aware of the positive public impression patronage of the translations of different kind of texts would create in Baghdad, from suggesting continuity with the Sasanian past to offering the integrative possibility of creating a new Arabo-Islamic corpus of knowledge which those of non-Arab origin or non-Muslim faith could still feel part of. Translation was also part of a wider research culture which aimed to produce knowledge of relevance and use to 'Abbasid society as a whole. For patrons below the rank of the caliph, commissioning scholarly works was a way to demonstrate commitment to the values of elite culture and to 'arrive' in polite society, something quite important to rough-edged military commanders from the provinces, or *nouveaux riches* administrators of humble origin.

What occurred in Baghdad was part and parcel of a much larger process happening at all levels of society as people began to convert to Islam. The risk, of course, was that Arab and Islamic identity as formulated during the first century of Islam with its poetic, literary and religious dimensions would be lost and that all semblance of unity within the Muslim community, the *umma*, would likewise vanish and be replaced by endless competing permutations of faith and knowledge. The 'Abbasids managed to steer a different path in which the knowledge of the Greeks, often described simply as 'those who came first' (*al-awwaliyyun*) in contrast to the 'later' scholars of Islamic times, was synthesized and offered back to the community in a new Arabo-Islamic form which everyone could share, regardless of their background. By 950 this new corpus of Arabo-Islamic knowledge was firmly entrenched and new generations interrogated earlier Arabic works rather than going back to Greek or Pahlavi Persian texts.

Knowledge and science after the translation movement

As the need to translate materials of Hellenic origin abated, the next task facing Muslim intellectuals was to organize and systematize the vast amount of sometimes disjointed information they had at their fingertips. The tenth to eleventh centuries thus witnessed the emergence of a new breed of Muslim scholar able to synthesize divergent works and present an overview of a particular discipline or disciplines. The earliest such compilations and encyclopedias appeared in the medical field from Baghdad to Cordoba, with philosophy following soon after. Some of the best-known intellectuals of this genre are al-Razi, known as Rhazes in the Latin West, al-Majusi, Ibn Sina (Avicenna) and Ibn Rushd (Averroes), but there were many more.

Abu Bakr Muhammad al-Razi (*c.* 854–935) came from the city of Rayy near modern Tehran and gained fame and some infamy as a physician, philosopher and alchemist. Like many boys of his era, his education included a firm grounding in the Greek sciences and, unusually for a Muslim boy, he may even have known some Greek as well as studying through Arabic translations. He began his career in Rayy, where he was a companion to the Samanid governor as well as head of the hospital. He then moved to Baghdad to head the hospital there, but returned often to Rayy where he eventually died at a ripe old age. Al-Razi was in many ways a radical and innovative thinker who placed great emphasis on observation and experimentation in his medical work and did not hesitate to question earlier authorities on medicine and philosophy. In fact he argued that such questioning was the very essence of philosophy and intellectual endeavour and that slavishly following a master showed a fundamental misunderstanding of the objective of scholarship and science. His contribution to medicine was enormous: not only was he a renowned and respected practitioner in the hospitals he headed, he also wrote two medical compendia, the *Kitab al-Hawi fi'l-Tibb* and the *Kitab al-Jami' al-Kabir*, numerous specialist treatises, the most famous on smallpox and measles, and a sustained critique of Galenic medicine entitled *Doubts about Galen*, most of which was subsequently translated into Latin and circulated widely in Europe. In a strikingly modern way, al-Razi also recognized the social dimension to medical treatment and wrote about why people resorted to faith healers and wise women rather than coming to see qualified doctors.

Al-Razi's attitudes to philosophy and religion were even more radical and gained him many critics including Ibn al-Qifti, who describes him as rather wayward in his attitude towards 'religious science' and someone who 'adopted foolish opinions and subscribed to offensive schools of thought', despite his indubitable excellence in medicine.[37] One of his more infamous comments was his response when asked if philosophy and revealed religion were compatible. In stark contrast to al-Kindi and al-Farabi, al-Razi replied, 'How can anyone think philosophically while committed to those old wives tales founded upon contradictions, obdurate ignorance and dogmatism?'[38] While not actually denying the underlying truth of religion, this was nonetheless the kind of intellectual elitism which so irritated religious scholars. However, his rejection of the special role of prophets in favour of every person's God-given ability to reason and to reach their destiny by thinking for themselves cannot help but strike a chord today.

In medicine, the *Complete Book of the Medical Art* by al-Majusi, a tenth-century doctor from Ahwaz in Iran who trained in Shiraz, was as popular as the works of al-Razi. It was dedicated to 'Adud al-Dawla, the Buyid *amir* who built the town library and hospital, and came to be a standard medical textbook until it was partially superseded by the work of the most famous polymath of the 'Abbasid era, Avicenna, known in Arabic as Abu 'Ali al-Husayn Ibn Sina (980–1037). We are lucky in the case of Avicenna to have an autobiography completed by his pupil and friend al-Juzjani, which adds colour and detail to the sometimes dry, laconic entries more commonly found in biographical dictionaries. It is a measure of Avicenna's great fame throughout the Islamic world that this extended biography found its way into the biographical dictionaries, including that of Ibn al-Qifti, an Egyptian who composed his work in Syria far from Avicenna's Transoxanian homeland.[39]

Avicenna was a Persian whose father served the Samanids of Khurasan and Transoxania as the administrator of a rural district outside Bukhara. Although Avicenna and his brother were born in the village of Afshana, their father ensured that his sons were educated in the Samanid capital of Bukhara, where Avicenna began with the memorization and study of the Qur'an and Islamic jurisprudence before engaging with geometry, logic, other aspects of philosophy and medicine. Already a child prodigy, Avicenna attracted the attention of the Samanid ruler Nuh b. Mansur when he managed to cure an illness from which the latter was suffering. The young man's reward was access to the Samanid library, one of the numerous excellent libraries in the Islamic world at that time. Today we have no catalogue of the Samanid collection, but it undoubtedly contained major Islamic works as well as a great deal of pre-Islamic material from the Iranian, Hellenic and Indic traditions. Access to it enabled Avicenna to discover many 'works of the ancients' which he had not previously read, several of which he memorized and referred to for the rest of his adult life.

This was the springboard for Avicenna: not only did his attendance at the Samanid court give him access to patronage and teach him the ropes of being a courtier but it also gave him the knowledge upon which he built his reputation as a philosopher and a physician. Unfortunately the demise of the Samanids and the jostling for power between rival *amir*s which ensued in Iran forced Avicenna to move frequently in search of new patrons. He spend some time wandering before securing a position as physician to the Buyid *amir*s Majd al-Dawla and Shams al-Dawla in Rayy and then 'Ala al-Dawla in Isfahan, whom he served until he died in 1037 at the relatively young age of 57, victim of his own desire to live life to the full according to al-Juzjani's testimony.

In addition to revealing the trials and tribulations facing a career academic in the early eleventh century, Avicenna's biography gives a rare taste of the way men such as he lived. During the day he attended his patron, performing whatever tasks he was required to in his capacity as advisor and physician. When he returned to his home, his students gathered to hear him lecture, or he settled down to read and write late into the night. He was a devout Muslim who sought inspiration by going to the mosque to pray but also drank wine to stimulate his creativity, seeing no contradiction in this:

> I returned to my house at night and placed a lamp in front of me and
> busied myself with reading and writing. Whenever sleep overcame me or
> I felt weak I restored my equilibrium by drinking a draft of wine in order
> that my strength would return to me.[40]

Despite his dedication to scholarship, Avicenna was not an anti-social man: he socialized with his students and enjoyed the company of women, often in a setting which was a scaled-down version of the *majlis* sessions held by caliphs and *amir*s. Al-Juzjani tells us:

> Seekers of knowledge gathered at his house each night. I used to read
> from the [*Book of*] *Healing* and someone else would read from the *Canon*
> [*of Medicine*]. When we finished, different types of singers joined us and a
> drinking party with the requisite utensils was prepared.[41]

Avicenna was as prolific as other famous Muslim philosophers and scientists but, as usual, only a proportion of his works survive. The most famous of them are the *Book of Healing* [*of the Soul*], a philosophical compendium, and the *Canon of Medicine*, a comprehensive medical work. He also wrote many treatises on specialist medical topics and more specific philosophical, mathematical and religious questions. In the philosophical realm Avicenna worked from an Aristotelian base but he was also galvanized by the works of Plotinus, which were attributed to Aristotle at the time. It has been suggested that it was the inexplicable contradictions between the ideas in Aristotle's works and pseudo-Aristotelian writings by Plotinus that actually drove Avicenna to new explanations for the relationship between man and God, the Creator and his creation.

The education, career and writings of Avicenna are testament to the extent to which sciences of Greek derivation, especially philosophy and medicine, had become part of the educational curriculum alongside the religious sciences. Although giants like al-Razi and Avicenna took their knowledge much further than the average person, even men like Avicenna's early teacher al-Natili had a smattering of philosophy, geometry and logic, and medicine was widely practised in city hospitals. An ordinary jurist was happy to commission a few works of philosophy from Avicenna when he was a young man and, as the latter's reputation grew, his ideas spread in the cities where he lived – Bukhara, Gurganj, Rayy and Isfahan – and were disseminated much further afield by means of correspondence. He exchanged views with another famous polymath, al-Biruni, who served Mahmud of Ghazna in Afghanistan, and with pupils such as Abu'l-Hasan Bahmanyar (d. 1067). By the end of the eleventh century, his teachings were an essential part of the philosophical curriculum in Baghdad, and less than a century later in Cordoba, Averroes and the great medieval Jewish philosopher Maimonides gave their responses to the works of the 'great master'.

Although al-Razi and Avicenna were men of the east, more westerly parts of the Islamic world also produced their own physicians and philosophers. In 1049 a Baghdadi Christian called al-Mukhtar b. Butlan travelled through northern Iraq and Syria to Cairo, where he became involved in a bitter medical controversy with another physician, Ibn Ridwan, which led to his eventual departure from Egypt for Constantinople and then Syria.

He later lampooned doctors like Ibn Ridwan in an amusing little tract on medical ethics and quack doctors called, in loose translation, *The Doctors' Dinner Party*. During the course of his career he also wrote the *Taqwim al-Sihha*, a highly original medical compendium of information on diet and hygiene arranged in tabular form, which was somewhat similar to a GP's manual. He justified his choice of presentation, more common in astronomy than medicine, as necessary because 'people are wearied by the prolixity of scholars and the many books composed and their need is for the benefit they can derive from the sciences not their proofs and definitions'.[42]

In Spain the provincial flavour of learning prior to the tenth century was superseded by a burst of independent activity which began in the realm of medicine and then moved to philosophy. 'Abd al-Rahman III's personal physician Abu'l-Qasim al-Zahrawi wrote a monumental 30-volume medical encyclopedia, the *Tasrif*, which included a chapter on surgery way ahead of its time in the Latin West, where its author was known as Abulcasis. Pharmacology was improved by the acquisition of a copy of Dioscorides' *Materia Medica* from Byzantium, although it proved so difficult for the Umayyads to find a Greek translator in Spain that a Byzantine monk called Nicholas had to assist with its translation. Once it was translated, however, it formed the basis for much of the pharmacological work of the caliph Hisham's physician, Abu Dawud Sulayman b. Juljul (*c.* 944–94), who meticulously identified the plants and drugs in the translation and wrote an oft-cited appendix to it called the *Treatise on Medicaments not Mentioned by Dioscorides*.

In terms of scope, however, it was Averroes (1126–98), a doctor, jurist, philosopher and astronomer, who most closely resembled the eastern polymaths, although he did not always agree with their ideas. In addition to writing a medical compendium, he wrote works of jurisprudence and philosophy, the most famous of which are his three levels of commentary on the works of Aristotle, supposedly commissioned by the Almohad caliph Abu Ya'qub Yusuf. What was unique about Averroes was his attempt to rediscover the 'true' Aristotle and strip away the Neoplatonic accretions accepted and developed by Avicenna, a project which may appear conservative or radical depending on one's standpoint. He also revisited al-Kindi to the extent that he too wished to avoid supposing an unbridgeable gulf between philosophy and religion, although he did not embrace the theologians as al-Kindi had but ranked them below philosophers because of the purely dialectical rather than syllogistic nature of the proofs they offered for their beliefs.

The writing of such masterful compendia was not restricted to medicine and philosophy but also occurred in the religious sciences, most notably in the work of Abu Hamid Muhammad al-Ghazali (1058–1111), a jurist,

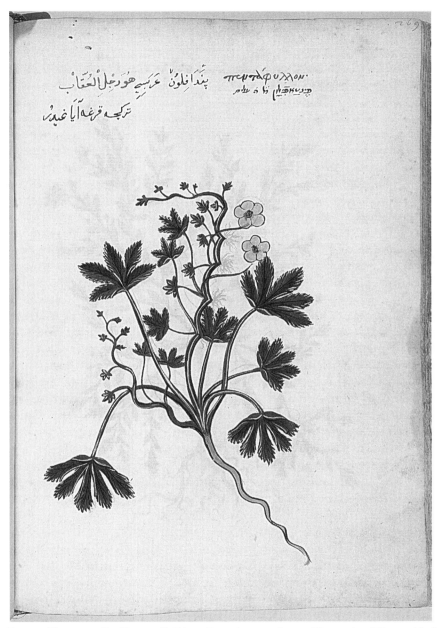

Fig. 26. The entry for Cinque Foil in a *Botanicum antiquum* illustrating Dioscorides' botanical dictionary with captions in Hebrew, Greek, Arabic and Turkish. (Manuscript Ee.5.7, p 269. Reproduced by kind permission of the Syndics of Cambridge University Library)

theologian and mystic who was also extremely well versed in philosophy and wrote the famous *Revivification of the Religious Sciences*. Al-Ghazali is of such towering stature in Sunni Muslim circles even today that it is all too easy to attribute to him all the developments in religious thought which occurred during the Saljuq sultanate. He does nonetheless seem to personify the intellectual atmosphere of his day in its positive and nega-tive aspects. On the one hand, al-Ghazali was one of the theologians at the forefront of the so-called Sunni revival, a movement which actually witnessed the emergence of Sunnism as it is understood today – a blend of Sunni law, Ash'ari theology, philosophy and mysticism. On the other hand, scholars like him helped confirm the break between Sunnism and Shi'ism and encourage a more imitative attitude in legal studies, captured in the common Muslim saying that the gate of *ijtihad*, rational enquiry, was closed from the time of al-Ghazali onwards. Practically speaking this was nonsense, and jurists and judges continued to respond to the situations presented to them, but it conveys an important aspect of Islamic thought in the ensuing centuries – the assumption that the great work of forming a tradition had been done and that al-Ghazali epitomized that culmination.

Al-Ghazali and his brother Ahmad, a famous mystic, came from Tus in Khurasan and were educated in Iran. Al-Ghazali was bright and soon reached the thriving cultural centre of Nishapur, where he studied with the famous al-Juwayni as well as many other scholars. From Nishapur he moved to Baghdad during the heyday of the Saljuqs and joined the circle of their chief minister Nizam al-Mulk, founder of the Nizamiyya theologi-cal colleges. Al-Ghazali lectured at the Nizamiyya college in Baghdad to hundreds of students for four years in the 1090s but then experienced what he describes as a nervous breakdown of some kind. This personal crisis may well have been compounded by the uncertain political climate in Baghdad after Nizam al-Mulk's assassination by an Isma'ili Shi'i in 1092 and the death of the sultan Malikshah in 1095. In any case, al-Ghazali stopped teaching, left Baghdad and, following the lead of his brother, became a peripatetic Sufi, wandering in Syria and the Hijaz around the time of the First Crusade. Some accounts say that he also went to Alexandria in Egypt and offered his services to the Almoravids, the new rulers of Morocco and Spain. He lived in partial seclusion for over a decade, during which he became convinced that religion without a mystical dimension had no mean-ing. In 1106 he returned to Nishapur and began to lecture in its Nizamiyya college, but soon after retired to his native city of Tus to work at a Sufi *khanqah* which he had already established to train Muslims in the mystical way.

Al-Ghazali wrote many books and many more have been attributed to him in order to partake of his aura, but a brief survey of the best known is sufficient to show how his thought developed in the course of his life. As a young man in Nishapur al-Ghazali studied jurisprudence, *kalam* and philosophy and he was especially influenced by the Muslim philosophers al-Farabi and Avicenna. During this period he wrote a book entitled *The Aims of the Philosophers*, which was a neutral explanation of philosophy. However, he became increasingly disillusioned with both philosophy and jurisprudence during his time in Baghdad. Shortly before abandoning his position at the Nizamiyya he wrote *The Incoherence of the Philosophers*, which demolished 20 philosophical tenets. Although this has often been seen as a blanket rejection of philosophy, it was more a case of rejecting some aspects of philosophy while bringing others, especially syllogistic logic, firmly within the religious fold for the benefit of theologians. It was countered nearly a century after it was written by Averroes' *Incoherence of the Incoherence*, which was part of his own project to reconcile religion and philosophy in the Spain of his day.

Al-Ghazali's dissatisfaction with jurisprudence related not to theoretical issues but to the corruption and worldliness of the religious scholars he had mingled with in Baghdad and other cities. He addressed this issue in his *Revivification of the Religious Sciences*, a book designed to show how Sunni Muslims must synthesize the inner and outer aspects of their faith and how they should apply faith in their daily lives. In a sense he defined an 'orthodoxy' which drew together the trends apparent in religion in the previous centuries and placed Sunnism on a new path. All the competing facets of knowledge came together in a new curriculum promulgated in the *madrasa*s of the east, which contained not only the standard legal fare but also Avicennan philosophy and Sufism. Meanwhile Neoplatonism flourished in an Islamized form in both Isma'ili and Twelver Shi'i circles.

Although the characteristic culture of the 'Abbasid age of learning came to a natural end, it was not replaced by a sudden and disastrous atrophy which persisted until modern European ideas began to circulate in the Middle East during the nineteenth century. Many sciences continued to flourish, despite the end of the translation movement and the move away from the study of self-consciously Greek philosophy. Mathematics, astronomy, astrology, engineering and medicine were fully naturalized within 'Abbasid society and advances in all areas were made for centuries to come. Meanwhile philosophy found a new home within religious studies. Nonetheless the kind of sustained imperial patronage which the 'Abbasids, their various 'protectors' and rivals had offered to knowledge production for so many centuries faded away after 1258. The new military regimes which succeeded them legitimized themselves in other ways: they waged *jihad* with enthusiasm and commissioned buildings and works of art which showed their commitment to Islam. As a result, illuminated Qur'ans, miniature painting and stunning architecture characterized the next phase in Islamic history, while many of the branches of learning favoured in the 'Abbasid centuries found a new audience in Latin Christendom where they were interrogated afresh.

≈ ∾

CHAPTER 6

The 'Abbasid Legacy

The end of this particular era in the history of Islam was first and foremost a political break – the destruction of the caliphate, an institution which had existed in some shape or form since the death of the Prophet in 632. However, the real change was not the termination of the caliphate, which had for centuries been a symbolic rather than an active political or religious role, but the occupation of much of the eastern Islamic world, the heartlands of the 'Abbasid caliphate, by the Mongols, who represented the most serious threat to Islamic hegemony that had ever occurred. In comparison with the devastating Mongol invasions which took place between 1222 and 1260, and which laid waste Transoxania, Khurasan and much of Iran and Iraq, the Crusades were a sideshow, affecting a very small part of the Islamic world, despite the symbolic importance of Jerusalem for Muslims, Christians and Jews alike. Moreover, in contrast to the Buyids and Saljuqs, who had been Muslim, and the Crusaders, who were at least Peoples of the Book, the Mongols were pagans who contacted the spirits via their shamans. That they should take over such a significant part of the Islamic world seemed to Muslims of the time an event comparable to the apocalypse. The Persian historian al-Juwayni (d. 1283) recounts the fate of Nishapur in the following emotive terms:

> They then drove all the survivors, men and women, out onto the plain; and in order to avenge Toghachar [Chinghiz Khan's son-in-law] it was commanded that the town should be laid waste in such a manner that the site could be ploughed upon; and that in the exaction of vengeance not even cats and dogs should be left alive.[1]

Of course the Mongol invasions were not the end of days: despite the Mongols' sense of martial superiority and disparagement of peasants and the sedentary cultures of which they were part, they soon succumbed to the civilizations of China and the Middle East. Al-Juwayni himself became governor of Iraq for the Mongols, and in 1295, 37 years after the fall of Baghdad and the Mongol execution of the last 'Abbasid caliph, the Mongol ruler of the Ilkhanid realm in Iraq and Iran, Ghazan Khan, converted to Islam, taking the Mongol elite with him. The khan of the Golden Horde in the Crimea had already adopted Islam and it spread rapidly too in the Chagatai khanate in Transoxania. Nonetheless the arrival of the Mongols irrevocably altered the geopolitics of the Islamic world, and the Fertile Crescent again became a frontier with the Mongol Ilkhanids in Iraq and Iran to the east and the Mamluks in Syria and Egypt to the west. This internal frontier was perpetuated into modern times by the formation of the Sunni Ottoman Empire from the Balkans around the Mediterranean to Algeria, and the rival Shi'i Safavid Empire in Iran in the early sixteenth century which transformed Iraq into a contested borderland. In North Africa west of Egypt, local Berber dynasties took control, and in the Iberian peninsula Ferdinand III of Castile (r. 1217–52) pushed the Muslims out of Cordoba and Seville into the enclave of Granada, while Jaime I of Aragon (r. 1213–76) conquered Muslim Valencia. Sultans, khans and kings with no serious pretensions to universal empire now ruled across the old Islamic lands.

The impact of all this on society and culture varied from place to place. For Iraq it was a disaster which compounded the agricultural problems of preceding centuries and led to the final collapse of the old irrigation systems of Sasanian provenance. War and unbearable Mongol taxation caused peasants to flee the land in desperation and the once fertile land which had fed Baghdad became a wasteland. Its complete disintegration was only prevented by the intervention of Rashid al-Din, a Persian Jew who converted to Islam and was chief minister to the Mongol ruler Ghazan Khan. According to Rashid al-Din's own – perhaps rather biased – testimony, he pointed out to the Mongols that they would cease to make any money out of Iraq at all if the peasants ran away *en masse* and single-handedly reformed the tax system and administration so that it was profitable but also tolerable for the beleaguered peasants.

Despite such straitened circumstances, scientific and cultural activity did not cease completely. Once the dust had settled, cultural influences from China stimulated a flowering of the arts, most notably in ceramics, tilework and miniature painting. Chinghiz Khan's grandson Hulegu killed the last 'Abbasid caliph but also patronized the foundation of a new observatory at Maragha in Azerbayjan at the instigation of the Persian Shi'i polymath Nasir al-Din Tusi. In the same region, a new monastery was established where the famous Christian clergyman Bar Hebraeus maintained the 'Abbasid scientific heritage by lecturing on Euclid and Ptolemy.[2]

For Syria and Egypt the change was less dramatic, although news of events to the east caused widespread panic and facilitated a political revolution. The descendants of Salah al-Din were replaced by their Turkish slave soldiers, the Mamluks, who came to power on the basis that they alone could prevent the Mongol advance – which they did at the Battle of 'Ayn Jalut in 1260 – and expel the last Latin descendants of the Crusaders from Syria – an ambition fulfilled by the Mamluk sultan Qalawun in 1291. However, in social and cultural terms, the Mamluks opted for policies which emphasized continuity with the past rather than any radical break in order to overcome the strange political reality of 'slaves' ruling as sultans. They welcomed an 'Abbasid refugee from Baghdad, and he and his descendants functioned as puppet caliphs, wheeled out by the Mamluks on special occasions, until the Ottoman conquest of Egypt in 1517. They also built the hospitals, theological colleges and trading facilities which made Cairo, Damascus and Aleppo the foremost cities of the day, and paid attention to the judicious rather than simply rapacious collection of taxes throughout their domains.

Further west the most traumatic aspect of the thirteenth century was not the Mongol invasions but the Christian capture of the historically important Muslim cities of Cordoba and Seville and the sudden reduction of Muslim political power in the Iberian peninsula to a small, rugged mountain area around the city of Granada in what is now Andalucía. Although the equally important city of Toledo had fallen to Castile in 1085, the Berber Almoravids and Almohads from North Africa had more or less held the frontier for 150 years and the sudden political reversal which struck the Muslims in the mid-thirteenth century was a major blow. It was, however, on this long Mediterranean frontier, which included the Balearics, Sicily, southern Italy and the Crusader enclaves in the Levant, that some of the most interesting cultural developments of the late 'Abbasid era took place and where the cultural riches of Islam began to find a new home.

Muslim contact with Orthodox Christendom, as opposed to the Latin world, was very old indeed. The Byzantines were the Muslims' neighbours and trading and raiding brought them into constant contact from the seventh century onwards. As we have mentioned, during the translation movement, subjects of the caliph went to Byzantium seeking manuscripts of little-known texts and this may well have stimulated a new interest in pagan Greek knowledge among the Byzantines themselves. In Byzantine history, the seventh and eighth centuries are a 'dark age' during which ancient learning appears to have died out completely and the empire was riven by iconoclasm. This was, however, followed by a revival of learning in the ninth century, which was probably stimulated in part by information about the translation movement in Baghdad brought by travelling scholars and 'Abbasid requests for manuscripts, since the manuscripts re-copied in Byzantium after 800 are almost identical to those being translated into Arabic in Baghdad at the same time.³ As the translation movement progressed and new works were written in Arabic, some of these found their way to Byzantium, as did the discoveries of the Maragha astronomers later on.

Latin Christendom only became aware of the intellectual, scientific and cultural achievements of Muslim society a little later through Castilian and Aragonese conquests in Spain, the Norman capture of Sicily and, briefly, the coast of Tunisia, and finally the Crusades to the Holy Land. Christian appreciation manifested itself first in greedy consumption of the material culture of the Muslims. Christian kings and churchmen wore and were buried in opulent robes stitched from luxury Muslim fabrics. Roger II of Sicily (r. 1130–54) commissioned his famous coronation cape from Muslims who used the weaving techniques and decorative styles of Islamic monarchs, including bands of Arabic calligraphy woven in red and gold thread. He also commissioned al-Idrisi's famous geography, written in Arabic but often known simply as the *Book of Roger*, and Arabic was one of the Sicilian chancery's official languages, alongside Greek and Latin.

Norman Sicilian architecture was similarly permeated with Islamic motifs, styles and decoration to the extent that Roger's pleasure palaces, the Cuba, Ziza and Favara in Palermo, are routinely described in books on Islamic architecture. Meanwhile the ceiling of his royal chapel, undeniably a Christian building, employed an eclectic range of decoration which juxtaposed Byzantine-inspired mosaics with an Islamic honeycomb ceiling of myriad pieces, embellished with paintings of figures taken straight from the artistic repertoire of Fatimid Cairo. Norman cathedrals in Sicily show the same inventive and unconstrained adoption of a mixture of Mediterranean styles which brings to mind the eclecticism of the Umayyads, the first Muslim dynasty to encounter the cultural riches of Byzantium and Persia.

As the Sicilian court shifted its gaze away from the Muslim south to the Christian north, composition in Arabic was gradually replaced by Sicilian Italian, and the translation of Arabo-Islamic learning began, reaching its apogee at the court of Frederick II, an exotic figure who inherited the kingdom of the two Sicilies (Sicily and Naples) via his mother Constance, the daughter of Roger II. Frederick became king in 1198, the year of Averroes' death, at the tender age of 14. His reign was characterized by the ambiguity and ambivalence Christians of the time felt towards Arabo-Islamic culture and Muslims. He established a court which sought to replicate the supposed hedonism of the 'Abbasid court, as well as its literary culture and science, but render it anew in Italian. He commissioned scientific translations and attracted translators and scholars to his circle in a similar way to Alfonso X, who ruled Castile at the same time. However, he also completed the purge of Muslims from Sicily, forcibly transferring them to Lucera in southern Italy, a closed settlement of Muslims who tilled the land for him and provided manpower for his army. Although his apparent 'protection' of Muslims scandalized the papacy, he had effectively enslaved the free Muslims of Sicily and cast them out of their land.

The fascinating multilingual and multicultural world of eleventh- to thirteenth-century Sicily was only matched by that of northern Spain, where previously Muslim cities such as Toledo, Saragossa, Tarazona and Tudela were steadily added to the crowns of Castile-Léon and Aragon, and their previous Muslim rulers' libraries opened to inquisitive Christian clergymen and scholars. This was certainly the case with the library of the Banu Hud, a dynasty of mathematicians and scholars who allowed Christians to borrow their books after they had lost Saragossa in 1118 and were pensioners living in a backwater called Rueda de Jalón. Up until this time, most transmission between Latin and Arabic cultures had taken place by word of mouth, but now translation of written materials began to gather impetus, focusing in the first place on the astrological lore which had initially appealed to the Muslims themselves in the eighth century. For early translators such as Hugh of Santalla, who used the library of the Banu Hud to make translations for the Bishop of Tarazona, this was occult material not to be revealed to the ordinary man, but in the next generation a new attitude to Arabo-Islamic knowledge developed and it began to be seen as relevant to all, as science to be acquired and a religious tradition to be argued against and dismissed.[4]

Translation activity occurred in many towns but the most renowned location was Toledo, which had become Castilian in 1085 but remained imbued with Arabo-Islamic culture for at least two centuries after that date. Alfonso VI, the 'conqueror' of Toledo, gained the city by ruse as much as by battle and had previously resided in the city as a guest of its Muslim masters and had married a Muslim wife. Unlike later Castilian monarchs who saw the conquest of Muslim lands in Spain as the precursor to the expulsion of Islam and Muslims from a Christian land, Alfonso's attitude followed the more pluralistic line of earlier Muslim monarchs, and he allowed Muslims, Jews and Christians to live and work together in Toledo. Although many Muslims preferred to leave, and the Christian population was swelled by the arrival of Arabized Christians from the south, the culture of the city remained firmly Arabo-Islamic, with Jews often providing the interface between existing Arabic and new Castilian elements in the city's society and culture.

Christian overlordship oriented the city towards a new audience, that of Latin Christendom, and it soon became a magnet for scholars from northern Spain, France, Italy and the British Isles who became part of a new translation movement, which frequently passes as unrecognized as the Baghdad translation movement which preceded it and is as important. It is not an exaggeration to say that across Europe, 'the vast corpus of Greek and Arabic Aristotelian works that were made available to Latin thinkers revolutionised education and systematic thought of all sorts'.[5] Like their 'Abbasid predecessors, the translators in Toledo and other cities were not passive recipients of knowledge but actively sought out what was most relevant to the needs arising in Latin Christendom at the time and built on the Arabo-Islamic knowledge they acquired. One can also detect some of the same ambiguities that marked the Byzantine and 'Abbasid responses to pagan knowledge, expressed most picturesquely by Dante's placing of the thirteenth-century translator Michael Scot in the eighth circle of hell with other 'sorcerers'. This is particularly ironic given the inspiration Dante himself drew from Muhammad's night journey to heaven in Latin translation and the influence of Arabic poetic forms on the emergence of Dante's own style of Italian poetry.

The translators of Toledo and northern Iberia more generally consisted of Arabized Jews and Christians from the region and Latin scholars from all over Europe who learnt Arabic to engage in translations or else used Jews, Christians and occasionally Muslims conversant with Arabic to help them. The Jews formed a natural set of intermediaries because of their trade networks, which extended from Islamic lands into Christian Europe, and because of their linguistic skills. They naturally knew the language of their host society, whether it was Arabic, Persian or Romance, as well as Hebrew. It was therefore relatively simple for a Jewish scholar from the Islamic world to translate from Arabic into Hebrew while getting a co-religionist to translate from Hebrew into Latin or one of the European languages derived from it. Some Jews translated from Arabic to Castilian, enabling Christians unfamiliar with Arabic to translate the Castilian versions into Latin, the European intellectual *lingua franca*. Although not completely representative owing to his conversion to Christianity, Petrus Alfonsi, previously Moses Sepharadi (1062–1110), is one of the best known of these scholars, alongside Abraham b. Ezra (d. 1164) and Judah Ha-Levi (d. 1141), who were renowned Hebrew poets but also scientists and philosophers. However, most of the Arabized Jews who assisted Latin scholars remained anonymous contributors to this cultural movement.

The same is true of many Christians, although some names have come down to us. John of Seville, which was still a Muslim city at the start of this new translation movement, is one of the first Arabic-speaking Christians mentioned. There is also mention of a Peter of Toledo and, later, Mark of Toledo, a Christian native of the city who learnt Arabic as a child and translated the Qur'an into Latin around 1210 for the purposes of proselytism and the galvanization of the population prior to a major Castilian campaign against the Muslim Almohads who ruled to the south. Later in the thirteenth century, the Castilian school of translators, by then based as much in Seville as Toledo, enjoyed a final flourish under the patronage of Alfonso X (r. 1252–84), nicknamed 'the wise' for his interest in scholarship. However, his purpose was very much to acquire Arabo-Islamic knowledge as a precursor to shutting the door on Islam forever, an attitude which prefigured that of Ferdinand and Isabella in the fifteenth century and inspired their crusade against Muslim Granada from 1482 until its successful completion in 1492.

Native Jews and Christians worked with scholars of various European backgrounds who came to Toledo and other cities from the late eleventh to thirteenth centuries specifically to translate Arabic works into Latin. Among the best known of these scholars are Adelard of Bath (*c.* 1080–1152), Robert Ketton and Hermann of Carinthia, who was active in the mid-twelfth century, Gerard of Cremona (1114–87) and Michael Scot (d. *c.* 1235), whose name suggests a British origin although we do not actually know where he came from. Much of what these Latin scholars found worth translating was naturally exactly the same fields that the 'Abbasids had found of interest and value in the Greek, Persian and Indian corpus three centuries before, and in a similar order. Astrology and alchemy were the first 'sciences' translated, followed by astronomy and mathematics, then medicine and more abstract works of philosophy and metaphysics. Some also translated the Qur'an and other Muslim religious literature such as the life of Muhammad as ammunition for debates against Muslims and, they hoped, their conversion to Christianity. These translators worked with their Iberian colleagues, often in teams patronized either by high-placed churchmen or monarchs, including Peter the Venerable of Cluny in France, Ferdinand II of Sicily and, of course, the kings of Castile-Léon.

The biographies of a few such scholars suffice to give the flavour of the era and the nature of the materials they translated. Petrus Alfonsi is most famous for his conversion to Christianity and for the *Dialogue* he wrote between his two selves, Jewish and Christian, to explain his choice. However, he also talks at length about Arabic science in the *Dialogue* and made one of the first translations of al-Khwarazmi's astronomical tables (*zij*), which he may well have taught in England and France before returning to Aragon in the last years of his life.[6] Adelard of Bath travelled from England to Salerno, Sicily and probably Toledo around 1105. He spent another extended period of travel on the Christian–Muslim frontier between 1109 and 1116, arriving finally in Crusader Antioch before returning to Bath where he made important translations of the astronomical tables of Khwarazmi corrected by al-Majriti for the meridian of Cordoba, Euclid's *Elements* and several astrological works. Using al-Majriti's work on astrolabes composed about 1000, he wrote a treatise on the astrolabe and promoted the use of Arabic numerals and zero in Europe, as well as making a living casting royal horoscopes and writing talismans to remove mice from properties![7]

Robert Ketton, a native of Rutland, spent his life in England and Spain and held ecclesiastical benefices in both countries, including the post of archdeacon in Pamplona. Although his primary interest was astronomy and mathematics and he translated al-Khwarazmi's manual on algebra into Latin, he is better known for his translation of the Qur'an, which was commissioned by Peter the Venerable of Cluny in 1142 to assist Christian proselytism among Muslims. Robert took the interesting step of consulting Arabic works of Qur'anic exegesis to give his rather 'exuberant' paraphrase of the Qur'an entitled the *Law of Muhammad, the Pseudo-prophet* a meaning consonant with living Muslim understandings of their holy text. His translation was very popular with the reading public, although it has been criticized for the liberties it takes with the Arabic original by scholars from Juan de Segovia (*c.* 1393–1458) – who produced his own Qur'an translation – onwards.[8]

With Gerard of Cremona (*c.* 1114–87) we see a shift towards medicine and philosophy which was replicated in Toledan circles by Dominicus Gundissalinus, his collaborator. Gerard, a native of Lombardy in Italy, went to Toledo to study Arabic in order to read and translate works of Muslim science and philosophy. Although there is some debate over whether it was Gerard of Cremona or someone of the same name who translated Avicenna's *Canon of Medicine*, he was undoubtedly an important conduit of Islamic philosophical works, especially those of al-Farabi and Aristotle in his Neoplatonic guise. He also translated some Avicenna, Ptolemy's *Almagest* and numerous astronomical, mathematical and medical works, including Hunayn b. Ishaq's *Medical Matters*, the great Arabo-Islamic compendia of al-Razi, al-Majusi and al-Zahrawi, and specialist treatises in the areas in which the Arabs excelled – ophthalmology, surgery and pharmacology. After his death his students estimated that he had translated 87 works, even though his humility had prevented him from signing several of them. His version of the *Almagest* was the sole one available in Latin for centuries and, as a result of his medical translations, Arabo-Islamic medicine began to circulate throughout Latin Christendom.

Michael Scot, who worked in Toledo and Bologna and spent the last years of his life at the court of Frederick II, was another translator of philosophy and medicine, although he has entered the popular imagination as an alchemist and magician through the possibly false attribution to him of various alchemical works. He translated al-Bitruji's *On the Principles of Astronomy* in Toledo in 1217, a mere 17 years after its composition, then a series of Arabo-Islamic medical works in the early 1220s in Bologna, before attracting the attention of Frederick II. His philosophical translations included works by Aristotle and several of Averroes' commentaries which were still cutting-edge Islamic philosophy given that Averroes had only died around three decades before in 1198. Scot also wrote a number of elementary handbooks based on Arabic learning which helped promote a new university curriculum in the Latin West, which began with 'a highly Arabised set of Aristotelian studies' in which the Arabo-Islamic element was a vital link between Greece and the Latin West.[9]

The combined translations of Gerard of Cremona and Michael Scot gave Latin schoolmen access to two competing views of Aristotle: the Neoplatonic view cultivated by al-Farabi and Avicenna which was based on the false – but stimulating – attribution of some Neoplatonic works to Aristotle, and the view of Averroes who had attempted to strip away this Neoplatonic veneer. Thomas Aquinas and other Latin scholars eagerly read and questioned the ideas of al-Farabi, Avicenna and Averroes, and in a strange twist of fate the last great philosopher of Muslim Spain, Averroes, found a much larger audience in Europe where Latin Averroism was all the rage than in the Islamic world where he left few disciples, a natural consequence perhaps of the sudden political collapse of Muslim power in Iberia which made philosophy one of many luxuries to be forgone.

Arabo-Islamic medicine had a similarly lasting impact on Latin Christendom. The School of Salerno used al-Majusi's section on surgery from the eleventh century, and his entire compendium was translated by Stephen of Antioch in 1127 and again by Gerard of Cremona. Its popularity endured for several centuries, as its printing in Venice in 1492 and Lyons in 1523 shows. Al-Zahrawi's work on surgery was indispensable for centuries, as was al-Razi's *Kitab al-Hawi fi'l-Tibb*, known as the *Continens* in Latin. Avicenna's *Canon of Medicine* was used in the medical school of Montpellier until at least 1557 and at other French universities into the seventeenth century. By the thirteenth and fourteenth centuries, Avicennan medical works were circulating throughout Europe, from Italy and France to Denmark. Equally well received was Ibn Butlan's *Taqwim al-Sihha*, which was partially translated for one of the kings of Sicily and Naples, either Manfred (d. 1266) or Charles of Anjou (d. 1285), entitled *Tacuini Sanitatis*. It was copied numerous times in northern Italy and ultimately printed in Strasbourg in 1531.

Naturally these Arabic materials did not go unquestioned, but in the same spirit as the Arab physicians European doctors also took medicine further and added a new layer in the accretion of knowledge and understanding that ultimately became modern medicine. After a hiatus, European doctors showed renewed interest in Arabo-Islamic medicine in the sixteenth century, and travellers began to bring back accounts of Middle Eastern medicine and pharmaceuticals. Al-Razi's treatise on smallpox and measles was even used during eighteenth-century European debates on the benefits of inoculation and variolation.[10] At the same time, Western medicine began to be translated into Arabic and Persian, and Islamic medicine began to be viewed, like Middle Eastern societies themselves, as a 'backward' folk tradition at variance with the 'modern' scientific medicine developing in Europe.

In the Middle Ages attitudes were very different. Although Byzantine and Latin churchmen could not help but see Islam as a heresy and Muhammad as a false prophet, neither Orthodox nor Latin Christians could fail to marvel at the material and intellectual riches of Islamic society, albeit rather grudgingly on occasion. The 'Abbasid caliphate as an institution and an ideal was central to the process whereby Muslims built upon the foundations laid by the Arabs during the conquest era and the Umayyad caliphate. The empire they crafted took much from the imperial pasts of the Mediterranean basin and Middle East – Greek, Roman, Byzantine and Persian – but emerged as something novel. New cities rose on the routes taken by Muslim armies, merchants and pilgrims, while many ancient cities received a fresh lease of life; commerce flourished as merchants of all religious persuasions travelled freely from Spain to China and down into sub-Saharan Africa. The new faith of Islam gradually won over the majority of the inhabitants of the Middle East, North Africa and Spain, but Christians and Jews continued to live in Islamic lands in keeping with Islam's acceptance of monotheistic pluralism. That is not to say that minorities did not suffer inhibitions on their freedom of worship or hostility on occasion, but they did have a legally recognized place in society in contrast to Jews, or indeed Muslims, in Christian lands at the same time.

Alongside the Muslim empire's geopolitical continuity with the past, and Islam's self-appointed role as the last Abrahamic monotheism, the 'Abbasid age also witnessed a flowering of knowledge and science, remarkable by any standard. Although it is common to see this as a Baghdad-centred movement, produced when caliphs rather than their military commanders or 'protectors' really ruled, it was much more than that in both time and space. Certainly Baghdad was the place where translation began in earnest and the early caliphs fostered the translation movement through their patronage of scholars, libraries and intellectual salons, but translation was a fashion which gripped the entire elite and complemented the intellectual activity already taking place elsewhere in Iraq, especially Basra. It quickly spread beyond the Baghdad court circle to the courts of governors all over the eastern Islamic world, from Rayy in Iran to Bukhara in Transoxania and to Ghazna in Afghanistan.

Moreover the constant diminution of the political power of the 'Abbasid caliphs did not immediately undermine the notion of the caliphate, which remained a cherished ideal, and the emulation of the Baghdad paradigm by rival caliphs played a vital role in taking knowledge and culture out to the furthest western frontiers of the Islamic world, the deserts of North Africa and the Pyrenees in Spain. Although it is common to see the 'Abbasids as a solidly Middle Eastern regime with their face turned towards Iran, Khurasan and Transoxania, this is really an imposition of the old East–West dichotomy between Rome and Greece on one side and the Persians on the other which is not borne out by the realities of the Islamic world at the time. It is easy to forget that troops from Khurasan established garrisons as far west as Tunisia and that the city-state of Tahert in Algeria was founded by a man of mixed Persian–Tunisian origin, that the Fatimids, who launched their bid to form a Shi'i caliphate in North Africa, began their career in Iraq, and that even the Umayyads of Cordoba, who never recognized the 'Abbasids politically, eagerly copied the habits of the Iraqi elite in dress, architecture and the promotion of the sciences.

This was a Mediterranean society stretching the length of the old Roman Empire and beyond. As in all pre-modern societies most people did not move that far from home, but certain quintessentially Islamic institutions – the pilgrimage and journeys 'in search of knowledge' – nurtured a striking level of mobility. All Muslims, men and women, were required to perform the pilgrimage at least once in their lifetime if they had the resources to do so, and poor pilgrims living on charity and peddling cheap trinkets rubbed shoulders with princesses and their entourages in the environs of Mecca and Medina. Scholars who sought knowledge often spent years moving from one city to another, studying with the eminent professors of each place before settling far from home, or returning imbued with an international Islamic ethos which transcended their original parochial outlook. The study of *hadith* reached Cordoba around 50 years after it had begun to galvanize the political and intellectual communities of Iraq, carried by such scholars. Astronomy, medicine and philosophy also travelled quickly from one end of the Mediterranean to the other and speedily breached confessional lines, as the fertile interactions between Islamic and Jewish philosophy, the prominence of Christian doctors and the later reception of Arabo-Islamic knowledge in Latin Christian circles show.

All this made the culture and society of the Islamic lands during the 'Abbasid caliphate vibrant, sophisticated and a source of admiration to outsiders. There was a dark side of poverty and deprivation, of the exploitation of slaves, and the depredations of military men with little concern for the people whose lives they ruined, but none of this is totally absent from any society, and neither Greece nor Rome had very good human rights records by the standards of today. Nevertheless this should not dent our appreciation of what they did achieve. The same should be true for classical Islamic civilization which built on the foundations of the Mediterranean and Middle Eastern empires which preceded it and ultimately transmitted its knowledge of both the mundane and sublime to Latin Christendom. It was then the achievement of Christian Europeans to take that knowledge in directions relevant to their own culture and society.

The Renaissance was a European phenomenon, but such a rebirth of classical knowledge depended in part on its preservation and elaboration by Arabic-speakers in Islamic lands. For European intellectuals of the twelfth to sixteenth centuries this was not really a contentious point: many scholars and scientists of the Arabo-Islamic world were household names in university circles, and Arabic was one of the languages all MA students at Oxford had to study in the seventeenth century. It is only in modern times that we have forgotten this connection. However, in reality, we are all part of the story of human civilization which began in the Middle East in the sixth millennium BCE and all those who insist upon the irreconcilable division between the 'West' and 'Islam' would do well to step down from their soapboxes to read a little history.

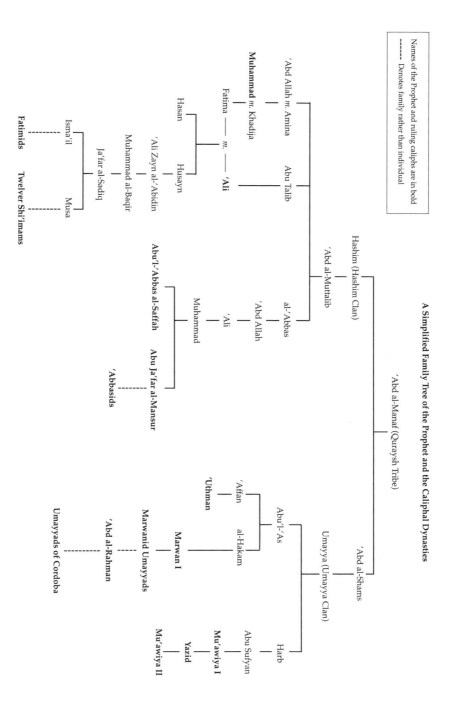

A Simplified Family Tree of the Prophet and the Caliphal Dynasties

Names of the Prophet and ruling caliphs are in bold
- - - - - Denotes family rather than individual

'Abd al-Manaf (Quraysh Tribe)

Hashim (Hashim Clan)

'Abd al-Muttalib

'Abd Allah *m.* Amina

Muhammad *m.* Khadija

Fatima ——— *m.* ——— **'Ali**

Abu Talib

Hasan

Husayn

'Ali Zayn al-'Abidin

Muhammad al-Baqir

Ja'far al-Sadiq

Isma'il

Musa

Fatimids

Twelver Shi'i imams

al-'Abbas

'Abd Allah

'Ali

Muhammad

Abu'l-'Abbas al-Saffah

Abu Ja'far al-Mansur

'Abbasids

'Abd al-Shams

Umayya (Umayya Clan)

Abu'l-'As

'Affan

'Uthman

al-Hakam

Marwan I

Marwanid Umayyads

'Abd al-Rahman

Umayyads of Cordoba

Harb

Abu Sufyan

Mu'awiya I

Yazid

Mu'awiya II

215

Notes

Introduction

1. Carl Ernst, *Following Muhammad: Rethinking Islam in the Contemporary World* (Chapel Hill: University of North Carolina Press, 2003), p 6.

Chapter 1. A Stormy Sea

1. Ibn Khaldun, *The Muqaddimah: An Introduction to History*, translated by Franz Rosenthal (New York: Pantheon, 1958), vol. 1, p 330.
2. See Hugh Kennedy, *The Early 'Abbasid Caliphate: A Political History* (London: Croom Helm, 1981) and Hugh Kennedy, *The Court of the Caliphs: When Baghdad Ruled the World* (London: Weidenfeld and Nicolson, 2004).
3. al-Tabari, *The History of al-Tabari (Tarikh al-rusul wa'l-muluk)*, edited by Ehsan Yar-Shater, 38 volumes (Albany: State University of New York Press, 1985–), vol. 9, p 188.
4. Qur'an 2:30–1.
5. Qur'an 38:26.
6. al-Tabari, *The History of al-Tabari*, vol. 15, p 197.
7. 'Ali b. Muhammad Mawardi, *The Ordinances of Government: al-Ahkam al-Sultaniyya wa'l-Wilaya al-Diniyya*, translated by Wafaa Hassan Wahba (Reading: Garnet, 1996, reprinted 2000), p 16.
8. al-Tabari, *The History of al-Tabari*, vol. 15, p 213.
9. *Ibid.*, vol. 15, p 216.
10. *Ibid.*, vol. 15, p 259.
11. *Ibid.*, vol. 17, pp 214–15.
12. *Ibid.*, vol. 17, p 225.
13. *Ibid.*, vol. 18, p 4.
14. *Ibid.*, vol. 18, p 185.
15. *Ibid.*, vol. 38, p 58.
16. *Ibid.*, vol. 19, pp 151–4.
17. *Ibid.*, vol. 26, p 127.
18. Patricia Crone, 'Mawla', *Encyclopedia of Islam* 2, vol. 6, p 876.
19. Hugh Kennedy, *The Prophet and the Age of the Caliphates* (London: Longman, 1986), pp 124–5.

20. al-Tabari, *The History of al-Tabari*, vol. 27, p 166.
21. *Ibid.*, vol. 27, p 175.
22. *Ibid.*, vol. 28, p 20.
23. *Ibid.*, vol. 28, p 19.
24. Adam Silverstein, *Postal Systems in the Premodern World* (Cambridge: Cambridge University Press, 2007), pp 81–2.
25. al-Tabari, *The History of al-Tabari*, vol. 30, p 42.
26. *Ibid.*, vol. 30, p 182.
27. *Ibid.*, vol. 31, p 22.
28. *Ibid.*, vol. 28, p 281.
29. *Ibid.*, vol. 32, p 61.
30. *Ibid.*, vol. 32, p 84.
31. *Ibid.*, vol. 32, p 211.
32. Charles Pellat, *The Life and Works of Jahiz*, translated into English by D.M. Hawke (London: Routledge and Kegan Paul, 1969), p 49.
33. al-Tabari, *The History of al-Tabari*, vol. 33, p 27.
34. *Ibid.*, vol. 33, pp 11–12.
35. *Ibid.*, vol. 33, pp 25–6.
36. Ibn al-Athir, 'Izz al-Din, *Annals of the Saljuq Turks: Selections from al-Kamil fi'l-Tarikh of 'Izz al-Din Ibn al-Athir*, translated and annotated by D.S. Richards (London: RoutledgeCurzon, 2002), p 178.
37. *Ibid.*, p 171.
38. *Ibid.*, p 187.
39. Amin Maalouf, *The Crusades through Arab Eyes* (London: al-Saqi, 2004), p 39.

Chapter 2. From Baghdad to Cordoba

1. Muhammad b. Ahmad al-Muqaddasi, *The Best Divisions of Knowledge of the Regions: A Translation of Ahsan al-taqasim fi ma'rifat al-aqalim*, translated by Basil A. Collins (Reading: Garnet, 1994), p 108.
2. *Ibid.*, p 208.
3. See Simon O'Meara, 'The foundation legend of Fez and other Islamic cities in light of the life of the Prophet', in Bennison and Gascoigne (eds), *Cities in the Pre-Modern Islamic World: The Urban Impact of Religion, State and Society* (London: RoutledgeCurzon, 2007), pp 27–41.
4. al-Isfahani, quoted in R. Hoyland, *Arabia and the Arabs* (London and New York: Routledge, 2001), p 241.
5. al-Tabari, *The History of al-Tabari*, vol. 13, p 63.
6. *Ibid.*, vol. 13, p 67.
7. *Ibid.*, vol. 13, p 68.
8. Robert Hillenbrand, *Islamic Architecture: Form, Function and Meaning* (Edinburgh: Edinburgh University Press, 2000), p 34.
9. al-Tabari, *The History of al-Tabari*, vol. 13, pp 69, 73.
10. Nezar Alsayyad, *Cities and Caliphs: On the Genesis of Arab Muslim Urbanism*

(New York, Westport, Connecticut and London: Greenwood Press, 1991), pp 95–6.

11.	al-Muqaddasi, *The Best Divisions of Knowledge of the Regions*, p 385.

12.	A. Guillaume, *The Life of Muhammad: A Translation of Ishaq's Sirat Rasul Allah* (London: Oxford University Press, 1955), p 182.

13.	*Ibid.*

14.	al-Muqaddasi, *The Best Divisions of Knowledge of the Regions*, p 146.

15.	See Donald Whitcomb, 'An urban structure for the early Islamic city: an archaeological hypothesis', in Bennison and Gascoigne (eds), *Cities in the Pre-Modern Islamic World*, pp 15–26.

16.	al-Tabari, *The History of al-Tabari*, vol. 28, p 243.

17.	*Ibid.*, vol. 28, pp 245–6

18.	Hillenbrand, *Islamic Architecture*, p 395.

19.	*Ibid.*

20.	al-Tabari, *The History of al-Tabari*, vol. 29, p 8.

21.	Ibn Hayyan, *Al-Muqtabis fi Akhbar Balad al-Andalus*, edited by Abdurrahman Ali al-Hajji (Beirut: Dar Assakafa, 1965), p 22.

22.	Ibn Hawqal, *Kitab al-Masalik wa'l-Mamalik*, edited by M.J. de Goeje (Leiden: Brill, 1873), p 77.

23.	al-Muqaddasi, *The Best Divisions of Knowledge of the Regions*, p 181.

24.	Ibn Jubayr, *The Travels of Ibn Jubayr*, translated by Ronald Broadhurst (first published London, 1952, republished by Goodword Books, New Delhi, 2001), p 226.

25.	al-Muqaddasi, *The Best Divisions of Knowledge of the Regions*, p 146.

26.	Nasir-i Khusraw, *Nāṣer-e Khosrow's Book of Travels (Safarnāma)*, translated by W.M. Thackston, Persian Heritage Series 6 (New York: Bibliotheca Persica, 1986), p 52.

27.	al-Muqaddasi, *The Best Divisions of Knowledge of the Regions*, p 182.

28.	'Abd al-Malik Ibn Sahib al-Salat, *Tarikh al-mann bi'l-imama*, edited by 'Abd al-Hadi al-Tazi (Beirut: Dar al-Andalus, 1964), p 474.

29.	al-Tabari, *The History of al-Tabari*, vol. 37, p 176.

30.	*Ibid.*, vol. 38, p 47.

31.	Nasir-i Khusraw, *Book of Travels*, p 16.

32.	Ibn Jubayr, *Travels*, p 277.

33.	Paul Wheatley, *The Places Where Men Pray Together* (Chicago: University of Chicago Press, 2001), p 247.

34.	al-Muqaddasi, *The Best Divisions of Knowledge of the Regions*, p 384.

35.	*Ibid.*, p 367.

36.	Nasir-i Khusraw, *Book of Travels*, p 13.

37.	*Ibid.*, p 53.

38.	Ibn Jubayr, *Travels*, p 33.

39.	al-Muqaddasi, *The Best Divisions of Knowledge of the Regions*, p 380.

40.	'Abd al-Rahman al-Shayzari, *The Book of the Islamic Market Inspector: Nihayat al-rutba fi talab al-hisba by 'Abd al-Rahman b. Nasr al-Shayzari*, translated by R.P. Buckley, *Journal of Semitic Studies*, Supplement 9 (Oxford: Oxford University Press, 1999), p 36.

41. Pellat, *The Life and Works of Jahiz*, p 109.
42. al-Muqaddasi, *The Best Divisions of Knowledge of the Regions*, pp 378, 182.
43. Nasir-i Khusraw, *Book of Travels*, p 52.
44. *Ibid.*, pp 46–7.
45. *Ibid.*, p 13.
46. al-Muqaddasi, *The Best Divisions of Knowledge of the Regions*, pp 383, 266.
47. Nasir-i Khusraw, *Book of Travels*, pp 19, 3.
48. *Ibid.*, pp 7–8.
49. *Ibid.*, pp 9, 13.
50. Ibn Jubayr, *Travels*, pp 226, 238.
51. *Ibid.*, pp 286–7.
52. al-Muqaddasi, *The Best Divisions of Knowledge of the Regions*, p 381.
53. Ibn Jubayr, *Travels*, pp 43–4.
54. 'Abd al-Wahid al-Marrakushi, *Al-Mu'jib fi Talkhis Akhbar al-Maghrib*, edited by Muhammad Sa'id al-Aryan (Cairo, 1963), p 364.
55. Lisan al-Din Ibn al-Khatib, *al-Ihata fi Akhbar Gharnata*, 2 vols. (Cairo: al-Tiba'a al-Masriyya, 1974), vol. 2, pp 50–1.
56. Ibn Jubayr, *Travels*, p 40.

Chapter 3. Princes and Beggars

1. al-Muqaddasi, *The Best Divisions of Knowledge of the Regions*, p 438.
2. Qur'an 5:69.
3. Qur'an 49:13.
4. James Monroe, *The Shu'ubiyya in al-Andalus: The Risala of Ibn García and Five Refutations* (Berkeley: University of California Press, 1970), p 24.
5. al-Muqaddasi, *The Best Divisions of Knowledge of the Regions*, p 198.
6. al-Tabari, *The History of al-Tabari*, vol. 38, p 45.
7. *Ibid.*, vol. 33, p 32.
8. Ibn Hayyan, *al-Muktabis III: Chronique du règne du caliphe umaiyade 'Abd Allah à Cordoue*, edited by P. Melchor Antuña (Paris: Geuthner, 1937), p 63.
9. *Ibid.*, p 66.
10. al-Tabari, *The History of al-Tabari*, vol. 29, p 258.
11. al-Muqaddasi, *The Best Divisions of Knowledge of the Regions*, pp 216–17.
12. al-Tabari, *The History of al-Tabari*, vol. 38, p 46.
13. *Ibid.*, vol. 30, p 321.
14. al-Muqaddasi, *The Best Divisions of Knowledge of the Regions*, p 79.
15. *Ibid.*, p 380.
16. al-Shayzari, *The Book of the Islamic Market Inspector*, p 176.
17. Philip Kennedy, *Abu Nuwas: A Genius of Poetry* (Oxford: Oneworld, 2005), p 61.
18. al-Tabari, *The History of al-Tabari*, vol. 31, p 238.
19. al-Mawardi, *The Ordinances of Government*, p 273.

20. Michael Dols, *The Black Death in the Middle East* (Princeton: Princeton University Press, 1977), p 23.
21. *Ibid.*, p 297.
22. al-Shayzari, *The Book of the Islamic Market Inspector*, p 115.
23. *Ibid.*
24. Michael Dols, 'The leper in medieval Islamic society', *Speculum* 58:4 (1983), pp 891–916.
25. Qur'an 6:151, 17:31.
26. Diana Richmond, *'Antar and 'Abla: A Bedouin Romance* (London: Quartet, 1978), p 40.
27. See Hugh Kennedy, *The Court of the Caliphs*, paperback edition (London: Phoenix, 2005), pp 166–72.
28. See Delia Cortese and Simonetta Calderini, *Women and the Fatimids in the World of Islam* (Edinburgh: Edinburgh University Press, 2006), pp 46–58.
29. See D. Fairchild Ruggles, 'Mothers of a hybrid dynasty: race, genealogy, and acculturation in al-Andalus', *Journal of Medieval and Early Modern Studies* 34:1 (2004), pp 65–94, pp 69–73.
30. al-Marrakushi, *Al-Mu'jib fi Talkhis Akhbar al-Maghrib*, p 84.
31. Ibn al-Athir, *Annals of the Saljuk Turks*, pp 203–4.
32. al-Marrakushi, *Al-Mu'jib fi Talkhis Akhbar al-Maghrib*, p 253.
33. al-Shayzari, *The Book of the Islamic Market Inspector*, p 39.
34. *Ibid.*, p 49.
35. *Ibid.*, pp 89, 90.
36. *Ibid.*, p 127.
37. *Ibid.*, pp 105–7.
38. al-Muqaddasi, *The Best Divisions of Knowledge of the Regions*, p 380.
39. Ibn al-Athir, *Annals of the Saljuk Turks*, p 272.
40. Ibn Khaldun, *The Muqaddimah*, p 22.
41. Cynthia Robinson, *Medieval Andalusian Courtly Culture in the Mediterranean: Hadith Bayad wa Riyad* (London and New York: Routledge, 2007), p 26.
42. *al-Muwatta of Imam Malik b. Anas*, translated by Aisha Abdurrahman Bewley (London and New York: Kegan Paul, 1989), p 108.
43. S. Goitein, *A Mediterranean Society: The Jewish Communities of the Arab World as Portrayed in the Documents of the Cairo Geniza* (Berkeley: University of California Press, 1967–), vol. 2, p 382.
44. al-Kindi, *Apology*, reproduced in N.A. Newman, *Christian–Muslim Dialogue: A Collection of Documents from the First Three Centuries of Islam (632–900 AD)* (Hatfield, PA: Interdisciplinary Biblical Research Institute, 1993), p 432.
45. *Ibid.*, p 387.
46. Camille Adang, *Muslim Writers on Judaism and the Hebrew Bible* (Leiden: Brill, 1996), p 25.
47. al-Jahiz, quoted in Newman, *Christian–Muslim Dialogue*, p 705.
48. Jessica Coope, *The Martyrs of Cordoba: Community and Family Conflict in an Age of Mass Conversion* (Lincoln and London: University of Nebraska Press,

1995), pp 7–8.

49. Paul Alvarus, quoted in Jessica Coope, *The Martyrs of Cordoba*, p 8.

50. Carleton Sage, *Paul Albar of Cordoba: Studies on His Life and Writings* (Washington DC: Catholic University of America Press, 1943), p 194.

51. al-Muqaddasi, *The Best Divisions of Knowledge of the Regions*, p 193.

52. *Ibid.*, p 152

53. al-Tabari, *The History of al-Tabari*, vol. 38, p 44.

54. al-Muqaddasi, *The Best Divisions of Knowledge of the Regions*, p 374.

55. *Ibid.*, pp 388–9.

56. Amin Tibi, *The Tibyan: The Memoirs of 'Abd Allah b. Buluggin, Last Zirid Amir of Granada* (Leiden: Brill, 1986), p 75.

57. Milka Levy-Rubin, 'New evidence relating to the process of islamisation in Palestine in the early Muslim period: the case of Samaria', *Journal of the Economic and Social History of the Orient* 43:3 (2000), pp 257–76.

58. *Risala* of Abu Dulaf, quoted in C.E. Bosworth, *The Medieval Islamic Underworld: The Banu Sasan in Arabic Society and Literature*, 2 vols. (Leiden: Brill, 1976), vol. 2, p 191.

59. *Ibid.*, vol. 2, p 207.

Chapter 4. The Lifeblood of Empire

1. Pellat, *The Life and Works of Jahiz*, p 44.

2. Hoyland, *Arabia and the Arabs*, p 108.

3. Guillaume, *Ishaq's Sirat Rasul Allah*, pp 79–80.

4. *Ibid.*, p 82.

5. Qur'an 2:275.

6. Eliyahu Ashtor, 'Prolegomena to the medieval history of Oriental Jewry', in *Jews and the Mediterranean Economy* (London: Variorum, 1983), p 56.

7. Guillaume, *Ishaq's Sirat Rasul Allah*, p 84.

8. Ibn Jubayr, *Travels*, p 26.

9. K.N. Chaudhuri, *Trade and Civilisation in the Indian Ocean: An Economic History from the Rise of Islam to 1750* (Cambridge: Cambridge University Press, 1985), p 36.

10. *Ibid.*, p 51.

11. al-Muqaddasi, *The Best Divisions of Knowledge of the Regions*, p 370.

12. al-Shayzari, *The Book of the Islamic Market Inspector*, pp 102–3.

13. Abu'l-Fadl Ja'far al-Dimashqi, *Beauties of Commerce*, quoted in R. Lopez, I. Raymond and O. Constable (eds), *Medieval Trade in the Mediterranean World* (New York: Columbia University Press, 2001), p 24.

14. S. Goitein, *A Mediterranean Society*, vol. 1, p 286.

15. Ibn Jubayr, *Travels*, pp 63–4.

16. *Ibid.*, p 103.

17. *Ibid.*, pp 116–17.

18. *Ibid.*, p 188.

19. *Ibid.*, p 132.

20. al-Mawardi, *The Ordinances of Government*, p 279.
21. Ibn Jubayr, *Travels*, p 131.
22. *Ibid.*, pp 189–90, 192.
23. *Ibid.*, p 30.
24. Benjamin Foster, 'Agoranomos and muhtasib', *Journal of the Economic and Social History of the Orient* 13:2 (1970), pp 128–44.
25. al-Shayzari, *The Book of the Islamic Market Inspector*, p 40.
26. *Ibid.*, p 43.
27. Eliyahu Ashtor, 'Banking instruments in East and West', *Journal of European Economic History* 1 (1972), pp 553–73, p 555.
28. *Ibid.*, p 557.

Chapter 5. Baghdad's 'Golden Age'

1. al-Farabi, *Alfarabi: Philosophy of Plato and Aristotle*, translated by Muhsin Mahdi with a foreword by Charles Butterworth (Ithaca, New York: Cornell University Press, 2001; first published in 1962 by the Free Press of Glencoe), p 1.
2. Erwin I.J. Rosenthal, 'The place of politics in the Philosophy of Ibn Rushd', *Bulletin of the School of Oriental and African Studies* 15:2 (1953), pp 246–78, p 254.
3. Quoted in Pellat, *The Life and Works of Jahiz*, p 47.
4. J. Pedersen [M. Rahman and R. Hillenbrand], 'Madrasa', *Encyclopedia of Islam* 2, vol. 5, p 1123.
5. Pellat, *The Life and Works of Jahiz*, p 139.
6. *Ibid.*, pp 113–14.
7. Muhammad b. Isma'il al-Bukhari, *Sahih*, 8 volumes in 4 (Cairo, 1879), vol. 3, p 29.
8. *Ibid.*, vol. 3, p 183.
9. Joseph Lowry, *Early Islamic Legal Theory: The Risala of Muhammad ibn Idris al-Shafi'i* (Leiden: Brill, 2007), p 24.
10. L. Gardet, "Ilm al-Kalam', *Encyclopedia of Islam* 2, vol. 3, p 1141.
11. Dimitri Gutas, *Greek Thought, Arabic Culture: The Graeco-Arabic Translation Movement in Baghdad and Early Abbasid Society (2nd–4th/8th–10th Centuries)* (London: Routledge, 1998).
12. George Saliba, *Islamic Science and the Making of the European Renaissance* (Cambridge, MA and London: MIT Press, 2007).
13. *Ibid.*, pp 58–64.
14. Roshdi Rashed, 'Greek into Arabic: transmission and translation', in J. Montgomery (ed), *Arabic Theology, Arabic Philosophy: From the Many to the One* (Leuven: Peeters, 2006), pp 157–98.
15. Gutas, *Greek Thought, Arabic Culture*, pp 53–60.
16. William Gohlman, *The Life of Ibn Sina: A Critical Edition and Annotated Translation* (Albany: State University of New York Press, 1974), pp 36–7.
17. al-Muqaddasi, *The Best Divisions of Knowledge of the Regions*, p 395.

18. Gohlman, *The Life of Ibn Sina*, pp 38–41.

19. Ibn al-Qifti, *Ta'rikh al-hukama'*, edited by Julius Lippert (Leipzig, 1903), p 323.

20. Gutas, *Greek Thought, Arabic Culture*, p 118.

21. *Ibid.*, p 61.

22. *Ibid.*, p 138; Bayard Dodge, *The Fihrist of al-Nadim: A Tenth Century Survey of Muslim Culture*, 2 vols. (New York and London: Columbia University Press, 1970), vol. 2, p 585.

23. Dodge, *The Fihrist of al-Nadim*, vol. 2, pp 586–90.

24. Ibn al-Qifti, *Ta'rikh al-hukama'*, p 441.

25. Dodge, *The Fihrist of al-Nadim*, vol. 2, p 645; repeated by Ibn al-Qifti, *Ta'rikh al-hukama'*, pp 315–16.

26. Ibn al-Qifti, *Ta'rikh al-hukama'*, p 174.

27. Dodge, *The Fihrist of al-Nadim*, vol. 2, pp 584, 693.

28. Ibn al-Qifti, *Ta'rikh al-hukama'*, p 173.

29. Ibn al-Qifti, *Ta'rikh al-hukama'*, pp 262–3; Dodge, *The Fihrist of al-Nadim*, vol. 2, pp 694–5.

30. Ibn al-Qifti, *Ta'rikh al-hukama'*, pp 394–5.

31. *Ibid.*, p 367.

32. Dodge, *The Fihrist of al-Nadim*, vol. 2, p 615.

33. Ibn Abi Usaybi'a, *Kitab 'uyun al-anba' fi tabaqat al-atibba'*, edited and introduced by August Müller (Konigsberg, 1884; reprinted by Gregg International Publishers, Farnborough, 1972), part 1, p 207.

34. Peter Adamson, *al-Kindi* (Oxford: Oxford University Press, 2007), pp 21–2.

35. J. Jolivet and R. Rashed, 'al-Kindi, Abu Yusuf Ya'kub b. Ishaq', *Encyclopedia of Islam 2*, vol. 5, p 122.

36. Richard Walzer, *al-Farabi on the Perfect State: Abū Nasr al-Fārābī's Mabādi' ārā' ahl al-madāna al-fādila* (Oxford: Clarendon, 1985), p 253.

37. Ibn al-Qifti, *Ta'rikh al-hukama'*, p 261.

38. L.E. Goodman, 'al-Razi, Abu Bakr Muhammad b. Zakariyya', *Encyclopedia of Islam 2*, vol. 8, p 476.

39. Ibn al-Qifti, *Ta'rikh al-hukama'*, pp 413–26.

40. Gohlman, *The Life of Ibn Sina*, pp 20–1.

41. *Ibid.*, pp 54–5.

42. Hosam Elkhadem, *Le Taqwīm al-Sihha (Tacuini Santitatis) d'Ibn Butlan: un traité médical du XIe siècle* (Louvain: Peeters, 1990), p 71.

Chapter 6. The 'Abbasid Legacy

1. Ala' ad-Din al-Juvaini, *The History of the World Conqueror*, translated from the text of Mirza Muhammad Qazvini by J.A. Boyle (Manchester: Manchester University Press, 1958), vol. 1, p 177.

2. V. Minorsky, 'Maragha', *Encyclopedia of Islam 2*, vol. 6, p 502.

3. Gutas, *Greek Thought, Arabic Culture*, pp 175–86.

4. Charles Burnett, 'The translating activity in medieval Spain', in Salma

Jayyusi (ed), *The Legacy of Muslim Spain* (Leiden: Brill, 1994), pp 1036–58, pp 1041–43.

5. Thomas Burman, 'Michael Scot and the translators', in M. Menocal, R. Scheindlin and M. Sells (eds), *The Cambridge History of Arabic Literature: The Literature of al-Andalus* (Cambridge: Cambridge University Press, 2000), pp 404–11, p 406.

6. Lourdes María Alvárez, 'Petrus Alfonsi', in Menocal, Scheindlin and Sells (eds), *The Literature of al-Andalus*, pp 282–91.

7. Burnett, 'The translating activity in medieval Spain', p 1038; 'Adelard of Bath, the first English scientist', Bath Royal Literary and Scientific Institution, www.brisi.org/adelard.htm, 10 March 2008.

8. See Thomas Burman, 'Tafsīr and translation: traditional Arabic Qur'ān exegesis and the Latin Qur'āns of Robert of Ketton and Mark of Toledo', *Speculum* 73:3 (1998), pp 703–32.

9. Burman, 'Michael Scot', p 406.

10. Emilie Savage-Smith, 'Tibb', *Encyclopedia of Islam* 2, vol. 10, p 458.

Bibliography

Reference works

Encyclopedia of Islam, new edition (Leiden: Brill, 1960–2002)
Encyclopedia of the Qur'an (Leiden: Brill, 2001)

Primary sources

al-Bukhari, Muhammad b. Isma'il, *Sahih*, 8 volumes in 4 (Cairo, 1879)
al-Farabi, *Al-Farabi on the Perfect State: Abū Nasr al-Fārābī's Mabādi' ārā' ahl al-madīna al-fādila*, revised text, introduction, commentary and translation by Richard Walzer (Oxford: Clarendon Press, 1985)
___, *Alfarabi: Philosophy of Plato and Aristotle*, translated by Muhsin Mahdi with a foreword by Charles Butterworth (Ithaca, New York: Cornell University Press, 2001; first published in 1962 by the Free Press of Glencoe)
al-Juvaini, Ala' ad-Din, *The History of the World Conqueror*, translated from the text of Mirza Muhammad Qazvini by J.A. Boyle (Manchester: Manchester University Press, 1958)
al-Marrakushi, 'Abd al-Wahid, *al-Mu'jib fi Talkhis Akhbar al-Maghrib*, edited by Muhammad Sa'id al-Aryan (Cairo, 1963)
al-Muqaddasi, Muhammad b. Ahmad, *The Best Divisions of Knowledge of the Regions: A Translation of Ahsan al-taqasim fi ma'rifat al-aqalim*, translated by Basil A. Collins (Reading: Garnet, 1994)
___, *Description de l'occident musulman au Ive-Xe siècles*, edited and translated by Charles Pellat (Algiers, 1950)
Gohlman, William, *The Life of Ibn Sina: A Critical Edition and Annotated Translation* (Albany: State University of New York Press, 1974)
Guillaume, A., *The Life of Muhammad: A Translation of Ishaq's Sirat Rasul Allah* (London: Oxford University Press, 1955)
Ibn Abi Usaybi'a, *Kitab 'uyun al-anba' fi tabaqat al-atibba'*, edited and introduced by August Müller (Konigsberg, 1884; reprinted by Gregg International Publishers, Farnborough, 1972)
Ibn al-Athir, 'Izz al-Din, *Annals of the Saljuq Turks: Selections from al-Kamil fi'l-tarikh of 'Izz al-Din Ibn al-Athir*, translated and annotated by D.S. Richards (London: RoutledgeCurzon, 2002)

Ibn Butlan, al-Mukhtar, *The Physicians' Dinner Party*, edited with an introduction by Felix Klein-Franke (Wiesbaden: Harrassowitz, 1985)

Ibn Hawqal, Abu'l-Qasim Muhammad, *Kitab al-masalik wa'l-mamalik*, edited by M.J. de Goeje (Leiden: Brill, 1873)

Ibn Hayyan, Abu Marwan, *Al-Muqtabis fi Akhbar Balad al-Andalus*, edited by Abdurrahman 'Ali al-Hajji (Beirut: Dar Assakafa, 1965)

___, *Al-Muktabis III: Chronique du règne du caliphe umaiyade 'Abd Allah à Cordoue*, edited by P. Melchor Antuña (Paris: Geuthner, 1937)

Ibn Ishaq, Hunayn, *The Book of the Ten Treatises on the Eye, Ascribed to Hunain ibn Ishaq*, translated by Max Meyerhof (Cairo: Government Press, 1928)

Ibn Jubayr, Muhammad, *The Travels of Ibn Jubayr*, translated by Ronald Broadhurst (first published London, 1952; republished by Goodword Books, New Delhi, 2001)

Ibn Khaldun, 'Abd al-Rahman, *The Muqaddimah: An Introduction to History*, translated by Franz Rosenthal (New York: Pantheon, 1958)

Ibn al-Khatib, Lisan al-Din, *al-Ihata fi akhbar Gharnata* (Cairo: al-Tiba'a al-Masriyya, 1974)

Ibn al-Qifti, Abu'l-Hasan 'Ali, *Ta'rikh al-hukama'*, edited by Julius Lippert (Leipzig, 1903)

Ibn Sahib al-Salat, 'Abd al-Malik, *Tarikh al-mann bi'l-imama*, edited by 'Abd al-Hadi al-Tazi (Beirut: Dar al-Andalus, 1964)

Malik b. Anas, *al-Muwatta of Imam Malik b. Anas*, translated by Aisha Abdurrahman Bewley (London and New York: Kegan Paul, 1989)

Mawardi, 'Ali b. Muhammad, *The Ordinances of Government: al-ahkam al-sultaniyya wa'l-wilaya al-diniyya*, translated by Wafaa Hassan Wahba (Reading: Garnet, 1996; reprinted, 2000)

Nasir-i Khusraw, *Nāṣer-e Khosrow's Book of Travels (Safarnāma)*, translated by W.M. Thackston, Persian Heritage Series 6 (New York: Bibliotheca Persica, 1986)

Tibi, Amin, *The Tibyan: The Memoirs of 'Abd Allah b. Buluggin, Last Zirid Amir of Granada* (Leiden: Brill, 1986)

Yar-Shater, E. (ed), *The History of al-Tabari (Tarikh al-rusul wa'l-muluk)*, 38 vols. (Albany: State University of New York Press, 1985–)

Secondary sources

Abu-Lughod, Janet, 'The Islamic city', *International Journal of Middle Eastern Studies* 19 (1987), pp 155–76

Abun-Nasr, Jamil, *A History of the Maghrib in the Islamic Period* (Cambridge: Cambridge University Press, 1987)

Adamson, Peter, *al-Kindi* (Oxford: Oxford University Press, 2007)

Adang, Camille, *Muslim Writers on Judaism and the Hebrew Bible* (Leiden: Brill, 1996)

Ahsan, Muhammad M., *Social Life under the 'Abbasids* (London and New York: Longman, 1979)

Alsayyad, Nezar, *Cities and Caliphs: On the Genesis of Arab Muslim Urbanism* (New York, Westport, Connecticut and London: Greenwood Press, 1991)

Alvárez, Lourdes María, 'Petrus Alfonsi', in Menocal, Scheindlin and Sells (eds), *The Literature of al-Andalus*, pp 282–91

Anderson, Glaire, 'Villa (*munya*) architecture in Umayyad Córdoba: preliminary considerations', in Anderson and Rosser-Owen (eds), *Revisiting Al-Andalus*, pp 53–79

___, and Mariam Rosser-Owen (eds), *Revisiting Al-Andalus: Perspectives on the Material Culture of Islamic Iberia and Beyond* (Leiden: Brill, 2007)

Arberry, Arthur, *The Koran Interpreted* (Oxford: Oxford University Press, paperback edition, 1983; first published by Allen and Unwin, 1955)

Ashtor, Eliyahu, 'Banking instruments in East and West', *Journal of European Economic History* 1 (1972), pp 553–73

___, 'Prolegomena to the medieval history of Oriental Jewry', in *Jews and the Mediterranean Economy* (London: Variorum, 1983)

___, *Social and Economic History of the Near East in the Middle Ages* (London, 1976)

Bacharach, Jere, 'African military slaves in the medieval Middle East: the cases of Iraq (869–955) and Egypt (868–1171)', *International Journal of Middle Eastern Studies* 13:4 (1981), pp 471–95

Barrucand, Marianne and Achim Bednorz, *Moorish Architecture* (Cologne: Taschen, 1992)

Bennison, Amira, 'Muslim universalism and Western globalization', in A.G. Hopkins (ed), *Globalization in World History* (London: Pimlico, 2002), pp 74–97; (New York: Norton, 2002), pp 73–98

___, 'Power and the city in the Islamic west from the Umayyads to the Almohads', in Bennison and Gascoigne (eds), *Cities in the Pre-Modern Islamic World*, pp 65–95

___, and Alison Gascoigne (eds), *Cities in the Pre-Modern Islamic World: The Urban Impact of Religion, State and Society* (London: RoutledgeCurzon, 2007)

Berkey, Jonathan, *The Formation of Islam: Religion and Society in the Near East, 600–1800* (Cambridge: Cambridge University Press, 2003)

Blankinship, Khalid Yahya, 'The tribal factor in the 'Abbâsid revolution: the betrayal of the Imâm Ibrâhîm b. Muhammad', *Journal of the American Oriental Society* 108:4 (1988), pp 589–603

Bloom, Jonathan, *Arts of the City Victorious: Art and Architecture in Fatimid North Africa and Egypt* (New Haven and London: Yale University Press, 2007)

___, 'Ceremonial and sacred space in early Fatimid Cairo', in Bennison and Gascoigne (eds), *Cities in the Pre-Modern Islamic World*, pp 96–114

___, (ed), *Early Islamic Art and Architecture* (Aldershot: Ashgate, 2000)

Bosworth, Clifford Edmund, *The Medieval Islamic Underworld: The Banu Sasan in Arabic Society and Literature*, 2 vols. (Leiden: Brill, 1976)

Brett, Michael, *Ibn Khaldun and the Medieval Maghrib* (Aldershot: Ashgate, 1999)

____, *The Rise of the Fatimids: The World of the Mediterranean and the Middle East in the Fourth Century of the Hijra, Tenth Century CE* (Leiden: Brill, 2001)

Brown, Daniel, *A New Introduction to Islam* (Oxford: Blackwell, 2004)

Buckley, R.P., *The Book of the Islamic Market Inspector: Nihayat al-rutba fi talab al-hisba by 'Abd al-Rahman b. Nasr al-Shayzari*, Journal of Semitic Studies Supplement 9 (Oxford: Oxford University Press, 1999)

____, 'The Muhtasib', *Arabica* 39 (1992), pp 59–117

Burman, Thomas, 'Michael Scot and the translators', in Menocal, Scheindlin and Sells (eds), *The Cambridge History of Arabic Literature: The Literature of al-Andalus*, pp 404–11

____, 'Tafsīr and translation: traditional Arabic Qur'ān exegesis and the Latin Qur'āns of Robert of Ketton and Mark of Toledo', *Speculum* 73:3 (1998), pp 703–32

Burnett, Charles, 'The translating activity in medieval Spain', in Jayyusi (ed), *The Legacy of Muslim Spain*, pp 1036–58

Canard, Marius, 'Le cérémonial fatimide et le cérémonial byzantin; essai de comparaison', *Byzantion* 21 (1951), pp 355–420

Chaudhuri, K.N., *Trade and Civilisation in the Indian Ocean: An Economic History from the Rise of Islam to 1750* (Cambridge: Cambridge University Press, 1985)

Constable, Olivia, *Housing the Stranger in the Mediterranean World* (Cambridge: Cambridge University Press, 2003)

____, *Trade and Traders in Muslim Spain* (Cambridge: Cambridge University Press, 1994)

____, R. Lopez and I. Raymond (eds), *Medieval Trade in the Mediterranean World* (New York: Columbia University Press, 2001)

Cook, Michael, *Commanding Right and Forbidding Wrong in Islamic Thought* (Cambridge: Cambridge University Press, 2000)

Coope, Jessica, *The Martyrs of Cordoba: Community and Family Conflict in an Age of Mass Conversion* (Lincoln and London: University of Nebraska Press, 1995)

Cooperson, Michael, *Al-Ma'mun* (Oxford: Oneworld Publications, 2005)

Cortes, Delia and Simonetta Calderini, *Women and the Fatimids in the World of Islam* (Edinburgh: Edinburgh University Press, 2006)

Coulson, Noel, *A History of Islamic Law* (Edinburgh: Edinburgh University Press, 1964)

Crone, Patricia, *From Kavad to al-Ghazali: Religion, Law and Political Thought in the Near East c.600–c.1100* (Aldershot: Ashgate, 2005)

____, *Meccan Trade and the Rise of Islam* (Princeton: Princeton University Press, 1987)

____, *Medieval Islamic Political Thought* (Edinburgh: Edinburgh University Press, 2005)

____, *Slaves on Horses: The Evolution of the Islamic Polity* (Cambridge: Cambridge University Press, 1980)

____, and Martin Hinds, *God's Caliph: Religious Authority in the First Centuries of*

Islam (Cambridge: Cambridge University Press, 1986)

Daftary, Farhad, *Isma'ilis: Their History and Doctrines* (Cambridge: Cambridge University Press, 1990)

___, *A Short History of the Isma'ilis: Traditions of a Muslim Community* (Edinburgh: Edinburgh University Press, 1998)

Dodge, Bayard, *The Fihrist of al-Nadim: A Tenth Century Survey of Muslim Culture*, 2 vols. (New York and London: Columbia University Press, 1970)

Dols, Michael, *The Black Death in the Middle East* (Princeton: Princeton University Press, 1977)

___, 'Insanity in Byzantine and Islamic medicine', *Dumbarton Oaks Papers* 38 (1984), pp 135–48

___, 'The leper in medieval Islamic society', *Speculum* 58:4 (1983), pp 891–916

Elkhadem, Hosam, *Le Taqwīm al-Sihha (Tacuini Santitatis) d'Ibn Butlan: un traité médical du XIᵉ siècle* (Leuven: Peeters, 1990)

Endress, Gerhard, 'Reading Avicenna in the madrasa: intellectual genealogies and chains of transmission of philosophy and the sciences in the Islamic east', in Montgomery (ed), *Arabic Theology, Arabic Philosophy*, pp 371–422

Ernst, Carl, *Following Muhammad: Rethinking Islam in the Contemporary World* (Chapel Hill: University of North Carolina Press, 2003)

Ess, J.V., *The Flowering of Muslim Theology* (Cambridge, MA: Harvard University Press, 2006)

Fierro, Maria Isabel and Samsó, Julio (eds), *The Formation of al-Andalus 2: Language, Religion, Culture and the Sciences* (Aldershot: Ashgate, 1998)

Forcada, Miquel, 'Astronomy, astrology and the sciences of the ancients in early al-Andalus (2nd/8th–3rd/9th centuries)', *Zeitschrift für Geschichte der Arabisch-Islamischen Wissenschaften* 16 (2004–5), pp 1–74

___, 'Ibn Bajja and the classification of the sciences in al-Andalus', *Arabic Sciences and Philosophy* 16 (2006), pp 287–307

___, 'Investigating the sources of prosopography: the case of the astrologers of 'Abd al-Rahman II', *Medieval Prosopography* 23 (2002), pp 73–100

Foster, Benjamin, 'Agoranomos and muhtasib', *Journal of the Economic and Social History of the Orient* 13:2 (1970), pp 128–44

Gabrieli, Francesco, *Arab Historians of the Crusades* (London: Routledge and Kegan Paul, 1969)

Garijo, Ildefonso, 'Ibn Juljul's treatise on medicaments not mentioned by Dioscorides', in Fierro and Samsó (eds), *The Formation of al-Andalus*, part 2, pp 420–30

Goitein, S., *A Mediterranean Society: The Jewish Communities of the Arab World as Portrayed in the Documents of the Cairo Geniza*, 6 vols. (Berkeley: University of California Press, 1967–)

Goldziher, Ignaz, *Muslim Studies*, translated by C.R. Barber and S.M. Stern (London and New Brunswick: Aldine Transaction, 2006)

Griffith, Sidney, 'Comparative religion in the apologetics of the first Christian Arab theologians', in Hoyland (ed), *Muslims and Others in Early Islamic*

Society, pp 175–200

Gutas, Dimitri, *Greek Thought, Arabic Culture: The Graeco-Arabic Translation Movement in Baghdad and Early Abbasid Society (2nd–4th/8th–10th Centuries)* (London: Routledge, 1998)

Halm, Heinz, *The Empire of the Mahdi: The Rise of the Fatimids* (Leiden: Brill, 1996)

Hamilton, Robert, *Walid and His Friends: An Umayyad Tragedy*, Oxford Studies in Islamic Art 6 (Oxford: Oxford University Press, 1988)

Hill, Donald, *The Book of Ingenious Devices (Kitab al-Hiyal) by the Banu Musa bin Shakir* (Dordrecht and London: D. Reidel, 1979)

___, *Islamic Science and Engineering* (Edinburgh: Edinburgh University Press, 1993)

Hillenbrand, Carole, *The Crusades: Islamic Perspectives* (Edinburgh: Edinburgh University Press, 1999)

Hillenbrand, Robert, *Islamic Architecture: Form, Function and Meaning* (Edinburgh: Edinburgh University Press, 2000)

Hodgson, Marshall G.S., *The Venture of Islam 1: The Classical Age of Islam* (Chicago: University of Chicago Press, 1974)

Hoyland, Robert (ed), *Arabia and the Arabs* (London: Routledge, 2001)

___, *Muslims and Others in Early Islamic Society* (Aldershot: Ashgate Variorum, 2004)

___, *Seeing Islam as Others Saw It: A Survey and Evaluation of Christian, Jewish and Zoroastrian Writings on Early Islam* (Princeton: Darwin Press, 1997)

Hurvitz, Nimrod, 'The Mihna as self-defense', *Studia Islamica* 92 (2001), pp 93–111

Jacoby, David, 'Silk economics and cross-cultural artistic interaction: Byzantium, the Muslim world and the Christian west', *Dumbarton Oaks Papers* 54 (2004), pp 197–240

Janssens, Jules, *Ibn Sina and His Influence on the Arabic and Latin World* (Aldershot: Ashgate Variorum, 2006)

Jayyusi, Salma (ed), *The Legacy of Muslim Spain*, 2 vols. (Leiden: Brill, 1994)

Johns, Jeremy, *Arabic Administration in Norman Sicily: The Royal Diwan* (Cambridge: Cambridge University Press, 2002)

___, and Julian Raby, *Bayt al-Maqdis*, 2 vols. (Oxford: Oxford University Press, 1992–)

Kaegi, Walter, *Byzantium and the Early Islamic Conquests* (Cambridge: Cambridge University Press, 1992)

Kennedy, Hugh, *The Court of the Caliphs: When Baghdad Ruled the Muslim World* (London: Weidenfeld and Nicolson, 2004)

___, *The Early Abbasid Caliphate: A Political History* (London: Croom Helm, 1981)

___, *The Great Arab Conquests* (London: Weidenfeld and Nicolson, 2007)

___, *Muslim Spain and Portugal: A Political History of al-Andalus* (London: Longman, 1996)

___, *The Prophet and the Age of the Caliphates* (London: Longman, 1986)

Kennedy, Philip, *Abu Nuwas: A Genius of Poetry* (Oxford: Oneworld, 2005)

Kraemer, Joel, *Humanism in the Renaissance of Islam: The Cultural Revival during the Buyid Age* (Leiden: Brill, 1992)

Larsson, Goran, *Ibn García's Shu'ubiyya Letter: Ethnic and Theological Tensions in al-Andalus* (Leiden: Brill, 2003)

Lassner, Jacob, 'Notes on the topography of Baghdad: the systematic descriptions of the city and the Khatib al-Baghdadi', *Journal of the American Oriental Society* 83:4 (1963), pp 458–69

___, 'Provincial administration under the early 'Abbâsids: the ruling family and the Amsâr of Iraq', *Studia Islamica* 50 (1979), pp 21–35

___, *The Shaping of 'Abbasid Rule* (Princeton: Princeton University Press, 1980)

___, *The Topography of Baghdad in the Early Middle Ages* (Detroit: Wayne State University Press, 1970)

Lazarus-Yafeh, Hava, 'Some neglected aspects of medieval Muslim polemics against Christianity', *Harvard Theological Review* 89:1 (1996), pp 61–84

Levy-Rubin, Milka, 'New evidence relating to the process of islamisation in Palestine in the early Muslim period: the case of Samaria', *Journal of the Economic and Social History of the Orient* 43:3 (2000), pp 257–76

Lowry, Joseph, *Early Islamic Legal Theory: The Risala of Muhammad ibn Idris al-Shafi'i* (Leiden: Brill, 2007)

Lyons, M. and D.E.P Jackson, *Saladin: The Politics of Holy War* (Cambridge: Cambridge University Press, 1982)

Maalouf, Amin, *The Crusades through Arab Eyes* (London: al-Saqi, 2004)

Madelung, W. and P. Walker, *The Advent of the Fatimids: A Contemporary Shi'i Witness* (London: I.B.Tauris, 2000)

Martin, R.C., M.R. Woodward and D.S. Atmaja, *Defenders of Reason in Islam: Mu'tazilism from Medieval School to Modern Symbol* (Oxford: Oneworld Publications, 1997)

Martinez-Gros, Gabriel, *L'idéologie omeyyade: la construction de la légitimité du Califat de Cordoue (Xe–XIe siècles)* (Madrid: Casa de Velázquez, 1992)

Mazzoli-Guintard, Christine, 'Remarques sur le fonctionnement d'une capitale à double polarité: Madinat al-Zahra'-Cordoue', *Al-Qantara* 18 (1997), pp 43–64

Menocal, M., *Ornament of the World: How Muslims, Jews and Christians Created a Culture of Tolerance in Medieval Spain* (New York and Boston: Little, Brown and Company, 2002)

___, R. Scheindlin and M. Sells (eds), *The Cambridge History of Arabic Literature: The Literature of al-Andalus* (Cambridge: Cambridge University Press, 2000)

Meyendorff, John, 'Byzantine views of Islam', *Dumbarton Oaks Papers* 18 (1964), pp 113–32

Momen, M., *An Introduction to Shi'i Islam: The History and Doctrines of Twelver Shi'ism* (New Delhi, 1985)

Monroe, James, *The Shu'ubiyya in al-Andalus: The Risala of Ibn García and Five Refutations* (Berkeley: University of California Press, 1970)

Montgomery, James E. (ed), *Arabic Theology, Arabic Philosophy: From the Many to the One. Essays in Celebration of Richard Frank* (Louvain: Peeters, 2006)

___, 'The empty Hijaz', in Montgomery (ed), *Arabic Theology, Arabic Philosophy*, pp 37–97

___, 'Ibn Fadlan and the Rusiyyah', *Journal of Arabic and Islamic Studies* 3 (2000), pp 1–25

Morony, Michael, 'Religious communities in late Sasanian and early Muslim Iraq', *Journal of the Economic and Social History of the Orient* 17:2 (1974), pp 113–35

Mottahedeh, Roy, *Loyalty and Leadership in an Early Islamic Society* (Princeton: Princeton University Press, 1980)

Navarro, J. and P. Jimenez, 'Evolution of the Andalusi urban landscape: from the dispersed to the saturated medina', in Anderson and Rosser-Owen, *Revisiting Al-Andalus*, pp 115–42

Nawas, John, 'The Mihna of 218 AH/833 AD revisited: an empirical study', *Journal of the American Oriental Society* 16:4 (1996), pp 698–708

___, 'A reexamination of three current explanations for al-Ma'mun's introduction of the Mihna', *International Journal of Middle Eastern Studies* 26:4 (1994), pp 615–29

Newman, N.A., *Christian–Muslim Dialogue: A Collection of Documents from the First Three Centuries of Islam (632–900 AD)* (Hatfield, PA: Interdisciplinary Biblical Research Institute, 1993)

Noth, Albrecht, 'Problems of differentiation between Muslims and non-Muslims: re-reading the "Ordinances of 'Umar" (*al-Shurut al-'Umariyya*)', in Hoyland (ed), *Muslims and Others in Early Islamic Society*, pp 103–24

O'Leary, De Lacey, *How Greek Science Passed to the Arabs* (London: Routledge and Kegan Paul, 1948)

O'Meara, Simon, 'The foundation legend of Fez and other Islamic cities in light of the life of the Prophet', in Bennison and Gascoigne (eds), *Cities in the Pre-Modern Islamic World*, pp 27–41

Pellat, Charles, *The Life and Works of Jahiz*, translated into English by D.M. Hawke (London: Routledge and Kegan Paul, 1969)

Peters, F.E., *Mecca: A Literary History of the Muslim Holy Land* (Princeton: Princeton University Press, 1994)

Phillips, Jonathan (ed), *The First Crusade: Origins and Impact* (Manchester: Manchester University Press, 1997)

Pipes, Daniel, *Slave Soldiers and Islam: The Genesis of a Military System* (New Haven and London: Yale University Press, 1981)

Pormann, Peter and Emilie Savage-Smith, *Medieval Islamic Medicine* (Edinburgh: Edinburgh University Press, 2007)

Rashed, Roshdi, 'Greek into Arabic: transmission and translation', in Montgomery (ed), *Arabic Theology, Arabic Philosophy*, pp 157–98

Raymond, André, 'Islamic city, Arab city: Orientalist myths and recent views', *British Journal of Middle Eastern Studies* 21:1 (1994), pp 3–18

Richmond, Diana, *'Antar and 'Abla: A Bedouin Romance* (London: Quartet, 1978)

Robinson, Chase (ed), *Empires and Elites after the Muslim Conquest: The Transformation of Northern Mesopotamia* (Cambridge: Cambridge University Press, 2000)

___, *Islamic Historiography* (Cambridge: Cambridge University Press, 2003)

___, *A Medieval Islamic City Reconsidered: An Interdisciplinary Approach to Samarra*, Oxford Studies of Islamic Art 14 (Oxford: Oxford University Press, 2001)

Robinson, Cynthia, *Medieval Andalusian Courtly Culture in the Mediterranean: Hadith Bayad wa Riyad* (London and New York: Routledge, 2007)

Rosenthal, Erwin I.J., 'The place of politics in the Philosophy of Ibn Rushd', *Bulletin of the School of Oriental and African Studies* 15:2 (1953), pp 246–78

Rosenthal, F., *The Classical Heritage in Islam*, (London: Routledge and Kegan Paul, 1975)

Ruggles, D. Fairchild, 'The mirador in Abbasid and Hispano-Umayyad garden typology', *Muqarnas* 7 (1990), pp 73–82

___, 'Mothers of a hybrid dynasty: race, genealogy, and acculturation in al-Andalus', *Journal of Medieval and Early Modern Studies* 34:1 (2004), pp 65–94

Safran, Janina, 'Ceremony and submission: the symbolic representation and recognition of legitimacy in tenth century al-Andalus', *Journal of Near Eastern Studies* 58:3 (1999), pp 191–201

___, 'Identity and differentiation in ninth-century al-Andalus', *Speculum* 76 (2001), pp 573–98

___, *The Second Umayyad Caliphate: The Articulation of Caliphal Legitimacy in al-Andalus* (Cambridge, MA: Harvard University Press, 2000)

Sage, Carleton, *Paul Albar of Cordoba: Studies on His Life and Writings* (Washington, DC: Catholic University of America Press, 1943)

Saliba, George, *Islamic Science and the Making of the European Renaissance* (Cambridge, MA and London: MIT Press, 2007)

Samsó, Julio, *Islamic Astronomy and Medieval Spain* (Aldershot: Variorum, 1994)

___, *Las ciencias de los antiguos en al-Andalus* (Madrid: MAPFRE, 1992)

___, and Josep Casulleras (eds), *From Baghdad to Barcelona: Studies in the Islamic Exact Sciences in Honour of Juan Vernet* (Barcelona: Instituto Millás Vallicrosa de Historia de la Ciencia Arabe, 1996)

Saunders, Paula, 'From court ceremony to urban language: ceremonial in Fatimid Cairo and Fustat', in C.E. Bosworth (ed), *The Islamic World from Classical to Modern Times: Essays in Honour of Bernard Lewis* (Princeton: Darwin Press, 1989), pp 311–21

Shatzmiller, Maya, *The Berbers and the Islamic State: The Marinid Experience in Pre-Protectorate Morocco* (Princeton: Marcus Wiener, 2000)

Silverstein, Adam, *Postal Systems in the Pre-Modern Islamic World* (Cambridge: Cambridge University Press, 2007)

Smith, Margaret, *An Early Mystic of Baghdad: A Study of the Life and Teaching of Harith b. Asad al-Muhasibi* (London, 1935)

Stierlin, Henri, *Islam 1: Early Architecture from Baghdad to Cordoba* (Cologne: Taschen, 1996)

Tibi, Amin, *The Tibyan: The Memoirs of 'Abd Allah b. Buluggin, Last Zirid Amir of Granada* (Leiden: Brill, 1986)

Toorawa, Shawkat M., *Ibn Abi Tahir Tayfur and Arabic Writerly Culture: A Ninth Century Bookman in Baghdad* (London: RoutledgeCurzon, 2005)

Turner, John P., 'The *abna' al-dawla*: the definition and legitimation of identity in response to the fourth *fitna*', *Journal of the American Oriental Society* 124:1 (2004), pp 1–22

Waines, David, 'The third century internal crisis of the 'Abbasids', *Journal of the Economic and Social History of the Orient* 20:3 (1977), pp 282–306

Wheatley, Paul, *The Places Where Men Pray Together* (Chicago: University of Chicago Press, 2001)

Whitcomb, Donald, 'An urban structure for the early Islamic city: an archaeological hypothesis', in Bennison and Gascoigne (eds), *Cities in the Pre-Modern Islamic World*, pp 15–26

Williams, Tim, 'The city of Sultan Kala, Merv, Turkmenistan: communities, neighbourhoods and urban planning from the eighth to the thirteenth century', in Bennison and Gascoigne (eds), *Cities in the Pre-Modern Islamic World*, pp 42–62

Wolf, Kenneth, *Christian Martyrs in Muslim Spain* (Cambridge: Cambridge University Press, 1988)

——, *Conquerors and Chroniclers of Early Medieval Spain* (Liverpool: Liverpool University Press, 1990)

Zaman, Muhammad Qasim, *Religion and Politics under the Early 'Abbasids: The Emergence of the Proto-Sunni Elite* (Leiden: Brill, 1997)

Ze'evi, Dror, *Producing Desire: Changing Sexual Discourse in the Ottoman Middle East* (Berkeley: University of California Press, 2006)

Index